CRITICAL
INSIGHTS

American
Multicultural Identity

CRITICAL

INSIGHTS

American
Multicultural Identity

Editors
Linda Trinh Moser
Missouri State University

Kathryn West
Bellarmine University

SALEM PRESS
A Division of EBSCO Information Services, Inc.
Ipswich, Massachusetts

GREY HOUSE PUBLISHING

Library of Congress Cataloging-in-Publication Data

American multicultural identity / editors, Linda Trinh Moser, Missouri
  State University, Kathryn West, Bellarmine University. — [First edition].

    pages ; cm. — (Critical insights)

  Includes bibliographical references and index.
  ISBN: 978-1-61925-407-7

  1. National characteristics, American, in literature. 2. Multiculturalism in literature. 3. Identity (Philosophical concept) in literature. I. Moser, Linda Trinh, 1964- II. West, Kathryn, 1962- III. Series: Critical insights.

PS169.N35 A44 2014
810.9

LCCN: 2014949120

Contents _____

About This Volume

Linda Trinh Moser & Kathryn West

Critical Insights: American Multicultural Identity features American literature that explores the implications for one's sense of identity while living within and between two or more cultures, whether that arises from immigration, being the child of immigrants, being mixed race, or some other circumstance. Taken together, the articles in this volume represent a variety of perspectives intended to foster an understanding of the way identity is highlighted in American literature and in interpretations of that literature.

The volume's first section, "Critical Contexts," contains four essays that introduce key concepts, contexts, and critical approaches, providing a foundation for studying the theme in greater depth. In the first essay, Annette Harris Powell provides a historical overview of those social and cultural factors affecting discussions of identity in the twentieth and twenty-first centuries. Powell highlights multiculturalism and the way racial and ethnic diversity have challenged earlier definitions, which equated American identity with white, male, middle- and upper-class values and practices. In particular, Powell traces changing social attitudes toward the idea of the "hyphen." In 1915, Teddy Roosevelt famously proclaimed, "There is no room in this country for hyphenated Americans." Roughly fifty years later, the call for civil rights led groups to proudly claim a hyphenated status; for example, African-American, Jewish-American, Asian-American, or Italian-American. Half a century after passing the Civil Rights Amendment, many Americans view the hyphen as obsolete. Nonetheless, as Powell argues, Americans still struggle over the idea of a multicultural American identity that embraces difference.

The second essay, by Jessica Boykin, surveys the history of critical approaches and captures the major trends and concerns in the treatment of identity in recent American literary scholarship. For example, Boykin notes a turn away from an emphasis on unitary versions of American identity after the Civil Rights Movement, just as critics become interested in identifying and examining literature by writers of color. While the emphasis on diversity challenged prejudice and bias, it also led to a focus on "authenticity," which, unfortunately, tended to rely on limited versions of American identity. More recent attention to the social construction of identity and an emphasis on "hybridity," hetereogeneity, and the intersection of multiple identity markers (such as race, class, gender, and sexuality) have, as Boykin notes, led to more inclusive and diverse notions of national identity.

Kathryn West's "Critical Lens" essay offers a close reading of Sherman Alexie's young adult novel *The Absolutely True Diary of a Part-Time Indian* through the lens of Ethnic Studies. The essay notes the preponderance of doubles and character- and event-doubling in the work, and it argues that this encourages readers to think in terms of the concept of double-consciousness—to understand what it meant for the protagonist to choose to attend high school off reservation, to choose a bicultural existence.

In the "Comparative Analysis" essay, Rickie-Ann Legleitner examines the connection between identity formation and parent-child relationships in poems by four writers: Natasha Trethewey, Rhina Espaillat, Anthony Hecht, and Shirley Geok-lin Lim. These writers feature identity development in terms of race, linguistics, religion, and gender, respectively. Applying W. E. B. Du Bois' notion of double-consciousness, Legleitner discusses the way children from ethnic American communities develop identities affiliated with both their familial roots and with the dominant culture. While each poet acknowledges the negative aspects of double-consciousness, their works celebrate the benefits of developing a plural identity. Doing so, Legleitner argues, expands definitions of American identity and helps to create the image of a new and more inclusive American family.

The opening three essays in the Critical Readings section take up issues of gender, sexuality, and identity, but each with a very different focus. Gad Guterman analyzes Larry Kramer's *The Normal Heart*, a play set in New York City at the start of the AIDS epidemic. While *The Normal Heart*'s ostensible goal is to recount the severe obstacles faced by victims of AIDS in a homophobic society, Kramer's play also demonstrates an attempt to redefine the term "gay" outside the context of sex and desire and within US legal structures. Situating his discussion historically, Guterman provides examples of the way US law has defined gayness in negative and criminal terms. The play's staging of a gay wedding in its final scene calls for a new legal identity (one that would be realized in New York State in 2011, the year of the play's stage revival). Guterman argues that the play not only brought attention to and changed attitudes about the AIDS crisis, it also helped to trigger more equitable legal treatment of gay men and lesbians.

In the next essay, Michael Gorman considers the effect of trauma and loss on male identity as depicted in works by Chang-rae Lee. Each of Lee's male protagonists evade their familial duties. Henry Pak from *Native Speaker* escapes family life in work; Franklin Hata in *A Gesture Life* drowns his responsibilities while swimming. In each novel, Lee explores the connections between trauma, fatherhood, and silence. In his comparison, Gorman demonstrates the way Lee undermines stereotypical notions about taciturnity. Race, gender, and culture are integral to identity issues, but they play a secondary role in these works. Understanding the impact of loss and trauma on identity is key in the process of grief and recovery.

Where Gorman's essay explores father/son relationships, Jessica Labbé turns the spotlight on mother/daughter interactions in her essay on the work of three Cuban American women writers. More specifically, Labbé demonstrates the way relationships between women serve as a foundation for female identity. In the work of Cristina García, Achy Obejas, and Alisa Valdes-Rodriguez, each female character tends to identify herself in relation to another as mother, daughter, granddaughter, sister, cousin, and friend. Furthermore, as Labbé notes, the characters' interactions operate as microcosms of the identity struggles experienced by multiple generations of Cuban American women. Second- and third-generation women, in particular, reveal both the difficulties and rewards of navigating between multiple cultures and the identities they produce. They must learn to embrace the past experienced by previous generations, while also remaining open to "life on the hyphen."

Joanna Davis-McElligatt's article picks up and continues the discussion of struggles between generations that so often occur when a family has immigrated to the United States, looking in particular at a young woman who must struggle with the very different cultural ambitions of her parents in Paule Marshall's *Brown Girl, Brownstones*. Selina Boyce, the protagonist, tries to reconcile two opposing impulses—identification with the immigrant's homeland or with the United States—represented by her father's hopes of building a home back in Barbados and her mother's efforts to purchase their rented brownstone in New York. Selina, Davis-McElligatt argues, resists her parents' either/or thinking. She rejects her mother's urge to assimilate and her father's nostalgia. Instead, as Davis-McElligatt shows, she accepts her own subject position as in-between, choosing a fluid and transnational identity.

Tina Powell's essay analyzing Bich Minh Nguyen's memoir *Stealing Buddha's Dinner* examines similar themes in the context of Vietnamese American life. She offers a less positive view of cultural hybridity. Highlighting conventions of the *Bildungsroman* genre, Powell argues that Nguyen's memoir challenges the myth of the melting pot and also the notion that it is easy to assimilate into mainstream American culture. Nguyen's efforts to develop a taste for American junk food, Powell argues, is her way of constructing an American identity, in which the norm is white. Although she increasingly abandons traditional Vietnamese food, along with her family and other cultural aspects, Nguyen is never fully accepted as American. In the end, Bich's *Bildung* remains unfinished; her bicultural identity leaves her hungry for a space to belong.

The notion of a hybrid identity provides a starting point for the next essay, in which Linda Trinh Moser examines "Mrs. Spring Fragrance" and "The Inferior Woman" by Edith Eaton, who wrote under the pseudonym Sui Sin Far. On the surface, these stories seem more like exotic fairytales than an attempt to depict an Asian American identity. Rather than viewing the stories as "real" or "fake," Moser argues, they should be looked at as an attempt to produce a hybrid sensibility influenced by the multiple cultures with which Eaton identified. Although Eaton was influenced by popular images of Asian immigrants, she also identified with her Chinese mother and the Chinese immigrants about whom she wrote. Despite her use of Chinese cultural stereotypes, Eaton's stories attempt to dismantle barriers constructed between Asian and Anglo American communities. By simultaneously conforming to and resisting Western thought and literary traditions, Eaton reveals the complexity of responses to the volatile and variable nature of American racism.

Leanne P. Day considers land rights and ownership as a marker of cultural identity. Day's analysis of Kaui Hart Hemming's *The Descendants* and its film adaptation examines a connection between *kanaka maoli* (Native Hawaiian) identity and access to land. Her essay uncovers a metaphorical correlation between marital infidelity and the sale of Hawaiian land held in trust. The protagonist Matt's discovery of his wife's affair parallels the impending decision about the sale of his family's inherited land, raising larger questions about Hawai'i's history, tourism, and complex social relationships. Matt must negotiate between the traditional relationship of *kanaka maoli* to the land, which is largely communal, and Western notions of the land as individual property. The personal and economic choices Matt faces allow for a meditation on the colonial history of Hawai'i, while opening up the possibility for a modern *hapa-haole*, or mixed-race identity.

Kyoko Matsunaga's essay on Leslie Marmon Silko's *Ceremony* likewise addresses connections between land and identity, while also exploring images of cultural hybridity and the continuing impact of colonization. Participation in World War II and alcoholism are the legacy of cross-cultural contact between Laguna and Anglo American societies, negatively affecting Tayo, the novel's protagonist, and his tribal culture and community. Matsunaga, through her reading of *Ceremony*, demonstrates that cross cultural contact did not just damage the lives of indigenous people in the past, but that colonialist forces continue in the Atomic Age through the development of nuclear technology and industry, which have scarred tribal lands.

Neither Western medicine nor traditional methods of healing provide a cure for either Tayo or the land. Recognizing the impossibility of returning to pre-contact days, Silko offers cultural hybridity as a tool for survival.

John C. Orr and Enid R. Spitz also highlight hybridity in an essay on the life and work of Salish writer, Mourning Dove. With supporting evidence from Mourning Dove's letters, Orr and Spitz demonstrate Mourning Dove's resistance to her editor/collaborator Lucullus McWhorter, who sought to revise her writing based on his own cultural assumptions. Like the title character of her only novel, *Cogewea*, Mourning Dove mediated between cultures. Her race and her gender created situations in which she had to accede to the dictates of McWhorter, but though both author and character were in their own way victimized, neither allowed herself to remain a victim. Mourning Dove clearly understood and identified with the dilemmas of the heroine of her novel and found ways to validate and bring awareness to Native culture.

Finally, Conor Picken's essay on Gish Jen's *Mona in the Promised Land* examines intersections between the American Dream and American multicultural identity. Jen's novel, which, like many discussed earlier, highlights generational differences and explores the ramifications of cultural hybridity, also offers a bit of a counterpoint. While the Changs, Chinese immigrants, purposefully work toward the American Dream and American identity, their daughter rejects their impulse to assimilate. She converts to Judaism instead, choosing to identify with her community's middle-class Jewish residents. Picken argues that Mona's adopted identity simultaneously resists and gives in to the pressure to assimilate. Bringing us back to our opening essay, we may once again consider the losses and gains inherent to a hyphenated identity.

On American Multicultural Identity␣␣␣␣␣␣␣␣␣␣

Kathryn West

In a 1955 interview with *Paris Review*, Ralph Ellison, noted author of *Invisible Man* (1952), was asked if he believed that the search for identity is primarily an American theme. He replied, "It is *the* American theme. The nature of our society is such that we are prevented from knowing who we are." Knowing, understanding, who we are has been the quest for countless American writers and readers. It has been dramatized on the individual, the family, the neighborhood, the community, and the national levels, as well as through intersections of those groupings. That quest for identity, for an understanding of identity and the nature of the society that shapes it, has produced some of the most moving and some of the most narratively innovative works of literature we have.

Maxine Hong Kingston perhaps best encapsulates the dilemma of identity for the child of immigrant parents in the opening section to her *The Woman Warrior: Memoirs of a Girlhood Among Ghosts* (1976). The narrator asks, "Chinese-Americans, when you try to understand what things in you are Chinese, how do you separate what is peculiar to childhood, to poverty, insanities, one family, your mother who marked your growing with stories, from what is Chinese? What is Chinese tradition and what is the movies?" (Kingston 5–6). In this passage, Kingston encapsulates the conundrum of identity for all of us, but most especially for those who grow up in bicultural or multicultural environments: how do we sort through the myriad influences that make us *us*, in our own eyes and in the eyes of those around us?

The factors that shape any person's sense of identity are multiplicitous and come from internal and external forces. We often at least partially define ourselves in reaction to how others see us, or how we want them to see us, as well as how we perceive ourselves. Race, ethnicity, gender, class, sexuality, religion, geography, language, mental illness, family size—these factors combine in varying proportions to create a sense of identity. Of all these myriad factors that may shape identity, which matters most for any one individual? In what proportion to others? Where and how do they intersect? While such questions are part of the human condition, in the United States they have taken on a particular complexity and come to define much about our national character, since all Americans, with the exception of American Indians, were immigrants at some point in every family history. When writers try to account for the prevalence or lack of any identity marker when they examine these intersections, they give us what it means to be human: infinitely complex, impossible to sum up, but fascinating to think—and write—about.

Identity and American History

Awareness of history is essential to engaging this literature. In paraphrasing one of the key conceptual understandings of the feminist movement, "the personal is political," we can say of this topic, "identity is historical." In other words, beliefs, manners, customs, religion, ethnicity, race—all of the things that go into what we call culture—are inherited, some genetically, some environmentally. Beliefs about gender and sexuality, whether we agree with them or react against them or land somewhere in between, are also inherited. Identity is certainly shaped in part by one's current environment, but we imperil our understanding of identity if we also fail to address the past that informs it.

A focus on identity has been with this nation since before it was a nation. John Winthrop, who was to become governor of the Massachusetts Bay Colony, set the stage in his sermon to those crossing the Atlantic to the "New World," entitled "A Modell of Christian Charity" (1630). Winthrop declared, "GOD ALMIGHTY in His most holy and wise providence, hath so disposed of the condition of mankind, as in all times some must be rich, some poor, some high and eminent in power and dignity; others mean and in submission" (Winthrop). While Winthrop makes no distinctions about race or ethnicity in this speech, he delineates strict differences between classes and points to his religion as the source of such beliefs. While many contemporary Christians will argue with Winthrop's interpretation of biblical texts, his perception was that the natural order decreed such distinctions among people. Yet in the body of this sermon, Winthrop carefully lays out principles for how the rich and eminent must treat the poor and mean, and vice versa. "A Modell of Christian Charity" becomes a treatise on love and relationships between human beings. In his summation, he states,

> For this end, we must be knit together, in this work, as one man. We must entertain each other in brotherly affection. . . . We must uphold a familiar commerce together in all meekness, gentleness, patience and liberality. We must delight in each other; make others' conditions our own; rejoice together, mourn together, labor and suffer together, always having before our eyes our commission and community in the work, as members of the same body. (Winthrop)

Winthrop made distinctions between people, particularly on the basis of class and social status, which many contemporary readers will find troubling. Yet, it is the second, less familiar part of his message that should perhaps give more cause for discomfort: that differences between people should not get in the way of working together in harmony. As colonial America became the United States and since that time, the country's history is rife with conflicts and lack of fair treatment from those in power toward those with less power.

Multiculturalism is often associated with the contemporary era, or at least the late nineteenth and twentieth centuries. In fact, this land was "multicultural" long before Columbus or the Vikings arrived. It is estimated that there were between 350 and 375 distinct Native tribes and at least thirty different languages in 1492. For centuries, scholars estimated that only five to ten, or perhaps at most 20,000,000 people lived in the Americas before 1492. New research gathered by Charles C. Mann in his groundbreaking book, *1491: New Revelations of the Americas before Columbus* (2005), estimates a low population figure of 100,000,000 and a possible high of 200,000,000. These peoples and their tribes sometimes lived in harmony, and sometimes waged ferocious, long-standing wars. Their reality was very different from both extremes of the major stereotypes: they were neither Noble Savages living in total harmony with nature and each other nor violent primitives living in a Stone Age. Indeed, in Europe in the decades up to and for many years after Christopher Columbus' voyages, what would become a terribly brutal Inquisition was established in Spain, while hordes of people would show up in London for public executions, including burnings at the stake and beheadings, such as those of two of the wives of Henry VIII. Some early American civilizations did practice human sacrifice, but when compared to their European counterparts, they were probably no more nor less brutal. While we can trace a few characteristics that were true of a majority of American Indian tribes—hospitality toward guests, respect for land and nature—there has never been a monolithic Native American culture. So, as varied peoples from other continents arrived, they encountered—even if they did not always realize it—many varied cultures.

As European settlement moved across this continent, disease and warfare decimated the Native American population until, by the 1880s, that population was reduced to around 275,000. Whole tribes, whole cultures, disappeared. The land base preserved for reservations was reduced by one-third due to the allotment policies of the 1880s. The belief in Manifest Destiny, the idea that white people were destined to spread across the North American continent, carried as its corollary the myth of the "Vanishing American."

Knowing this history heightens our understanding of the prevalence of themes of loss in literature by Native American authors, such as Sherman Alexie, Louise Erdrich, Leslie Marmon Silko, and James Welch, among others. For instance, these authors have all been criticized at times for their frequent inclusion of depictions of alcoholics in their works. Yet alcoholism is widespread on contemporary reservations and among urban Indians, at least in part as a reaction to despair over lack of opportunities, and thus plays an important role in dramatizing Native identity. These authors and others also respond to the legacies of their history through strategies such as humor, environmentalism, spiritualism, oral storytelling traditions, and explorations of the possibility of hybridity for Native identity.

In more recent history, depictions in film, television, and sports mascots create other troublesome role models for the development of a strong, positive sense of identity. As award-winning Ojibwe writer Erdrich illustrates in her story "The Plunge of the Brave," when Native American actors were used in films (often white actors were given the work instead), their roles were overwhelmingly confined to looking "stoic," speaking in monosyllables, and falling dead off of a horse. Alexie has also written about the fraught nature of such filmic role models, particularly in his essay, "I Hated Tonto, Still Do."

Africans and later African Americans also experienced the loss of their homelands, but rather than having it taken from them, they found themselves torn from it. Centuries of being treated as slaves and then as second-class citizens, of having little to no link to or knowledge of - ancestors, created another form of loss to be worked through. Early to mid-twentieth century African American literature often concentrated on identity through documenting oppression and depicting the full range of human emotion and experience in African American characters, in the face of prejudices that denied them a full humanity. These strategies can be found in such writers as Charles Chesnutt, Ralph Ellison, James Baldwin, Langston Hughes, Zora Neale Hurston, and Chester Himes, among many others. Chesnutt and Hurston offer examples of writers who reached back to African traditions by employing trickster figures in many of their short stories and novels. The 1970s and the appearance of more African American women writers (Toni Morrison, Alice Walker, Gloria Naylor, Rita Dove) signaled a shift, with a somewhat lessened emphasis on racism from whites and more focus on the strengths and weaknesses within African American communities themselves. Ancestral figures, culture bearers, make frequent appearances in work by these African American writers. Walker's Pulitzer Prize–winning novel *The Color Purple* (1982) offers a significant example of acknowledging the role of loss, rootlessness, and lack of opportunity in African American lives, while also honoring the struggle and the strategies people go through to build satisfying lives. Two sisters are separated early on, with one going to Africa as a missionary and the other living in an abusive relationship in the Deep South. By the end of the novel, Walker has explored the ramifications of connecting with an African homeland as well as providing a complex portrait of how Celie, the sister who stays in the United States, comes to understand, appreciate, and value herself as an individual, as a black woman, as a sister, a lover, and eventually, as an entrepreneur.

Asian intersections with American identity offer still another historical variation, beginning with differences between Chinese American, Japanese American, Korean American, and Vietnamese American experiences, despite often being lumped together as "Orientals" or "yellow races" in the collective consciousness of the United States. A particular challenge for Asian Americans had to do with immigration laws that began in the nineteenth century and severely limited Asian immigration up until the passage of the 1965 Immigration and Nationality Act. These immigration laws were shaped in such a way as to take advantage of the labor of Asian men (most notably for building the transcontinental railroad system), but also to avoid providing them with the opportunity to establish permanent residence and families. For instance, the Page Act of 1875 severely limited the number of Asian women who could enter the United States.

Early stereotypes of Asian Americans defined them as inscrutable and alien. In the early twentieth century, Chinese Americans were generally more discriminated against than were Japanese Americans, as evidenced in part by the Chinese Exclusion Act of 1882. This act forbade immigration of any Chinese "labor" on the grounds that it endangered the "good order" of some localities. An example of literary responses to the prejudice against Chinese in particular can be seen in the choices of two sisters, Winnifred Eaton and Edith Maud Eaton, children of a Chinese mother and English father. From England, the family emigrated, living alternately in Canada and the United States. Winnifred published many novels about *Japanese* life, taking as her pseudonym Onoto Watanna, which was read as

Japanese, hoping for a more friendly audience through that avenue. Edith Eaton published short stories, journalism, and essays, choosing the pen name Sui Sin Far, a Chinese name. In her autobiographical essay, "Leaves from the Mental Portfolio of an Eurasian," Eaton/Sui Sin Far writes about the prejudice she encounters as a person with Chinese heritage, first from childhood playmates in England and later from "cultivated" people she meets in her travels around the United States. She ends the essay with a striking image: "I give my right hand to the Occidentals and my left to the Orientals, hoping that between them they will not utterly destroy the insignificant 'connecting link.' And that's all" (Sui Sin Far).

The US cultural preference for Japanese people over Chinese reversed somewhat during World War II, after the Japanese attack on Pearl Harbor. At its most extreme, it saw the US government confine over 100,000 Japanese people in internment camps; over sixty percent of these people were citizens. Several important memoirs and novels have delineated what this experience meant for Japanese American identity, including Yoshiko Uchida's *Journey to Topaz: A Story of the Japanese-American Evacuation* (1971), Julie Otsuka's *When the Emperor was Divine* (2002), Monica Sone's *Nisei Daughter* (1979), Jeanne Wakatsuki Houston and James D. Houston's *Farewell to Manzanar* (1973), and John Okada's *No-No Boy* (1957).

A Korean American presence began most notably in Hawai'i at the beginning of the twentieth century. The population expanded significantly during and after the Korean War in the 1950s, with marriages between Korean women and US military men and adoptions of Korean children. As with major Chinese American writers, such as Maxine Hong Kingston and Amy Tan, Korean American authors Nora Okja Keller and Chang-rae Lee explore identity issues and struggles between generations of immigrant families, while Mary Paik Lee and Younghill Kang focus on the immigrant experience for Korean Americans. Much Vietnamese American literature pays particular attention to the experiences of refugees, reflecting the growth of Vietnamese and Vietnamese American populations fleeing war and persecution in the late 1960s and the 1970s. Along with Bich Minh Nguyen, particularly notable are such writers as Lan Cao (*Monkey Bridge*, 1998) and Andrew Pham (*Catfish and Mandala: A Two-Wheeled Voyage through the Landscape and Memory of Vietnam*, 1999).

As with Asian American immigrants, those of Latino heritage were often welcomed to the United States only for their labor, not as families and citizens, and often on a temporary basis. Also similar to Asian Americans, Hispanics and Latinos are a diverse group coming from many different countries. These terms refer to ethnicities, not races, with Hispanic referring to people having a link to Spain, through language or colonization, and Latino referring to those with heritage and ancestry in Latin American countries. The experiences of Mexican Americans, Cuban Americans, Puerto Rican Americans, those from the Dominican Republic and Latin American countries, are vastly different from each other, according to the history and culture of the ancestral home, their reasons for immigrating, and the reception that met them when they arrived in the United States. Again we find literature that explores generational differences, experiences of bias, and struggle for economic opportunities as pressures on identity. Chicano writer Rudolfo Anaya, with *Bless Me, Ultima* (1972), probes cultural hybridity across intersections of religion, family, and spirituality. The protagonist, Antonio Márez y Luna, is torn between the lifestyle of the family of his mother—people of the sea—and the family of his father, people of the land. His mentor is Ultima, a *curandera,* or practitioner of herbalism and folk magic; she guides him through a spiritual journey that seeks to combine Catholicism with folk spirituality and myth. Other important explorations of Mexican American and Chicano/a identity can be found in works by Ana Castillo, Sandra Cisneros, Denise Chávez, José Antonio Villareal, and Tomás Rivera. Some works by Latino/a writers engage magical realism as a way to negotiate the differing perceptions of a rural or ethnic way of life in contact with a highly industrialized society. Particularly notable in this regard are Cuban American Cristina García's *Dreaming in Cuban* (1992) and Castillo's *So Far From God* (1993).

Piri Thomas' memoir *Down These Mean Streets* (1967) recounts growing up in Spanish Harlem as a Puerto Rican often mistaken for African American; he finds himself struggling with identity formation due to racial prejudice toward both Latinos and African Americans. Nicholasa Mohr's *Nilda* (1973) offers a similar tale from a female perspective. Julía Alvarez and Junot Díaz, Dominican American writers, offer fiction trained on identity and cultural hybridity in selections such as, for Alvarez, *How the García Girls Lost Their Accents* (1991), *¡Yo: A Novel!* (1997), and *In the Time of the Butterflies* (1994, set in the Dominican Republic during the Trujillo regime), and for Díaz, *Drown* (1996, short stories) and *The Brief Wondrous Life of Oscar Wao* (2007). Both authors highlight intersections between gender and ethnicity, and Díaz in particular employs humor to dramatize hybrid situations.

South Asian Americans, originating from India, Pakistan, Bangladesh, and Sri Lanka, have been a presence in American literature for a shorter span of time than most other groups discussed here, but have produced some very powerful works that speak to their experience of American identity. Bharati Mukherjee, author of numerous novels and short story collections, has lived in India, Canada, and the United States. Much of her writing has focused on the experiences of women as immigrants and their experiences uprooting and re-rooting, most especially *The Tiger's Daughter* (1971), *The Middleman and Other Stories* (1988), and *Jasmine* (1989). She has noted that Indian American writers before her still considered their roots in India, but that she represents a shift: "I'm the first among Asian immigrants to be making this distinction between immigrant writing and expatriate writing. . . . now my roots are here and my emotions are here in North America" (Meer). She asks that she be considered an American writer of Bengali-Indian origin. Jhumpa Lahiri, of Bengali descent, has the distinction of having her first book, the collection of short stories *Interpreter of Maladies* (1999), win the Pulitzer Prize for fiction. The stories in *Interpreter* feature first-generation Indian immigrants, their second-generation Indian American children in the United States and visiting India, and in two examples, South Asians still living in India or Bengali. In particular, she pays attention to marriages—arranged, by choice, and a hybrid sort somewhere in between—and food and foodways as markers of Bengali American identity. She has since published two novels and one more collection of short stories, all well received.

Of course, American literature also comprises many works written by white writers that investigate identity formation up against borders and boundaries, particularly in the circumstance of immigration. For that loss of the homeland, the ancestral land, to be a choice, albeit one made under political or financial pressures, is still loss. Again it takes on varied shapes and may result in a variety of different themes and forms. A landmark of the immigrant identity novel is Henry Roth's *Call It Sleep* (1934), the story of a Jewish immigrant family living in New York's Lower East Side in the early twentieth century, viewed through the perspective of a young boy, David. As he attempts to find his place in the world, David must struggle with his parents' pre-immigrant past, during which his mother may have had an affair with a non-Jewish man. In addition to poverty and the shadow of the past, David's education in his faith and in Hebrew play an important role in his development. Willa Cather's *My Ántonia* (1918) plays out on the Nebraska prairies, with a young Bohemian woman striving to overcome boundaries imposed by gender and financial hardship. Cather introduces a noteworthy element in that the lives of the characters before immigration are shown in brief flashbacks. O. E. Rolvaag writes about the hardships faced by Norwegian immigrants in such works as *Giants in the Earth* (1934). While Stephen Crane is often most remembered for his story of a young man facing war in *The Red Badge of Courage* (1895), his *Maggie: A Girl of the Streets* (1893) offers a powerful story of a young Irish woman from an immigrant family who becomes a prostitute in response to the violence and poverty surrounding her. Erdrich, of Ojibwe/German descent, has published extensively on the Ojibwe; however, in *The Master Butchers Singing Club* (2003), she draws on her German heritage to dramatize the experiences of Fidelis Waldvogel and his family and friends; he emigrates from Germany shortly after World War I. These works and many others describing immigrant life and the challenges it poses to identity offer a rich and complex terrain.

Identity and Genre

These many traditions of literature about American multicultural identity have tended to begin with the *Bildungsroman*, sometimes in the form of memoir or semi-autobiography. A *Bildungsroman* is a novel of initiation, the story of a young protagonist growing up and facing temptations or obstacles that he or she must overcome in order to establish a mature sense of identity and become a productive member of society. Short fiction of this type may be referred to as rite-of-passage stories, initiation stories, and growing-up stories. A special form of *Bildungsroman* often encountered in this literature is the *Künstlerroman*, the story of a young person finding his or her identity as an artist or writer. Such works make sense as the beginnings of these traditions, for in many respects, the story of the protagonist working through obstacles such as racism, ethnocentrism, financial pressures, learning a new language or set of beliefs or customs, parallels in microcosm the trajectory of the immigrant group, or, in the case of Native Americans, of those displaced from their lands and threatened by the erasure of their traditional cultures. Introduced into the traditional *Bildungsroman* pattern, we find struggles with language differences and many more female protagonists on a *Bildungsroman* trajectory than ever before.

Narratively, many authors of American multicultural identity have been particularly innovative with structure and style, using vignettes, inserting photographs and drawings, telling stories in reverse, and playing with the conventions of many different genres. Often, they use code-switching, the inclusion of words from languages other than English without translating them, in part to give readers a sense of what it is like to be bilingual in a society that does not always welcome that ability.

Cisnero presents the *Künstlerroman* of Esperanza Cordero, daughter of Mexican and Mexican-American parents, through a series of vignettes in *The House on Mango Street*. Filled with colorful, striking imagery, the barely 100-page novella manages to depict, with great emotional clarity and detail, struggles with language, domestic violence, poverty, class stratifications, neighborhood life, and sexual abuse. Esperanza, through all these contacts, the urging of mentors, and the support of family, comes to realize that she *will* leave the poor housing she has longed to put behind her, but will carry her neighborhood and her heritage in her heart, to recreate them in her writing.

Kingston's *The Woman Warrior*, introduced at the beginning of this essay, subverts our expectations of genre. Subtitled "Memoirs of a Girlhood Among Ghosts" and originally published as nonfiction, *The Woman Warrior* consists of six sections that include childhood memories, but also stories Maxine heard from her mother about Fa Mu Lan and other mythical Chinese figures doing such seemingly impossible things as flying. The family stories and her mother's version of Chinese legends combine to present a psychological biography of Maxine, a sense of how not just events, but *stories* shaped her sense of identity. Similarly, in her *China Men*, Kingston combines family stories, legends, a copy of the Chinese Exclusion Act, and other unexpected formats to delineate the lives of her male ancestors.

Michael Dorris' *A Yellow Raft on Blue Water* (1987) purportedly features the first biracial protagonist who is not part white, but rather is the daughter of an African American man and a Native American woman from an unspecified tribe. By starting with the youngest generation and working back through three female generations, Dorris powerfully limns each woman's identity and successively reveals events that have impacted that sense of identity, even though those events remain unknown to the younger characters.

Amy Tan also offers insight into how the events of a parent's life, even if unknown to the children, impact the identity of those children in her highly structured *The Joy Luck Club* (1988). Her sixteen-part structure contrasts four stories from four different mothers with four stories from their daughters, interweaving the past and the present and the identities of the different generations.

The quest is one of the oldest patterns in Western literature. In *Song of Solomon*, Nobel Prize–winning author Morrison performs several reversals of the traditional form by creating a rather dissolute and extremely selfish young African American man and sending him on a quest that he believes is for gold. In fact, he finds himself on a quest to discover his family's history and heritage and even his very self. Late in the novel, on a hunt in the woods in the deep South, lost and out of breath, he finds himself cradled in the roots of a huge tree. All the trappings of civilization are gone, and it is only at this extreme that he realizes his selfishness and lack of a true sense of self. From here, he rebuilds an identity worthy of the struggles of generations of African Americans and of his own family, including their identity as "flying Africans" who refused to succumb to slavery. Thus Morrison also incorporates a magical realism that, rather than copying that of Latin America, comes organically out of African American folk beliefs.

In a 1967 essay appearing in *The Atlantic*, John Barth argued that the genre of the novel might well be exhausted and that the only thing left to do was play with form and conventions. In this essay, "The Literature of Exhaustion," Barth posits that perhaps all the stories are used up. Through his short story published the next year, "Lost in the Funhouse" (1968), Barth hones in specifically on the initiation story to illustrate how such a narrative has already been told over and over and that perhaps the only thing to still make it amusing are metafictional musings and intellectual game-play. Ironically, it was also in the late 1960s that voices from myriad different identity positions, especially multicultural, exploded onto the literary scene, giving us stories we had not heard before, using innovative storytelling techniques.

Jhumpa Lahiri, in the final story of *Interpreter of Maladies*, titled "The Third and Final Continent," sums up beautifully what American multicultural identity can be, despite hard transitions, loss, re-learning, and even encountering prejudice: "While the astronauts, heroes forever, spent mere hours on the moon, I have remained in this new world for nearly thirty years. I know that my achievement is quite ordinary. I am not the only man to seek his fortune far from home, and certainly I am not the first. Still, there are times I am bewildered by each mile I have traveled, each meal I have eaten, each person I have known, each room in which I have slept. As ordinary as it all appears, there are times when it is beyond my imagination" (198).

Works Cited

Barnes, Ian. *The Historical Atlas of Native Americans*. New York: Chartwell, 2010.

Kingston, Maxine Hong. *The Woman Warrior: Memoirs of a Girlhood Among Ghosts*. New York: Knopf, 1976.

Lahiri, Jhumpa. *Interpreter of Maladies*. Boston: Houghton Mifflin, 1999.

Mann, Charles C. *1491: New Revelations of the Americas Before Columbus*. New York: Vintage, 2005.

Meer, Ameena. "Literature: Interview—Bharati Mukherjee." *Bomb: Artists in Conversation*. 29 (Fall 1989). Web. 14 Aug. 2014. <http://bombmagazine.org/article/1264/>.

Nabokov, Peter. *Native American Testimony: A Chronicle of Indian-White Relations from Prophecy to the Present, 1492–2000*. Rev. ed. New York: Penguin, 1999.

Pelaud, Isabelle Thuy. *This is All I Choose to Tell: History and Hybridity in Vietnamese American Literature*. Philadelphia: Temple UP, 2010.

Sui Sin Far. "Leaves from the Mental Portfolio of an Eurasian." 1890. *Quotidiana*. Ed. Patrick Madden. 1 Jun. 2008. Web. 27 July 2014. <http://essays.quotidiana.org/far/leaves_mental_portfolio>.

Takaki, Ronald. *A Different Mirror: A History of Multicultural America*. Boston: Little, Brown, 1993.

_____. *A Larger Memory: A History of Our Diversity, with Voices*. Boston: Little, Brown, 1998.

Winthrop, John. "A Modell of Christian Charity." 1630. *Hanover Historical Texts Project*. Hanover College History Department. Aug. 1996. Web. 3 May 2014. <https://history.hanover.edu/texts/winthmod.html>.

CRITICAL
CONTEXTS

The Hyphenated American in Twentieth- and Twenty-first Century America

Annette Harris Powell

Despite the efforts of multiculturalism to increase awareness and tolerance of racial and ethnic diversity, as well as hyphenated (implicit and explicit) identities, American national identity has always been fraught. If you are an American who identifies with a non-white race or ethnicity and who engages the languages, customs, and practices of multiple cultures, living on two sides of the hyphen is, indeed, a difficult dance. Do you recognize your religious or ethnic inheritance, or embrace your ancestral lands? If you do, does this mean that you are somehow indifferent or disloyal to your American identity? Does an acknowledgement or affinity for one's 'originary' culture suggest that difference is not possible without an imposed hierarchy?

Certainly, the American experience can be described as hybridized—rich with possibility, desire, anxiety, and complexity. Although cultural hybridity is most commonly referred to as "the creation of new transcultural forms within the contact zone produced by colonization" (Ashcroft, et al. 118), quite a bit of the discourse around hybridity is ambivalent and contested, viewed both as a space of "loss" and "dilution," where colonialist discourse gets reproduced, and as a space where the "mixture," Paul Gilroy has said, "remains assertively and insubordinately a bastard" (117). There is also the suggestion that if engaged appropriately, hybridity "offers an opportunity to celebrate the vigorous cosmopolitanism endowed in modernity by transgressive and creative contacts with different people" (Gilroy 217). Many also draw on Homi K. Bhabha's classic notion of cultural hybridity, in which he suggests that it is the process of mutuality between the colonizer and the colonized (the immigrant and the "parent" country) that results in the cultural creations or transformations taking place in the space "in between," or what Bhabha calls the "Third Space of Enunciation" (Ashcroft 209).

But, "mutuality" typically requires those individuals seeking entry to a particular culture to adopt the customs, cultural practices, and values of that culture, while sacrificing some aspects of their own. Acculturation, particularly during politically inauspicious times, is often a hasty process for immigrants to the United States, many of whom have been compelled to abandon their native language, dress, and habits, in order that they might adapt to their new environs.

In the early twentieth century, before and during World War I, "hyphenated American" was a slang term typically viewed with suspicion. An ideologically charged marker, the hyphen (the adjectival phrase, the slash or the actual hyphen) continues to generate tension and challenge ideas about what it means to be American. Traditionally represented as one of shared social, cultural, and political ideals, American identity troubles or, in some instances, displaces the hyphen because there is a singularity, an exceptionalism that underpins American experience, suggesting that there is only *one* American identity. A common early view of core American identity precludes the hyphen. Differences had to be subsumed under this notion of singularity, making assimilation the touchstone of American experience. In fact, some early American leaders tried to erase the hyphen rhetorically, in order to create the idea of one America.

Early Constructions of American Identity

During the revolutionary period, Patrick Henry emphasized the US national motto *e pluribus unum*—out of many, one. In his address to the First Continental Congress, Henry advanced the idea of singular Americanness: "The distinctions between Virginians, Pennsylvanians, New Yorkers, and New Englanders are no more. I am not a Virginian, but an American" (Garraty 134). This idea of a singular American identity was at the core of the Founders' conception of an American nation. Benjamin Franklin, concerned with America being overrun by "aliens," expressed early views promoting America as an exclusively white, racially pure nation. In his 1755 "Observations Concerning the Increase of Mankind" Franklin states:

Why should Pennsylvania, founded by the English, become a Colony of aliens, who will shortly be so numerous as to Germanize us instead of our Anglifying them, and will never adopt our language or customs, anymore than they can acquire our complexion? (Perea, et al. 104)

Colonial apprehension about the potential assimilation of Germans in Pennsylvania resonates with contemporary anxieties regarding recent immigrants. This apprehension is a hallmark of American history, and the American historical periods discussed below illustrate how this authentic brand of American apprehension serves to reinforce Americanism and label as threats those who are being excluded.

The 1890s through 1920s was a period of massive immigration to the United States. In the midst of strong suspicion of foreigners, many Native-born Americans were keen on fostering national citizenship. In his 1915 Columbus Day address to the Knights of Columbus, early Progressive Theodore Roosevelt said: "There is no room in this country for hyphenated Americans. When I refer to hyphenated Americans, I do not refer to naturalized Americans. A hyphenated American is not an American at all. The only man who is a good American is the man who is an American and nothing else" (Link 166). As political scientist Stanley Renshon suggests: American national identity had long been "synonymous with single white, male, middle-class culture—a collusion of race, gender, and class" (82). Assimilation, then the basis for citizenship, became the standard for joining the national family (Rodriguez). Various ethnic and racial groups voluntarily embraced mainstream values by assimilating culturally, through language, religion, and dress, and structurally, through political participation and employment. The diversity of American experiences was neutralized by one singular vision of Americanism—*whiteness.* In "Old Poison in New Bottles," Joe Feagin illustrates the indifference that immigrants of darker complexion experience. His analysis highlights the "one-way assimilation" to Anglo-Protestant culture that has become a reality for recent immigrants (352).

While immigrant identity centered around the drive to adopt Anglo-American values and practices, and on occasion, to engage with other nonwhites, there was a degree of complexity and apprehension to the "inbetweenness" or liminal space that immigrants occupied. Since the nation's founding, the normative framework for American citizenship has been whiteness. There has been a consistent progression of ethnic groups, from Greek Americans to Polish Americans, who shed their Otherness and moved across the hyphen to whiteness and full American citizenship. Indeed, these previously ethnic groups were readily accepted because they were not marked by color, and they could all be unified in their efforts to exclude African Americans, Asian Americans, Latinos, and American Indians who could not easily traverse this racial divide. For example, "Polish workers may have developed their very self-image and honed their reputation in more or less conscious counterpoint to the stereotypical *niggerscab*" (Perea, et al. 511).

As depicted above, central to what it means to be American is, whiteness. Some groups were more easily transformed into the white norm than others. Assembling all of these attributes made it easier for new European immigrants to become white. In *Racing Justice,* john a. powell offers an interesting discussion of whiteness as a new concept that came out of the New Deal, which he argues created new meaning, structure, and practices of whiteness once identity markers were traded in for white. He conceptualizes race as a verb, rather than how it is typically perceived—as a noun or adjective, a descriptor. So, people perform race, which means that groups formally construct their identities around the singularity of whiteness—every hyphenated difference is subsumed into the concept of one America. In all of the previous examples, "the Other" is never white. No longer Irish-American or Polish-American, once they became white, these groups characterized everyone else as "Other," and fiercely embraced the singularity of American identity. This single story potentially excludes those who cannot perform this vision of Americanism.

The single story creates the tension surrounding definitions of American identity. Hyphenated American identity encompasses the full complexities and nuance of identity; it explodes the narrow concept of an American identity rooted in a single culture. Historically, the tension between hyphenation and authenticity, then, is the result of a compelled choice between the multiplicities of diverse American identities—the "hyphen" and assimilation. American policy towards indigenous people graphically illustrates the tension between multiple identities and the compulsion of American identity.

The US treatment of American Indians evinces a cyclical posture that reinforces the conception of American singularity and exceptionalism. Federal policy towards Indians shifted from outright conquest and extermination in the name of expansion (1790–1834); to allotment policies designed to obliterate tribal lands through land redistribution (1870–1887); to numerous contrived attempts at preserving Indian sovereignty (1928–1945); to termination of American Indian sovereignty and coerced assimilation (1945–1961). The termination policy was abandoned in the 1960s and 70s, and the United States again embraced a policy of self-determination for Indian peoples. This brief history demonstrates the oppressive dominance of US Indian policies, which never gave American Indians any significant independence because to do so would mean relinquishing massive parcels of property acquired through the doctrines of discovery and conquest and acknowledging that American identity is multi-faceted.

Indeed, the United States adopted a uniform policy of exclusion, revealing racial bias dating back to the founding period up to the present. In *Opening the Floodgates: Why America Needs to Rethink Its Borders and Immigration Laws*, noted immigration and critical race theory scholar Kevin Johnson offers a critical overview of the Chinese Exclusion Act (1882), which barred all Chinese immigration, and an overview of the National Origins Quota Act (1924), which used the 1890s census to limit immigration from Eastern and Southern Europe on the grounds that these "immigrant others" were not assimilating as the Western Europeans had:

Before 1952, immigrants from Asia . . . still were barred from citizenship, refused full membership in U.S. society, and denied the right to vote. National identity was a primary justification for those measures, as the nation attempted to preserve its predominantly white, Anglo-Saxon, Protestant roots. (Johnson 51)

The structure and underlying policies of immigration law perpetuate the categorization of "Otherness" by adapting the impact of the law to exclude or include depending on the expediency of the circumstances.

While racial and ethnic (group) identity continues to be a central element for many Americans, American identity, largely defined by cultural, social, and political locations, has shifted from a sense of common culture to shared values and continues to change over time. Wars and national crises also serve as catalysts for anti-hyphenation sentiment and collective national identity. For example, America's entry into World War I heightened suspicion and fear of foreigners and radicals. This suspicion fueled the notion that there was *one* America and that any form of radicalism threatened American identity. Sentiment during World War II was no different.

After the Japanese attacked Pearl Harbor, there was a general feeling that Japan was the enemy. Therefore, Japanese immigrants and Japanese-Americans, seen as potential saboteurs, capable of engaging in espionage, were also proclaimed the enemy. Italians, the largest group of American immigrants, were also marked as "alien enemies" (Wucker 81). Yet notably, only those who held Italian citizenship were interned in camps, unlike those of Japanese ancestry—regardless of citizenship—who were all subject to removal. Thus, the Second World War was characterized by what Nelson Lichtenstein refers to as a period of "patriotic assimilation," and historian Eric Foner describes as "pluralistic acceptance of cultural diversity as the only real source of harmony in a heterogenous society" (237). Foner goes on to say that by the end of World War II, "the new immigrant groups had been fully accepted as ethnic Americans, rather than members of distinct and inferior races" (237). Rather than the coercive rhetoric of the World War I period, the new rhetoric became more inclusive, reflecting a broader view of American identity.

Although postwar America of the 1950s ushered in an era of conformity, shared experiences, and conventional values, the 1960s certainly presented its own challenges. However, it was during this period that conceptions of citizenship and American identity solidified, and immigrants were really able to embrace their cultural heritage (Rodriguez). The success of the Civil Rights Movement led to significant congressional action, specifically the Immigration and Nationality Act of 1965, which "eliminated the discriminatory national-origin quota system and embraced colorblindness in immigrant admissions" (Johnson 51).

The Civil Rights Movement, along with the prominence of the multiculturalism movement of the 1970s, quelled some resistance to ethnic and racial difference and direct challenges to expanded versions of American identity. Still, multiculturalism presents what James Bond aptly calls "America's enduring challenge." Bond demonstrates the tension between popular notions of multiculturalism—"melting pot" and "tossed salad" versions. The former, he says, supports assimilation, "view[ing] racial and other differences as a danger to be kept at arm's length, rather than a value to be embraced," while the latter favors "hyphenated Americanism" as it seemingly "emphasizes the primacy of separate identities, inherited or self-constructed, over a common identity as citizens" (Bond 59). Both metaphors illustrate just how polarized contemporary views of American identity continue to be.

Conceptualizing Modern (Post-9/11) Americanism

And, just as the early founders erased the hyphenated American identity rhetorically, so, too, does the law and history. In the 1995 Supreme Court case *Adarand Constructors, Inc. v. Peña*, Justice Scalia concurred with the Court in its rejection of a federal Disadvantaged Business Enterprise program that used race as one factor in awarding highway guardrail contracts, stating that there can be no race-based remedies to assist minority construction contractors: "In the eyes of government, we are just one race here.

It is American" (Perea, et al. 635). This is a provocative assertion because it literally erases any notion of the distinct aspects that make up American identity. Scalia presents an exclusionary conception of a single American identity devoid of race and any culture deemed "un-American."

The September 11, 2001 terrorist attacks on the World Trade Center in New York City and the Pentagon in the nation's capital have fostered intense nationalism and re-focused the discussion around what it means to be American. The events of 9/11 have contributed to increased suspicion of and discomfort with the "Other," reinforcing the appeal of American singularity in identity and patriotism and movement to only one side of the hyphen. US policy toward noncitizen immigrants has led to increased naturalization—either "you're a citizen" or you will be denied active/full membership in American society. Within this context, Barack Obama's 2008 presidential campaign message—*Hope* and *Change*—is particularly appealing because it unites all Americans under a common umbrella. At a time when there is a national longing for unity and profound skepticism of anything "un-American," Obama tapped into the post-9/11 need to construct one America. This is precisely why his message resonated so well with most American voters; both displace any difference, representing one America united by hope and change. But this constructed sense of unity only creates another tension between who is American—who belongs and who does not. Obama himself is a case study of how hybridization is working now in a "post-racial" United States because he is the most powerful and visible example.

In his 2004 DNC address, "The Audacity of Hope," Obama reinforced a singular conception of national identity: "There is not a black America and a white America and Latino America and Asian America. There's the United States of America." This singular vision of America erases all of the complexity and vibrancy that *is* America. This seeming post-racial declaration of singularity obscures, to a certain extent, the American experience. Race is displaced for a revised history of American homogeneity based on nationality. Slaves and immigrants are transposed. The story can be adopted universally for any purpose without race:

> It's the hope of slaves sitting around the fire singing freedom songs; the hope of immigrants setting out for distant shores; the hope of a young naval lieutenant bravely patrolling the Mekong Delta; the hope of a millworker's son who dares to defy the odds; the hope of a skinny kid with a funny name who believes that America has a place for him, too. (Obama)

The fire is notably located on the grounds of a plantation. These immigrants cannot set out for distant shores! Obama not only parallels his life and the history of African Americans with that of the underclass of America, he conflates the experience of slaves singing freedom songs with that of immigrants seeking distant shores, so that the history of oppression and subjugation is read out of black experience and slavery becomes an immigrant story of hope: "Americanism" is central and shared. Inclusion, the touchstone, equalizes all experiences of exclusion, and racism and the present day effects of past discrimination are submerged. Obama equates racism with the schoolyard bully ("hope of a skinny kid with a funny name") and racial discrimination to a career opportunity ("hope of a millworker's son") so that racism is about economics and opportunity, and the individual will to fight. It is much easier to conceptualize a pluralistic society where individualism, hope, choice, and upward mobility are valued when race is neutralized in the societal equation. Liberal Individualism, the notion that the rights of the individual are always celebrated, is an essential feature of the singularity of American identity—all *Americans* have the same opportunity. By erasing the hyphen, there is the danger of removing difference and its underlying complications and restoring a facile conception of American identity. Still, the hyphen might also be seen as a grammar that, while it seemingly joins two words, conveys a balance that does not necessarily exist. Rather, the hyphen can also be seen as neutralizing one or the other terms rather than meshing them. In some instances, the slash is seen as a productive grammar, a true unifier that is representative of a more vital and interchangeable relationship.

Contemporary Influences

What it means to be American continues to be shaped by current immigration policies, which reflect continuing efforts to mandate assimilation, and signal limited commitment to individual rights and distinct ethnic identities. In *Opening the Floodgates*, Johnson argues that "At various times, the U.S. government has attempted to coerce immigrants and people of color [and "noncitizens"] to assimilate into the mainstream and adopt 'American' ways" (47). This strand of Americanism has been at the core of American history, policy initiatives, culture, and the law. And although there has been a shift in explicit articulations of a single American identity, Johnson makes clear that there is still subtle endorsement of singularity that is balanced with a purported tolerance of diverse cultures: "The national rise of a civil rights consciousness, and a public commitment to respect and tolerance for different cultures and peoples, changed everything. Today, it is much more difficult, although not impossible, to adopt coercive measures that mandate assimilation" (47). These coercive policies have forced non-citizens to speak English, for example, and denied or limited their membership in American society.

Voter initiative measures, such as Proposition 187 (1994), which made it illegal for undocumented workers to receive public services or benefits, and Proposition 227, which banned bilingual education in California public schools (1998), are linked by their common coercive effect. Both advance a singular American identity that those who wish to be included must choose. Proposition 187 leads to *forced assimilation,* which compels one choice—to be American. Whatever you are must blend with what it means to be American. We define that in any number of ways, but when you move from undocumented to documented status, it makes you eligible for inclusion. It is important to note, however, that *Plyer v. Doe* does hold that it is unconstitutional for children to be penalized because of their parents' status. Proposition 227 implies that upward mobility in America goes hand in hand with English fluency. Both measures act as contemporary "nationalistic narratives" that reaffirm English as America's 'public language,' and 'foreignness' as a rationale for exclusion. Acceptance is conditioned on particular cultural practices—speaking English or acquiring proper documentation for citizenship.

Standing on *Either* Side of the Hyphen?

Today, the hyphen is used by many people, for various reasons, and it works in several ways. Teresa Heinz Kerry, wife of former presidential candidate John Kerry, voiced her right to be called African American because she was born in Mozambique. Former New Jersey governor Jim McGreevey shared his orientation with the country—"My truth," he said, "is that I am a Gay American." In both cases, the hyphen is implicit. It creates a physical demarcation, as well as a political and ideological one. Heinz Kerry uses the hyphen to place herself squarely in the middle, to claim an identity that is not obvious, while McGreevey uses the hyphen to avow connection and sameness. Yet, he also clearly chooses to identify with the *other* side of the hyphen. While some see descriptors like African-American, Jewish-American, Latin-American, or Asian-American as bureaucratic words that don't take history and context into consideration, perhaps they do because these terms and self-identifications all strive to bridge the gap between distinct cultural histories and the neutralizing effect of the monolithic American. This is the true irony of the American experience; it embraces difference, while simultaneously seeking to homogenize it—the very essence of crossing the hyphen.

Disrupting homogeneity and singularity, contemporary cultural discourses embrace the concept of a complex, multifaceted American identity as central to the American experience. This rupture underscores the true resonance of identity—it is lived on many levels outside of a singular conception. In her 2009 TED Talk, "The Danger of a Single Story," celebrated Nigerian novelist Chimamanda Ngozi Adichie highlights this seminal feature—the complexity of the hyphenated identity. Adichie speaks powerfully about the need to reject a single narrative in favor of a "balance of stories" that reflect experience and expression, and while Adichie speaks specifically about the problem with defining what it means to be "authentically African," her analysis underscores what has been central to the discussion of what it means to be American: "The single story creates stereotypes, and the problem with stereotypes is not that they are untrue, but that they are incomplete. They make one story become the only story" (Adichie). Adichie cautions against showing people as one thing, or that is what they will become, and she suggests that what it means to be American has always been defined by those in power. Given this nation's history, disregard for overlapping stories, for the multiplicity of experiences, often results in a compelled choice between the diverse identities—the "hyphen" and assimilation.

The true promise of the American experience and identity must mean that this compulsory choice will be rejected. What makes the American experience unique is not a narrow conception of inclusion, but a broad-based embrace of everything that contributes to a national identity that is truly pluralistic. Crossing the hyphen should not be a barrier to inclusion—the hyphen connects a multiplicity of experiences that are truly American. That is the hope of the twenty-first century.

Works Cited

Adichie, Chimimanda Ngozi. "The Danger of a Single Story." *TED*. TEDGlobal. Jul. 2009. Web. 10 May 2014. <http://www.ted.com/talks/chimamanda_adichie_the_danger_of_a_single_story>.

Ashcroft, Bill, Gareth Griffiths, & Helen Tiffin. *Post-Colonial Studies: The Key Concepts*. London: Routledge, 2003.

_____. *The Post-Colonial Reader*. London: Routledge, 1995.

Bond, James E. "Multiculturalism: America's Enduring Challenge." *Seattle Journal for Social Justice*. 1.1 (2002): 59.

Feagin, Joe R. "Old Poison in New Bottles: The Deep Roots of Modern Nativism." *Critical White Studies: Looking Behind the Mirror*. Eds. Richard Delgado & Jean Stefancic. Philadelphia: Temple UP, 1997. 348–53.

Foner, Eric. *The Story of American Freedom.* New York: W.W. Norton, 1998.

Garraty, John A. *The American Nation: A History of the United States.* New York: Harper and Row, 1966.

Gilroy, Paul. *Against Race: Imagining Political Culture beyond the Color Line.* Cambridge: Belknap/Harvard UP, 2000.

Johnson, Kevin R. *Opening the Floodgates: Why America Needs To Rethink Its Borders and Immigration Laws.* New York: NY UP, 2007.

Link, William A., & Susannah J. Link, eds. *The Gilded Age and Progressive Era.* Malden, MA/Oxford, UK: Wiley-Blackwell, 2012.

Obama, Barack H. "The Audacity of Hope." *2004 Democratic National Convention Keynote Address.* Fleet Center, Boston. *American Rhetoric Online Speech Bank.* 27 Jul. 2004. Web. 22 Aug. 2012. <http://www.americanrhetoric.com/speeches/convention2004/barackobama2004dnc.htm>.

Perea, J. R. Delgado, A. Harris, J. Stefancic, & S. Wildman, eds. *Race and Races: Cases and Resources for a Diverse America,* 2nd ed. St. Paul, MN: Thomson/West, 2007.

Plyer v. Doe. 457 US 202. Supreme Court of the United States. 15 Jun. 1982.

powell, john a. *Racing to Justice: Transforming Our Conceptions of Self and Other to Build an Inclusive Society.* Bloomington: Indiana UP, 2012.

Renshon, Stanley A. *The 50% American: Immigration and National Identity in an Age of Terror.* Washington, DC: Georgetown UP, 2005.

Rodriguez, Gregory. "Identify Yourself: Who's American? *New York Times.* 23 Sept. 2001. Web. 22 Aug. 2012.

Sekhon, Nirej. "A Birthright Rearticulated: The Politics of Bilingual Education." *New York University Law Review.* 74.5 (November 1999): 1407–1450.

Torres-Padilla, José, & Carmen Haydee Rivera, eds. "Introduction: The Literature of the Puerto Rican Diaspora and Its Critical Practice." *Writing off the Hyphen: New Perspectives on the Literature of the Puerto Rican Diaspora.* New York UP, 2008. 1–28.

Wucker, Michele. *Lockout: Why America Keeps Getting Immigration Wrong When Our Prosperity Depends on Getting It Right.* New York: Public Affairs, 2006.

Intersecting Lives: Critics and the Literature of American Multicultural Identity_____

Jessica Boykin

Since Israel Zangwill's play *The Melting Pot* debuted in 1908, its title phrase "has become the most popular, positive description of American diversity of the twentieth century" (Carter 13). The image suggests a blending of all cultures into a common one. While the melting pot metaphor may have seemed positive or welcoming, many find it objectionable for its promotion of assimilation, erasure of disparate ethnic identities, and its exclusion, as Carter notes, of certain racial groups, such as African and Asian Americans, whom Zangwill cut from the original version of the play. Scholars have more recently turned to the image of a "salad bowl" or "mosaic." Like the word "multiculturalism," these metaphors draw attention to culturally diverse identities, but can be problematic in their suggestion that the different strands that make up American identity exist alongside of, but are separate from, one another. No single metaphor or word has been universally accepted to describe the relationships between cultural groups in the United States and the complex identities and literary forms in which they result. To draw attention to cross-cultural interaction, mixture, and negotiation, literary critics, especially since the 1990s, have deployed words, such as hybridity, hyphenation, creolization, and *mestijaze*, while also making use of images related to borders and other contact zones. These terms draw attention to the idea of inhabiting and identifying with multiple cultures and reflect not only the immigrant experience, but also that same position shared by, for instance, Native Americans, who did not immigrate, but still find themselves in a position of being "in-between" and/or of two worlds, growing up and living in the larger US culture, but also in a home or root culture that often possesses different values, mores, customs.

Literary critics invoke identity as a way of conceptualizing the relationship between an individual and the historical, cultural, and social conditions in which they live as represented in imaginative works. In doing so, they pay particular attention to the interplay between subjectivity (an individual's understanding and experience of self) and public identity (how society defines an individual). While the melting pot and cultural pluralism debate no longer dominates the conversation about identity, questions about the nature of identity have not disappeared. On one end of the spectrum are critics who posit the notion of continuous and fixed identities; on the other are those who embrace the idea that identities are fluid and constructed. And, many more positions exist in between. Despite the variety of viewpoints, there is an overlap of approaches, including close textual analysis and attention to identity markers, such as race, ethnicity, class, gender, sexuality, and national origin—and the attempt to situate texts in their particular literary, historical, and social contexts. More important, this body of criticism shares an interest in expanding the literary canon, social justice, and combating racial and ethnic stereotypes.

Authenticity: Insiders and Outsiders

The American literary landscape radically changed in the course of the Civil Rights Movement of the 1960s, when minority groups drew attention to their claim to American identity in pursuit of legal and social progress. The activism of minority groups encouraged ethnic American writers to draw from their experiences in shaping their work and to pursue more opportunities to publish.

At the same time, literary scholars began focusing their attention on defining previously ignored or neglected history, traditions, and identity. While challenging racism and ethnocentrism, however, critics initially promoted a type of literary nationalism that relied on very narrow versions of identity. For some, insisting on a unitary identity seemed an effective means of opposing and defending oneself against political and social marginalization and stereotypes. In their definition of Asian American literature, the editors of *Aiiieeeee! An Anthology of Asian American Writers* (1974) and its expanded 1991 version, *The Big Aiiieeeee!*, for example, privilege masculine, non-immigrant, and non-Christian writers to counter

Western stereotypes of inscrutable, unassimilable, and passive Asians. The introduction to the later anthology distinguishes "the real, from its sources in the Asian fairy tale and the Confucian heroic tradition" to "the fake—from its sources in Christian dogma and in Western philosophy, history, and literature" (Chan, et al. xv). The version of identity offered by the *Aiiieeeee!* editors left little room for cultural overlap; a writer was either Asian American or not.

While the movement away from racist and ethnic stereotypes started with good intentions, the insistence on authenticity proved to be limiting. In *The Romance of Authenticity: The Cultural Politics of Regional and Ethnic Literatures,* Jeff Karem argues that authenticity is "highly problematic as a category of literary analysis" (6). Determining whether a literary text is authentic or not is "always contingent; whether made by a cultural 'insider' or 'outsider,' [judgments] depend on the interpreter's own horizon of expectations regarding the culture in question" (Karem 7). The critique of David Henry Hwang's play *M. Butterfly as* "the fulfillment of white male homosexual fantasy" (Chan xiii), for example, ignores the play's interest in combating heterosexism in addition to racism. Karem also notes how "intense political and economic interests determined which aspects of . . . works would be deemed authentic, not only constraining *what* [writers] could publish but also shaping *how* their works were received and interpreted" (Karem 3). These constraints are rooted in essentialist and racist concepts of identity as illustrated in Karem's discussion of Frederick Douglass, who promoted abolitionism by sharing his experiences as a former slave. Although Douglass was an excellent speaker, the white abolitionist William Lloyd Garrison asked him to pretend to be less articulate in anticipation of an audience who might question the authenticity of Douglass' speeches and his identity as a former slave. Based on a clearly arbitrary notion of black identity that does not include literacy, Garrison's notion of authenticity ignored the complexity of Douglass' individual experience.

In *Beyond Ethnicity: Consent and Descent in American Culture,* Werner Sollors notes the connection between an emphasis on authenticity and the tendency to group writers by shared ethnicity.

This results in the separation of American literary texts rather than in an examination across cultures. By doing so, Sollors notes, readers might overlook more significant connections between writers, such as stylistic similarities, major influential works, and other "cultural interplays" (*Beyond Ethnicity* 14). Sollors also points to the problem inherent in identity politics in his observation that:

> [Ethnic American] literature is often read and evaluated against an elusive concept of authenticity, and the question of who is entitled to interpret the literature is given undue emphasis. The belief is widespread among critics who stress descent at the expense of consent that only biological insiders can understand and explicate the literature of race and ethnicity. (*Beyond Ethnicity* 11)

Sollors warns that this type of separatist perspective "assumes that there is no shared history and no human empathy, that you have your history and I have mine—in which case it becomes quite pointless to give lectures on ethnic literature" (*Beyond Ethnicity* 13).

Ethnic Invention and Social Construction

Most contemporary literary critics readily embrace the notion of fluid and contextualized identities. They highlight creativity in order to challenge narrow visions of identity and either/or thinking that create divisions and hierarchies between ethnic groups. In their depiction of identity as fluid, these critics also challenge the kind of monoculturalism inherent in the melting pot image. By stressing mutuality and highlighting the possibility of negotiation between ethnic groups, they replace the notion of assimilation where one culture is subsumed by another with the possibility of multidirectional transculturation. In *The Invention of Ethnicity,* Werner Sollors clarifies that his use of the term *invention* to describe the social construction of these categories is "not meant to evoke a conspiratorial interpretation of a manipulative inventor who single-handedly makes ethnics out of unsuspecting subjects, but to suggest widely shared, though intensely debated, collective fictions that are continually reinvented" (*Invention* xi). According to Sollors, these collective fictions are largely unconscious and unintentional in individuals, but are deeply embedded in American culture and even literary studies. Sollors describes how these fictions about the inherent differences between groups are present in the work of some "literary critics [who] easily succumb to the danger of resorting to an implicit 'good vibes' methodology. . . grounding close readings of texts on static notions of descent and on primordial, organicist, sometimes even biological—but in all cases largely unquestioned—concepts of ethnic group membership" (*Beyond Ethnicity* 11). In response to the stereotypes present in scholarship and society more generally, Sollors encourages readers to investigate the process of *imagining* ethnic identity rather than "settling on a fixed encyclopedia of supposed cultural essentials" (*Beyond Ethnicity* xv, my emphasis).

In *Loose Canons: Note on the Culture Wars*, Henry Louis Gates, Jr., also highlights the "imagining" or social construction of identity categories, but unlike Sollors, he turns his attention to race. He urges scholars to undertake detective work to unearth underlying prejudices and assumptions within literary theory: "We must, of course, analyze the ways in which writing relates to 'race,' how attitudes toward racial differences generate and structure literary texts by us and about us; we must determine how critical methods can effectively disclose the traces of racial difference in literature" (Gates 69). Reading texts with a critical eye can show readers how identity categories like race have been socially constructed and can lead to new techniques for revealing these constructions to readers. Gates calls on scholars to scrutinize "the language of contemporary criticism itself, recognizing that hermeneutical systems, especially, are not 'universal,' 'color-blind,' or 'apolitical,' or 'neutral'" (69).

Gates uncovers the Western bias and racial prejudice in conversations about the American literary canon: which works of literature are most influential and representative of our culture. He argues that "once the concept of value became encased in the belief in a canon of texts whose authors purportedly shared a 'common culture' inherited from both the Greco-Roman and the Judeo-Christian traditions, no one need speak of matters of 'race' since 'the race' of these authors was 'the same'" (Gates 47). By calling into question the validity of a "common culture" proposed by Western scholars, Gates highlights how social construction has contributed to the distortion of the canon. Many scholars have criticized formulations of the literary canon, which present only a homogenous group of white, Protestant, male writers. To counteract this tendency, they have developed interpretive theories of inclusion, which allow minority cultures and multicultural voices to be seen and heard.

The investigation of race and ethnicity as markers of identity has also led to a re-examination of the meaning of "whiteness." As Maria Lauret notes in the introduction to *Beginning Ethnic American Literatures*, ethnic identity "tends to come about through the experience of marginality (economic and political, as well as cultural)—which is why dominant groups usually do not conceive of themselves in ethnic terms at all" (Lauret 4). Dominant groups tend to think of themselves as normal or universal because of their ability to regulate definitions of normality and universality. Mat Johnson illustrates this perfectly in his graphic novel *Incognegro: A Graphic Mystery* (2008). The novel's journalist-protagonist, Zane Pinchback, crosses identity borders because he understands the ways identity is socially constructed. While he recognizes that social roles are performed, members of the dominant culture do not: "That's what white folks never get. They don't think they have **accents**. They don't think they eat **ethnic** foods. Their music is **classical**. They think they're just **normal**. That they are the **universal**, and that everyone else is an odd **deviation** from form" (Johnson 19).

Working against the narrative of universality are critics who examine the social construction, normalization, and domination of "whiteness." In *Playing in the Dark*, Toni Morrison participates in the deconstruction of white identity through her examination of "American Africanism," or "the denotative and connotative blackness that African peoples have come to signify, as well as the entire range of views, assumptions, readings, and misreadings that accompany Eurocentric learning about these people" (Morrison 7). Morrison explains her aim to illuminate deeper interpretations of literature by revealing how critics have ignored or covered up black presence in classic American works (9). Through her examination of "willful critical blindness" (18), Morrison intends to ascertain "the nature—even the cause—of literary 'whiteness'" and answer the question, "What parts do the invention and development of whiteness play in the construction of what is loosely described as 'American'?" (9). Pursuing these incisive questions into the creation of white American hegemonic culture, Morrison destabilizes Eurocentric constructions and calls into question notions about universality.

Hybridity and Multicultural Identity

The term "hybridity" has been especially popular in literary studies focused on identity issues. Borrowed from the field of biology, in which it refers to the product of a cross-species union, it was used pejoratively in nineteenth-century racial discourse. Associated with the idea of miscegenation, "hybrid" described individuals whose parents were from different racial groups, and it implied impurity, degradation, even inferiority. Following the lead of cultural and postcolonial critic Homi K. Bhabha, the image of hybridity has more recently been recuperated from its association with racial categories and applied to culture, particularly "the creation of new transcultural forms within the contact zone produced by colonization" (Ashcroft 108). For Bhabha, hybridity is not merely the co-existence of cultures or the erasure of one or both. Instead it refers to an interaction or blending that results in what he calls the "Third Space of enunciations." Characterized by creativity, Bhabha's third space enables a variety of identities and challenges narrow visions of identity and either/or thinking that create divisions and hierarchies between ethnic groups. In its depiction of identity as fluid, hybridity also challenges monoculturalism.

Despite the popularity of hybridity as a framework for understanding multicultural American identity, the term has been criticized for its lack of specificity. Invocations of hybridity by literary critics are often contradictory and are sometimes conflated with notions of universality. Asserting that all cultures and identities are hybrid does not allow for very deep analysis. Making sense of the competing uses can be challenging. In general, criticism concerned with literary representations of hybridity and other forms of cross cultural contact present two conflicting, but equally convincing "narratives." One emphasizes plurality and creativity (in form and identity) and tends to be optimistic. In this version, hybridity expressed in literature is presented as evidence of agency and resistance to racism and ethnocentrism. Holly E. Martin, in *Writing Between Cultures: A Study of Hybrid Narratives in Ethnic Literature of the United States,* draws upon this positive vision of hybridity in her comparative exploration of narrative forms and tropes, which bridge and synthesize multiple cultures. Citing *The Woman Warrior* as an example, Martin highlights how Maxine Hong Kingston "goes beyond the two worldviews [Chinese and American] to a third alternative—one that allows her not only to accept both cultures and their interactions, but also to perceive what it is to live beyond the limitations of any one particular cultural view" (Martin 1).

In "North America as Contact Zone: Native American Literary Nationalism and the Cross-Cultural Dilemma," a survey of literary criticism concerned with Native American literature, Christopher Taylor describes an approach similar to that of Martin, which he describes as "outward-facing cosmopolitanism"; in opposition are "theorists favoring an inward-facing nationalism" (Taylor 26). While cosmopolitanism tends to be comparative in its attempt to draw out the relationships of a particular ethnic group with others, the latter focuses on one particular group in its attempt to identify specific cultural contexts from which literary texts emerge. The latter group's version of hybridity is less positive. Framing interpretation within the history of colonialism, slavery, anti-immigration legislation, and racism, this version reminds us that not all cultural contact is intentional nor beneficial for people of color. Here, hybridity threatens to erase difference and maintain the status quo. Taylor notes: "In their rush to destabilize identity, [critics interested in hybridity], risk erasing First Nations survival in and contributions to North American history" (31). Taylor, himself, proposes a "middle ground" in his reading of Sherman Alexie's *Reservation Blues,* one that will "account for both the internal, national aspects of Native texts and the multicultural milieu that has affected North American cultures so profoundly" (43).

Intersectionality: Race, Class, Gender, and Sexuality

The insistence on an authentic or unitary identity unfortunately reproduces the marginalization it sought to dismantle. Black feminists, for example, argued that attempts to define identity in masculine terms denied the importance of gender and sexuality to identity. In "Toward a Black Feminist Criticism," Barbara Smith calls for "a Black feminist approach to literature that embodies the realization that the politics of sex as well as the politics of race and class are crucially interlocking factors in the works of Black women writers" (170). Gloria Anzaldúa likewise discusses the necessity of linking ethnicity and gender when analyzing marginalized identities. In *Borderlands/La Frontera,* she describes "machismo" as an "Anglo invention," a projection of their own feelings of insecurity onto Chicano identity. "Machismo," she argues, is not an innate trait and is instead prompted by "oppression and poverty and low self-esteem. It is the result of hierarchical male dominance" (Anzaldúa 105). In a similar vein, King-Kok Cheung's *Articulate Silences: Hisaye Yamamoto, Maxine Hong Kingston, Joy Kogawa* undermines the stereotype of Asian female passivity by demonstrating the power of silence. In doing so, Cheung challenges patriarchy in both Asian and Anglo American cultures.

While Anzaldúa and Cheung highlight the importance of looking for connections between gender and ethnic stereotypes, Paula Gunn Allen urges readers to employ multiple cultural perspectives when analyzing cultural representations, especially those with which they have no or little familiarity. The cultural bias of the translator inevitably shapes his or her perception of the materials being translated, often in ways that he or she is unaware. Culture is fundamentally a shaper of perception, after all, and perception is shaped by culture in many subtle ways" (Allen 225). In her essay on the translation of Native American writing, Allen argues that "male bias has seriously skewed our understanding of tribal life and philosophy, distorting it in ways that are sometimes obvious but are most often invisible" (222). As a corrective, Allen prescribes an interpretive strategy that takes into consideration multiple perspectives. As a model, she provides three readings of the traditional Keres yellow woman story, which Allen describes as: Keres, "modern feminist," and "feminist-tribal." Approaching American Indian literature with a feminist-tribal reading, one that takes into consideration gender, sexuality, race, and culture, allows Allen to show "not only the exploitations and oppression of the tribes by whites and white government but also areas of oppression within the tribes and the sources and nature of that oppression" (223). This multi-layered approach provides an example of how an individual is influenced and informed by multiple identity categories, all of which contribute to their perception of literature and the world.

Leslie Petty, in "The 'Dual'-ing Images of la Malinche and la Virgen de Guadalupe in Cisneros' *The House on Mango Street*," focuses on representations of women—one bad, the other good— in the interplay between culture and gender that form women's identities. Petty explains that the novel's dichotomous archetypes which she finds,

> embodied in the stories of la Malinche, the violated woman, and la Virgen de Guadalupe, the holy Mother, sharply define female roles in Mexican culture based on female sexuality; however, as historical and mythical figures, these two archetypes take on both political and social significance that also influence perceptions of femininity in the Latin American world. (Petty 120)

Though the novel sets up binary prototypes for the women in the story, Cisneros ultimately resists them: "Esperanza is neither 'good' nor 'bad'; she encompasses traits of both the Virgin and la Malinche . . . she sees her life, like her dream house, as a space 'clean as paper before the poem' (108), with potential for creativity, autonomy, and most importantly, self-definition" (Petty 131). Esperanza exists outside the dichotomy set out for her, innovatively constructing her own identity.

Scholars also note the intersections of race, ethnicity, gender, and/or sexuality on literary form. In *Unsettling the Bildungroman:*

Reading Contemporary Ethnic American Women's Fiction, Stella Bolaki examines the way female writers adapt and change a genre devoted to tracing identity development. In a discussion of *The House on Mango Street*, Bolaki explores Cisneros' use of a "hybrid" form of the *Bildungsroman,* which highlights the tensions between self and family or community, a common trope in the genre that finds new significance in ethnic writing and women's writing, as these groups have historically faced pressure to assimilate to mainstream culture:

> While the traditional *Bildungroman* traces a young hero's development by portraying his journey out into the world, many ethnic American texts . . . examine their protagonists' complicated attachments to the spaces and communities in which they already live. Individualisation . . . takes place within an ethnic framework, and instead of idealizing movement, they often explore more nuanced forms of mobility mediating the appeal of individualism. (88)

Invoking Anzaldúa's work, Bolaki suggests that *The House on Mango Street* opens "an intermediate or 'third space,' in other words, 'a consciousness of the borderlands,' needs to be invented for our readings, one that makes room for a clash of interpretations and in which contradictions turn out to be productive" (Bolaki 131).

Conclusion

Recognizing that the traditional representation of American identity is outmoded is the first step to creating a more inclusive national narrative. Investigating the construction of American identity through the homogenous representations in the literary canon, prejudiced language in literature and theory, and perhaps most importantly, what perspectives are not represented, can reveal holes within the national narrative. As scholars and writers address the problematic representations, or lack of representations, in the field of literature, they work to construct a more cohesive and multicultural narrative of American experience. As more works of multicultural literature are written and added to theoretical discourse, they open new spaces and opportunities for explorations of American identity.

Works Cited

Allen, Paula Gunn. *The Sacred Hoop: Recovering the Feminine in American Indian Traditions.* 1986. Boston: Beacon, 1992.

Anzaldúa, Gloria. *Borderlands/La Frontera.* 2nd ed. San Francisco: Aunt Lute, 1999.

Ashcroft, Bill, Gareth Griffiths, & Helen Tiffin. "Hybridity." *Post-Colonial Studies: The Key Concepts.* 1998. London & New York: Routledge, 2000. 96–99.

Bolaki, Stella. *Unsettling the Bildungsroman: Reading Contemporary Ethnic American Women's Fiction.* New York: Rodopi, 2011.

Carter, Greg. *The United States of the United Races: A Utopian History of Racial Mixing.* New York & London: New York UP, 2013.

Chan, Jeffrey Paul, Frank Chin, Lawson Fusao Inada, & Shawn Wong, eds. *The Big Aiiieeeee! An Anthology of Chinese American and Japanese American Literature.* New York: Meridian, 1991.

Gates, Henry Louis, Jr. *Loose Canons: Notes on the Culture Wars.* New York: Oxford UP, 1992.

Johnson, Mat, & Warren Pleece. *Incognegro.* New York: DC Comics, 2012.

Karem, Jeff. *The Romance of Authenticity: The Cultural Politics of Regional and Ethnic Literatures.* Charlottesville: U of Virginia P, 2004.

Lauret, Maria. Introduction. *Beginning Ethnic American Literatures.* Eds. Helena Grice, Candida Hepworth, Maria Lauret, & Martin Padget. Manchester: Manchester UP, 2001.

Martin, Holly E. *Writing Between Cultures: A Study of Hybrid Narratives in Ethnic Literature of the United States.* Jefferson, NC: McFarland, 2011.

Morrison, Toni. *Playing in the Dark: Whiteness and the Literary Imagination.* Cambridge, MA: Harvard UP, 1992.

Petty, Leslie. "The 'Dual'-ing Images of la Malinche and la Virgen de Guadalupe in Cisneros' *The House on Mango Street*." *MELUS* 25.2 (2000): 119–132. Web. JSTOR. 5 Apr. 2014.

Smith, Barbara. "Toward a Black Feminist Criticism." *The New Feminist Criticism.* Ed. Elaine Showalter. New York: Pantheon, 1985. 168–85.

Sollors, Werner. *Beyond Ethnicity: Consent and Descent in American Culture*. New York: Oxford UP, 1986.

_____. *The Invention of Ethnicity*. New York: Oxford UP, 1989.

Taylor, Christopher. "North America as Contact Zone: Native American Literature and the Cross-Cultural Dilemma." *Studies in American Indian Literatures* 22.3 (Fall 2010): 26–44.

Sherman Alexie and the Absolute Truth of Double-Consciousness

Kathryn West

> I will tell you something about stories
> [he said]
> They aren't just entertainment.
> Don't be fooled.
> They are all we have, you see,
> all we have to fight off
> illness and death.
>
> You don't have anything if you don't have the stories.
> (Leslie Marmon Silko, *Ceremony*)

The Absolutely True Diary of a Part-Time Indian (2006), Sherman Alexie's first young adult novel, brought the author his first National Book Award, but has also been banned by a number of school boards and libraries in several states, such as Idaho, Kentucky, Missouri, Oregon, Washington, and Wisconsin, among others, for its strong language, discussion of masturbation, and depictions of alcoholism. These challenges were not Alexie's first brush with controversy—that has followed him throughout his career, in part due to his outspoken and often sharply sarcastic persona. First, a little about Alexie that illuminates his connection to the protagonist of this novel, known as Junior on the reservation and Arnold when off it.

Like Arnold, Alexie is of Spokane/Coeur d'Alene heritage and grew up on the Spokane reservation, where his father drove trucks and his mother was an elementary school teacher; his father was an alcoholic. Also Alexie was born hydrocephalic and was not expected to survive the operations that he had to undergo as an infant. However, he exceeded all expectations, and, although left with some brain scarring that caused seizures and other childhood problems, he reports that he first read John Steinbeck's *The Grapes of Wrath* at age five (and fell in love with it). In *The Absolutely True Diary*, at age fourteen, after being given a math textbook that had his mother's maiden name recorded in it as an earlier user, Arnold becomes so disgusted that he throws the book at Mr. P, his math teacher, and hits him in the face with it. After Arnold is suspended from school, Mr. P visits him at home to tell Arnold he must leave the reservation, that there is no hope for him there: "You have to take your hope and go somewhere where other people have hope" (Alexie, *Absolutely True* 43). It is a ringing indictment of the lack of opportunity and sense of hopelessness that has plagued many reservations for over a century. Arnold transfers to an off-reservation school twenty-two miles away, in the small, rural white town of Reardan, as did Alexie when he was a teenager.

As these brief facts suggest, *The Absolutely True Diary* is heavily autobiographical, but it is not strictly so. Alexie's decision to go to school off reservation was made in order to earn the credits necessary to apply to colleges as much as it was in reaction to the math book. At the age of fourteen, within the space of four months, Alexie witnessed the death not of three people close to him, as does Arnold in the novel, but of *seven* family members and friends. The novel is set in the late 1990s rather than during Alexie's own teenage years of the 1970s and early '80s. This allows, among other things, the exchange of emails between Arnold and friends and family members, especially Arnold's sister, Mary, after she unexpectedly runs away from the reservation to marry. This change in timeframe also allows Alexie to invoke a mode of communication familiar to contemporary teenagers, while not being required to adjust to any significant change in circumstances on the Spokane reservation between the 1970s/80s and the late 1990s.

Alexie, in his life, and his protagonist Arnold, in the novel, both *choose* a heightened state of double-consciousness by transferring to an off-reservation school. In other words, Arnold places himself— self-awarely—in a position of increased psychological discomfort, alienation, and isolation. What would bring someone to choose such a fraught position? Indeed, he experiences some physical danger as well as cognitive dissonance through this choice. The more typical move for human beings is to seek consonance, to choose situations that represent comfort, safety, and a minimum of conflicting beliefs. Arnold's choice is, arguably, made easier by his long experience of being bullied on the reservation. Yet the primary answer, of course, is that he does it to break away from poverty and the prevalence of poor health and alcoholism on reservations and to open up new opportunities for a better—both material and self-fulfilled—life.

Through the insistent presence of doubles in the novel, Alexie explores the realities of poverty and the complicated ramifications of Arnold's (and his own) choice to try to leave it behind. This decision to break from the geographical location of one's own culture in search of better economic opportunities echoes in microcosm that made by millions of immigrants throughout US history. Although the off-reservation school is only twenty-two miles from his home, culturally it represents as much distance as has crossing oceans for others. Reading *The Absolutely True Diary* through the lens of ethnic studies, with its understandings of hybridity, multiculturalism, and double-consciousness, demonstrates that one does not have to be mixed race or an immigrant to the United States in order to face such concerns, and it helps us to discern the distinctive shape they take for contemporary American Indians. An ethnic studies approach to literary texts draws from multiple disciplines, including history, anthropology, and psychology to highlight the particular perspectives and experiences of those who have been underrepresented in the United States. For instance, to better understand Arnold, we can invoke the oral history/memoir of Gabriel Horn, contemporary Native writer and teacher, who similarly describes his identity struggles as a young man: "Are you a real Indian? . . . I was only a kid trying to find a niche in the world and escape the government and self-inflicted cultural genocide that one day in the not too distant future may show the Indian on paper as not existing at all" (67).

A Legacy of Loss

Ethnic studies approaches emphasize the particular experience of a minority group. So it is important to understand how Native peoples of the North and South American continents are positioned differently from all other ethnic and racial groups when considering hybridity and the American experience. Toni Morrison, Ralph Ellison, Alice Walker, James Baldwin, Langston Hughes—all eminent voices of the African American experience—come primarily from people whose ancestors were forced into a hybrid life on this continent, a life made up of what could be preserved from ancestral African traditions, of what was forced on African Americans by slaveholders and, later, segregationist and unequal practices, of what was chosen by individuals sorting their way through the values and habits and manners available to them. By the mid- to late nineteenth and into the twentieth century, Asian American immigrants, South Asian immigrants, and most Latino/a peoples found themselves in a country that had amalgamated and created a sense of "American" culture, one each new group had to accommodate to some degree or another, engaging hybridity. And each ethnic group faced discrimination particular to it. Native Americans, despite their centuries-long presence on these lands, found themselves faced with the expectation of either assimilating to the "American" way of doing things or, literally, vanishing. Disease and centuries of wars with European settlers decimated the population to approximately 275,000 by the 1880s. Once no longer under physical attack, after being settled on reservations, Native American cultures and ways of life remained targets for obliteration through the boarding school system, the Allotment Acts, and laws forbidding native religions. In the (probable) words of Colonel Richard Pratt, a veteran of the "Indian wars" and founder of the boarding school system, "Kill the Indian and Save the Man." In 1915, at the Panama-Pacific International Exposition in San Francisco, James Earle Fraser, a noted sculptor, exhibited a huge version of his piece "The End of The Road," a statue of an Indian man slumped over his horse. Zane Grey, noted author of Westerns, published *The Vanishing American* in 1925, recording the injustices faced by Navajos despite their voluntary service for the United States in World War I. It was made into a popular silent film shortly after publication. These works of art epitomized the most prevalent belief about American Indian identity at the time: they were a defeated people, soon to vanish from the earth. As Arnold notes, "Reservations were meant to be prisons, you know? Indians were supposed to move onto reservations and die. We were supposed to disappear" (Alexie, *Absolutely True* 216).

Horrific physical and psychological violence accompanied the re-positioning of Native Americans from their own ancestral lands, just as with those who came from other lands, but the historical and geographic differences created a different reality for American Indians. Can the phenomenon and dilemma so cogently outlined by W. E. B. Du Bois as double-consciousness in 1903 offer any resonance for understanding Native American identity? In his often quoted passage from *The Souls of Black Folk*, Du Bois noted that African Americans found themselves "always looking at one's self through the eyes of others, of measuring one's soul by the tape of a world that looks on in amused contempt and pity" (299). This produces what Du Bois calls a "twoness . . . two souls, two thoughts, two unreconciled strivings; two warring ideals in one dark body" (299). How does one reconcile growing up in (at least) two different communities—the ethnic home and the so-called mainstream United States? How to reconcile their different customs, values, manners, goals? How to operate within both when the larger has historically looked down upon one's skin color, one's race, one's very existence? Comparative ethnic studies tells us to read with care the distinctions, historical and cultural, between races and ethnicities. However, it also points us toward the valuable comparisons to be drawn, particularly in terms of the psychological ramifications for identity when living a multicultural life or living in a second-class position, according to the biases of many in a society. What does it mean for identity when one is growing up on a native reservation within and surrounded by, but also carefully delineated from, the United States? Might the concept of double-consciousness help us understand that position? A scene from *Smoke Signals* (1998), a film written by Sherman Alexie, offers some quick insight into how he views it. As two young Spokane men board a bus to Arizona, two female friends tell them to be sure they have their passports because they are going "into a whole different country." When they reply,

"But it's the United States," they are told: "Damn right it is. That's as foreign as it gets. Hope you two got your vaccinations!"

Drawing Bicultural Identities

Alexie "doubles" his narration of *The Absolutely True Diary* by using two media: he writes a traditional novel, but also includes cartoons and pictures drawn by Ellen Forney. Arnold hopes to become a cartoonist and Forney's pictures represent his work. In a striking illustration early in the text, we see a teenage boy split down the middle (Alexie, *Absolutely True* 57). The left-hand side represents a white teenager, with a Ralph Lauren shirt, ergonomic backpack, and the latest Air Jordans. According to captions, he has "a bright future," "positive role models," and "hope." The other side of the split body depicts an Indian teenager, wearing canvas tennis shoes and a Kmart t-shirt and carrying his books in a Glad garbage bag. He also carries "a vanishing past," "a family history of diabetes and cancer," and "bone-crushing reality." Forney and Alexie report working closely together on the illustrations, and on display here are his trademark combination of sharp humor and even sharper critique of the way the United States has shaped Indian life (Alexie prefers "Indian" to "Native American" or "American Indian," terminology often used by academics). The white teenager faces a bright future built on positive role models and hope, supported by nice clothes and technology. The Indian teenager, rather than perceiving a future, feels himself a product of a vanishing past and looks forward to bone-crushing reality, while garbed in cheap clothes and bearing only a garbage bag for his possessions—after all, in comparison, they are cheap and relatively worthless. He faces more poverty, lack of opportunity, and poor health from the family history of diabetes and cancer. Although a growing problem in our population as a whole, diabetes is absolutely rampant on reservations across the country, thanks, in no small part, to commodity foods. According to the CDC, men and women living on reservations are more than two-and-a-half times as likely to be diagnosed with diabetes compared to the rest of the US population, and they are almost twice as likely to die from it. Poverty rates on reservations across the country range from fourteen to eighty-six percent; the Spokane Reservation poverty rate in 2009 (three years after the publication of *The Absolutely True Diary*) was forty-three percent, with sixteen percent at extreme poverty levels.

Alongside that image of the split teenager and slightly earlier in the text is a smaller illustration depicting Arnold standing by a road sign with one arrow pointing toward the "Rez," where he has lived all of his fourteen years and, thus, is "home," while the opposite arrow offers Hope, but also uncertainty, indicated by "? ? ?" (Alexie, *Absolutely True* 43). The reservation or "rez" is not an easy place for Arnold; beyond poverty and lack of educational opportunity, he is perceived as different and, thus, often bullied. Yet the arrow pointing toward Hope might be even more dangerous—it leads to the unknown. The two-sidedness and doubles inherent in these and many other illustrations point up the almost overdetermined presence of doubles in Alexie's novel. These external doubles reflect Arnold's inner turmoil as he negotiates living on the reservation and going off reservation to the small white town for school.

In other words, doubles abound within Alexie's largely autobiographical text. Karen Jorgensen has noted in Alexie's first novel, *Reservation Blues* (1995) a similar strategy of using doppelgängers, one from the white world and one from the Native, to highlight the connections and differences in cultural conditions. In *The Absolutely True Diary*, the doubling leads us also to consider how this intersects with the concepts of double-consciousness and hybridity, and what it reflects about Arnold's—and his creator's— life. A key point that makes this exploration so valuable and compelling is that Alexie and Arnold *choose* to live lives poised around double-consciousness. What does it mean for W. E. B. Du Bois' important conceptual insight into the pressures placed on the psyches of African Americans and those of other of mixed racial or cultural heritage in the United States to become a choice a person takes on, in order to better his or her opportunities?

The Power of Poverty Versus the Strength of Imagination

Much earlier than *The Absolutely True Diary*, Alexie had landscaped characters' imaginations against backgrounds of poverty and documented how it limits and warps perceptions of possibilities. In *The Lone Ranger and Tonto Fistfight in Heaven* (1993), imagination, represented by the reservation storyteller, Thomas Builds-the-Fire, occupies a vexed place: storytelling, an imaginative endeavor, is often avoided and derided by people on his reservation, for it stands for community and reminds them that, with so many individuals suffering from alcoholism and poverty, they may not be functioning as a real community. Even more telling, in regard to the fear and contempt with which his communities often view Thomas, is the problematic oscillation of imagination toward nostalgia. Thomas' stories often draw on American Indian history. When personal history includes the decimation and genocide of much of one's ancestral population and the loss of the majority of the land upon which they once lived, being reminded of it may be more of a paralyzing than empowering experience. In "The Trial of Thomas Builds-the-Fire," Thomas is described as "dangerous" because of his "storytelling fetish accompanied by an extreme need to tell the truth" (Alexie, *The Lone Ranger* 93). Thomas is dangerous to the Bureau of Indian Affairs (BIA) and the white judicial system that condemns him to "back-to-back life sentences" because he so vividly describes the injustices visited upon his people. On other occasions, however, he is viewed as equally dangerous by his fellow Spokanes because his stories, combining past, present, and future, remind them of what they've lost, what they currently live without, and what they sometimes fear to hope for. Riding in a bus to Walla Walla State Penitentiary, Thomas is accompanied by:

> six other prisoners: four African men, one Chicano, and a white man from the smallest town in the state. . . . Thomas looked at these five men who share his skin color, at the white man who shared this bus which was going to deliver them into a new kind of reservation, barrio, ghetto, logging-town tin shack. (Alexie, *The Lone Ranger* 103)

Alexie dramatizes the vested interest of those in power to quash and repress Thomas, the storyteller and the imagination of his community, for Thomas not only recognizes the inequities of the economic system that depends upon the labor of the brown-skinned and the poor, but he may hold the key to alternate possibilities, alternate realities, through his storytelling. In this story, Alexie most straightforwardly suggests the danger of imagination on the part of the oppressed to those in power and perhaps also dramatizes the double position he sees himself occupying: dangerous to the reservation he left behind, telling stories that aren't always flattering about them and reminding them of their histories of loss; dangerous to mainstream US readers by reminding the country of the injustices visited upon its first inhabitants.

In the closing passage of "Imagining the Reservation," also from *The Lone Ranger*, Alexie alternates between the concrete and the abstract:

> Imagine every Skin on the reservation is the new lead guitarist for the Rolling Stones. . . . Imagine forgiveness is sold 2 for 1. . . . Didn't you know? Imagination is the politics of dreams; imagination turns every word into a bottle rocket. . . . Imagine an escape. Imagine that your own shadow on the wall is a perfect door. Imagine a song stronger than penicillin. . . . Imagine a story that puts wood in the fireplace. (153)

Here is the concrete magazine cover to the abstract dream. Alexie reminds us of the double-edged nature of imagination: potentials and escapes, both double-edged in their own right. Precisely the dilemma that Arnold faces in his decision to attend the off-reservation, white high school, where other than the school mascot, he will be the only Indian. And yet, Arnold dares to not only imagine, but seek out a different reality for himself, although in that process he will exacerbate the double-consciousness he already feels.

When Arnold reflects on poverty in *The Absolutely True Diary*, Alexie offers a less lyrical, but just as powerful, description:

> But we reservation Indians don't get to realize our dreams. We don't get those chances. Or choices. We're just poor. That's all we are.
>   It sucks to be poor, and it sucks to feel that you somehow *deserve* to be poor. You start believing that you're poor because you're stupid

and ugly. And then you start believing that you're stupid and ugly because you're Indian. And because you're Indian you start believing you're destined to be poor. It's an ugly circle and *there's nothing you can do about it.*

Poverty doesn't give you strength or teach you lessons about perseverance. No, poverty only teaches you how to be poor. (13)

Thus, Arnold makes the choice to oscillate between reservation life and the white town, to live with a double-consciousness, in order to learn how to be something other than poor.

Structural Doubling and Basketball

In addition to employing a number of doubled or mirrored characters in *The Absolutely True Diary*, Alexie also weaves in a number of concepts and events that are replayed differently later in the novel. His parents are depicted in only one image each on page twelve, but there is an inherent doubleness: the title for the illustration is "Who My Parents Would Have Been If Somebody Had Paid Attention to Their Dreams." The reality of their lives is not depicted; the drawing concentrates on what they could have been: Arnold's mother is not Spokane Falls Community College Teacher of the Year 1992–1998, with a stylish bob from Vidal Sassoon, and his father is not the Fifth Best Jazz Sax Player West of the Mississippi. Their lived reality stays undelineated, but is nevertheless quite present, again suggesting a two-sidedness to the message and highlighting the force of poverty in their lives. Mr. P of the math book incident is drawn in caricature as very short ("4' tall") with large ears and nose (Alexie, *Absolutely True* 29); "Coach" at Reardan High is "maybe 5' tall" and similarly sports large ears and nose (Alexie, *Absolutely True* 137). Paralleling the crucial advice from Mr. P to leave the reservation for better schooling and better opportunities, Coach spends the night in Arnold's hospital room after Arnold has been injured in a basketball game. Notably, Arnold does not share with us any advice he may have received from Coach:

We told each other many stories.
But I never repeat those stories.

That night belongs to just me and my coach. (Alexie, *Absolutely True* 149)

Here Alexie represents the deep importance of mentors to teenagers, one on the rez and one off.

On the reservation, Arnold's best friend is Rowdy, a young boy whose violent home life is reflected by the violence with which he faces the world around him. Yet Arnold knows that Rowdy loves and laughs uproariously at *Archie* comic books. Rowdy serves as Arnold's defender as they grow up, until Arnold starts attending the white school. Rowdy reacts with rage, even seriously injuring Arnold in a basketball game, when Arnold plays for his new school. At Reardan, Arnold becomes friends with Gordon—Gordy, even the names suggesting a doppelgänger effect. Gordy teaches Arnold how to study and how to take pleasure in the "metaphorical boners" to be had from intellectual pursuits. On reservation, Arnold looks up to and cares deeply for his sister Mary; at Reardan High, he develops a crush on Penelope, one of the most popular high school girls. Mary suffers from very low self-esteem and spends most of her time in the family basement before she elopes. Although popular, Penelope suffers from bulimia. As Jorgensen notes in regard to Alexie's use of doppelgängers in *Reservation Blues*, they "illustrate the dynamics Alexie observes between the Indian and the non-Indian worlds" (26). The depressed Spokane girl tries to hide from the world, while the insecure white girl tries to shape herself to meet a consumer-oriented ideal of body size. Neither avenue is healthy, but there is an active aspect to Penelope's approach that contrasts with the passivity of Mary's.

When Arnold's grandmother dies, he is re-admitted to his tribal community as they mourn and celebrate a woman all considered authentic and "real" in the best senses of those words. Her opposite appears at her funeral: Billionaire Ted. He has spent millions collecting Indian artifacts and proclaiming his spiritual affinity for native life. He comes bearing a pow wow dress he believes belonged to Arnold's grandmother, but he is sent away amid much laughter when told it isn't even from their tribe. Billionaire Ted works as a doppelgänger of the evil twin brand to Arnold: he, too, chooses a more bicultural way of life, but he does so in an obnoxious and self-serving way, buying up artifacts of a heritage that isn't his own.

Characters are not the only doubled presences in the novel. In particular, two important basketball games between Welpinit and Reardan high schools mirror each other. In the first, held on reservation, the entire tribe turns its back on Arnold when he enters the gym with the Reardan team. "It was a fricking awesome display of contempt," as Arnold says (Alexie, *Absolutely True* 144). He is injured by Rowdy, and Rearden loses by thirty points. A series of deaths of people close to Arnold occurs between the two games. When Arnold's grandmother is killed by a drunk driver, her death signals the end of a symbol of his physical heritage on the reservation, and his re-admittance, albeit never to be wholly accepted, back into the community. The Billionaire Ted episode then highlights how his choice to identify with Indians differs so dramatically from Arnold's part-time Indian identity. On the reservation, a close family friend dies, and Arnold's sister burns to death in her new home, while in Reardan, Arnold begins making friends and growing closer to Penelope. In the second basketball game, held at Reardan, Arnold's team beats Welpinit soundly, and he is the hero of the game. However, in the midst of the celebration, he becomes sick at the realization of what the loss means for HIS people. An illustration highlights his moment of double-consciousness (Alexie, *Absolutely True* 182): "Who AM I?" He imagines himself as a devil in the Wellpinit gym and an angel in the Reardan gym. In the narration, he looks over at Rowdy and the Wellpinit team:

> I knew that two or three of those Indians might not have eaten breakfast that morning. No food in the house. I knew that seven or eight of those Indians lived with drunken mothers and fathers. I knew that one of those Indians had a father who dealt crack and meth. I knew two of those Indians had fathers in prison. I knew that none of them were going to college. Not one of them. . . . I was suddenly ashamed that I'd wanted so badly to take revenge on them. I was suddenly ashamed of my anger, my rage, and my pain. (Alexie, *Absolutely True* 195)

In the final chapter, Arnold and Rowdy talk, and Rowdy admits he always knew Arnold would and should leave the reservation, but couldn't help being enraged by that fact. Like the protagonist of another young adult novel, Sandra Cisneros' Esperanza in *The House on Mango Street*, Arnold will leave his childhood home, but will always have the reservation in his heart and as a part of his identity, and will report the reality of reservation life even when he is no longer living there. Once that is established, he can again play basketball with best friend Rowdy, this time without keeping score. Both young men have come to accept Arnold's identity as a part-time Indian, with all the pain and the possibility that entails.

Works Cited

Alexie, Sherman. *The Absolutely True Diary of a Part-time Indian.* New York: Little, Brown, 2007.

_____. *The Lone Ranger and Tonto Fistfight in Heaven.* New York: Grove, 1993.

_____. "Sherman Alexie." Official website. Fallsapart.com. Web.

Barnes, Patricia M., Patricia F. Adams, & Eve Powell-Griner. "Health Characteristics of the American Indian and Alaska Native Adult Population: United States, 2004–2008." *National Health Statistics Report* 20 (9 Mar. 2010): 3–5.

Du Bois, W. E. B. *The Souls of Black Folk.* 1903. Chicago: A.C. McClurg, 2001. Kindle E-book.

Horn, Gabriel. "The Genocide of a Generation's Identity." *Genocide of the Mind: New Native American Writing.* Ed. MariJo Moore. New York: Nation, 2003: 65–75.

Jorgensen, Karen. "White Shadows: The Use of Doppelgangers in Sherman Alexie's *Reservation Blues.*" *SAIL* 9.4 (Winter 1997): 19–26.

Four American Poets Explore Hybrid Identity Formation and Familial Relationships_____

Rickie-Ann Legleitner

In the poetry of Natasha Trethewey, Rhina Espaillat, Anthony Hecht, and Shirley Gcok-lin Lim, we find complex explorations of the sometimes fraught relationships between parents and children who inhabit seemingly different cultural spaces. This biculturalism leads to a negotiation of identity that occurs internally between parent and child and, ultimately, with the world at large. Children who belong to multiple cultures may be torn between the identities of their parents and a more fluid one comprised of a public persona strongly affiliated with the dominant culture and a domestic identity strongly tied to familial roots. While this cultural plurality may allow for the enhancement of self, it can also cause one's sense of self to become unstable. A child's identity may become split, or they may experience a complex form of double-consciousness. W. E. B. Du Bois in *The Souls of Black Folk* defines "double-consciousness" as:

> . . . a sense of always looking at one's self through the eyes of others, of measuring one's soul by the tape of a world that looks on in amused contempt and pity. One ever feels his twoness . . . two souls, two thoughts, two unreconciled strivings; two warring ideals in one dark body, whose dogged strength alone keeps it from being torn asunder. (14)

While Du Bois was originally writing about the plight of African Americans following the Reconstruction era, this sense of personal division applies to all Americans who identify with multiple cultures and feel pressured to assimilate. Instead of becoming wholly Americanized or entirely dismissing American culture in preference for ancestral ties, we find authors who carefully explore the precarious and enriching journey of, to borrow Homi K. Bhabha's term, the "hybridized" individual who attempts to embrace a plural identity.

By comparing the varied journeys to selfhood in Trethewey's "White Lies," Espaillat's "Bilingual/Bilingüe," Hecht's "The Vow," and Lim's "Learning to Love America," we can develop deeper understandings of the connection between familial relationships, identity formation, and the hybridized self.

The historical, cultural, and social contexts are different for each of these poems, revealing the multifariousness of hybridity within American spaces. Nonetheless, each of these poems examines familial relationships and their role in identity formation. Trethewey's and Espaillat's narrators are children who attempt to identify their cultural place in the midst of conflicting social pressures and parental desires. In "White Lies," Trethewey focuses on race as an issue of hybridity in African American contexts, specifically in relation to miscegenation laws in the South and the troubling message these laws gave to children who were the products of illegal unions. In "Bilingual/Bilingüe," Espaillat draws attention to language and the potential that bilingualism has to unite differing cultures, even when the dominant language may threaten to silence one's native tongue. Hecht's and Lim's poems offer the perspective of parents who strive to see beyond their traditional sense of cultural belonging, in order to better comprehend the struggles of their children. These speakers each realize that their offspring's journey to find a place of belonging will be fraught in a society that lauds what it considers "purity." In "The Vow," Hecht examines how trauma can force one to confront and combat ethnic and religious stigmatization and potentially lead one to embrace the hybridized experience. In "Learning to Love America," Lim's narrator-mother traces her immigration, recognizing empowerment in her transnational connections and in the strength of her son, despite any potential discrimination he might face. Each poem results in a different strategy to resist the pressure to choose a single identity over another, and each provides us with differing insights into hybridized identity formation and the rewards and struggles of biculturalism.

In "White Lies" and "Bilingual/Bilingüe," each child speaker's confused development stems from her liminal position between two worlds, impacting the shape and the language of these poems.

Trethewey and Espaillat experiment with combining languages, playing with double and shifting meanings of words, and revising how readers perceive traditional symbols and images, in order to convey the unique experiences and struggles of racial and ethnic hybridity. These poems do not express hybridity as wholly enriching, but often rather as disjointed, resulting from the confusion experienced by the divided child. The process of accepting one's "twoness" is further complicated by American notions of race/language/ethnicity/nation, which claim that, in order to be an American citizen, one should speak English, embrace American culture (while forsaking all others), and ultimately "look" American—or, traditionally, Western European. If one succumbs to these pressures, internalized racism can lead to the desire to forsake one part of the self in favor of the culturally preferred Other. This desire, however, often comes with the loss of one's cultural heritage and history, creating a disconnected sense of self.

This complicated coming of age is apparent in Trethewey's "White Lies" and Espaillat's "Bilingual/Bilingüe." The strain of hybridity causes these children to feel that they are betraying their parents, but ultimately, they come to recognize the value of their hyphenated status, expanding our notions of who should be included in the construct of the American family.

Pulitzer Prize winner Natasha Trethewey was born in Mississippi in 1966 to a black mother and a white father. At this time in the American South, anti-miscegenation laws forbade interracial marriage, relationships, and sexual intercourse. Trethewey's place of birth had a profound impact on her writing, as she explained in a lecture at Emory University: "I am tethered to a place whose Jim Crow laws rendered my family . . . second-class citizens, whose laws against miscegenation rendered my parents' marriage illegal, my birth illegitimate not only in the customs but also in the constitution of the state. Thus, I write to claim my native land even as it has forsaken me, rendered me an outsider" ("Why I Write"). William M. Ramsey contends that, "Because her biracial identity links her to both the white and black groups, she has felt quite personally the unnatural, alienating exclusion of the black narrative by the white"

(129–30). In her poetry, Trethewey explores the pressure she felt to embrace her father's white heritage because of its cultural privilege and power. Although cultural hybridity is a potential source of social and political exclusion, Trethewey deploys it in her poetry to criticize a social environment that perpetuates internalized racism. This is apparent in her poem "White Lies," in which she reveals how language can hide alternative narratives.

The title "White Lies" immediately provides a pun that plays with the idea of insignificant, small lies as well as telling lies related to race or color—calling attention to the double meaning found in the narrator's identity as a girl of mixed race. In the first stanza, she has difficulty pinning down her color, revealing the instability of supposedly fixed labels: "light-bright, near-white, / high-yellow, red-boned" (3–4). Although the narrator entertains the idea of passing as white, she knows this, too, is a lie, when she is "part" black. In the second stanza, the narrator describes a fantasy space, in which she can shake off her blackness and poverty: "I could act like my home-made dresses / came straight out the window of *Maison Blanche*. I could even / keep quiet, quiet as kept, / like the time a white girl said, / squeezing my hand, 'now / we have three of us in our class'" (11–18). Here, Trethewey outlines the exclusive cultural associations of whiteness: affluence, privilege, opportunity, and belonging. The narrator can seemingly possess these ideals as long as she keeps quiet, lying by omission and hiding her hybridity. Yet by denying her blackness, she accepts the racial hierarchy that deems her inferior. This damaging acquiescence helps to explain her mother's response: "But I paid for it every time / Mama found out. She laid her hands / on me, then washed out my mouth / with Ivory soap" (19–22). The soap is yet another cultural association with whiteness: purity. This pureness, too, is desired by the poem's speaker who swallows the suds willingly, "thinking they'd work / from the inside out" (25–26). The implicit irony in the mother's attempts to punish her child for lying about her race—a punishment that only reinforces the child's desire to become entirely white—speaks to the narrator's longing to change her exterior appearance while capturing the dilemma of choosing between two racial identities, especially when one of those identities is socially privileged above the other.

In an interview, Trethewey describes how her own sense of duality was further fueled by labels that highlighted racial tension. Her parents' divorce when she was young added an additional layer of complexity to her inherent feelings of dividedness: "My parents divorced when I was a child and I, too, rarely saw my father— only in the summers: that circumstance creat[ed] for me a dual existence" (Trethewey, "Why I Write"). Trethewey's father called her a "crossbreed child" (Alexander 33). This labeling disturbed Trethewey, and she aimed to correct such limiting perspectives in her own writing: "I write to tell a fuller version of American history, to recover the stories and voices of people whose lives have been marginalized, forgotten, erased, overlooked" ("Why I Write"). Trethewey's poem exposes the "white lies" regarding the superiority of whiteness and the supposed opposition of white and black embodied in terms like "crossbreed," which convey the sense that races are at odds. Her poem captures the distress a child experiences when caught between two worlds, two parents, and two possible selves, and is not given a clear, positive example of hybrid identity from which she can learn to accept both sides of her heritage and the unique construct of her own family. Even though the hyphenated identity has been overlooked by national and popular history, Trethewey's work reaffirms her young narrator's quest for a socially-accepted and acknowledged existence.

Rhina Espaillat's autobiographical poem "Bilingual/Bilingüe" features another young female speaker who feels divided, but in contrast to Trethewey's narrator, Espaillat's does not opt to select one identity and is able to blend her bicultural heritage in a space where they can productively coexist. Espaillat, born in the Dominican Republic in 1932, immigrated to the United States as a young girl. Drawing from both her native and adopted languages in her poetry, she strives to combine her cultural selves and provides a resolution to bicultural tensions through bilingualism.

Beginning with the title, Espaillat foregrounds the languages that represent cultural hybridity: English and Spanish. She plays with these two languages throughout the poem, inserting Spanish words in parenthesis to show the speaker's knowledge and love of both languages and cultures. As Espaillat explains in an interview with Roy Scheele, "Spanish-speaking poets are more playful with the rules than English-language poets are, by and large, and I've tried to bring that over—that sense of play, that sense of having fun with what you're doing" (27). The child's fun and experimentation with language is highlighted within "Bilingual/Bilingüe," as a way to challenge notions about the separateness of cultures. Like the mother in "White Lies," the father in this poem attempts to control the speaker's view of her identity: "My father liked them separate, one there, / one here (allá y aquí), as if aware // that words might cut in two his daughter's heart" (Espaillat 1–3). The father fears his daughter will be overly influenced by American culture and demands she speak only Spanish at home, in an attempt to preserve his own history and heritage within his daughter. This attitude promotes a monocultural and monolingual identity and a world structured in binaries that unfairly limits the daughter's bicultural development. Her world becomes literally divided between the outside and inside via language (and the symbolic stanza break), yet she secretly finds a way to mend this forced segregation: "late, in bed, / I hoarded secret syllables I read / until my tongue (mi lengua) learned to run // where his stumbled. And still the heart was one" (Espaillat 11–14). The child, despite her father's trepidation, is able to stay whole while embracing both English and Spanish language, culture, and heritage.

Moving beyond her father in language does not cause her to break in two, nor does it lead her to betray her cultural heritage. Yet her father's stubbornness causes him to lose out on a significant part of his daughter's life: "he stood outside mis versos, half in fear / of words he loved but wanted not to hear" (Espaillat 15–18). Throughout the poem, Espaillat provides her audience with the Spanish equivalents to English words, actively translating so her readers can find meaning, yet in the final stanza, she incorporates Spanish language directly, without translation. Furthermore, Espaillat does not italicize "mis versos," going against English language convention to italicize foreign words. This emphasizes that, for the speaker, English is not the dominant language, but both languages maintain equal standing. In doing this, Espaillat simultaneously confronts her audience's possible fear of cultural hybridity and blending as the narrator confronts her father, attempting to reveal the benefits of hybridity, cultural multiplicity, and bilingualism. As her father falls in love with the beauty of her English words, she attempts to inspire this same love of Spanish language in her Anglophone audience.

Espaillat resists the notion that either the dominant or the minority culture should be rejected, creating what Homi K. Bhabha describes as, "the historical movement of hybridity as . . . a contesting . . . a space between the rules of engagement" (277). In this sense, a dialog or back-and-forth between Spanish and English enriches both languages; this interplay is a two-way exchange rather than a mono-directional invasion on either side. Through her poetry, Espaillat foregrounds a hyphenated status to show that neither culture nor language is privileged and that both sides benefit from this engagement. For Espaillat, each culture and language is equal, beautiful, and limiting in its own way—no language is superior, and no language or culture should be dismissed, resisted, or privileged. At the same time, Espaillat resists the use of "Spanglish," as it has the potential to diminish each culture:

> It's dangerous, however, to accept the inevitable melding of languages over time as a justification for speaking, in the short run, a mix that impoverishes both languages by allowing words in one to drive out perfectly good equivalent words in the other . . . it represents . . . a loss to both cultures. (Scheele 68)

For her, languages and cultures should be appreciated in their entirety, in order to preserve their integrity and unique cultural contributions. In Espaillat's version of hybridity, cultural traits are not blurred, but each retains its own distinctive qualities.

Ultimately, within "Bilingual/Bilingüe," the separation of cultures that the father strives for is impossible, so the speaker instead attempts to inspire love and respect rather than fear and bitterness of difference, as the colliding and mixing of these worlds is inevitable—and not necessarily negative. Although Trethewey's poem accentuates black identity to challenge racial hierarchy, Espaillat's representation of the linguistic benefits of biculturalism instead celebrates each part of the speaker's cultural identity. Her father's reluctance to embrace a culture that differs from his own prevents him from fully enjoying the advantages of cultural and linguistic hybridity demonstrated in his daughter's hybridized poetry. Yet Espaillat understands the father's reluctance as a symptom of his insecure status as an immigrant in the United States: "Nostalgia, a confusion of identity, the fear that if the native language is lost the self will somehow be altered forever: all are part of the subtle flavor of immigrant life . . . Guilt, too, adds to the mix, the suspicion that to love the second language too much is to betray those ancestors" (68). Despite these sympathies, Espaillat emphasizes the loss and disjointedness of denying the pleasure that can be found in cross-cultural appreciation.

"White Lies" and "Bilingual/Bilingüe" sympathize with a parents' point of view, while being told through the eyes of a child. Conversely, Hecht's "The Vow" and Lim's "Learning to Love America" are both told from the perspective of parents who are ridden with anxiety about their children who are growing up in the liminal space between two distinct worlds—the new and the old. Nostalgia, fear, and identity confusion, those characteristics identified by Espaillat, mark these works as well. While Hecht explores the dangers and potential beauty of the child of an interethnic marriage, Lim ponders what life will hold for the child of a first-generation immigrant. Each parent-speaker hopes that his or her child will come to recognize the unique beauty present in cultural hybridity, though, as we see in Hecht's work, societal pressure can cause the parent to struggle to find this beauty as well.

"The Vow," by Jewish American poet Anthony Hecht, recounts the tragedies surrounding a miscarriage. The first tragedy is the loss of a pregnancy that would have produced the child of an Irish American mother and Jewish American father (the latter is the poem's speaker); the second is the ethnocentrism and binary thinking that encourages the parents to perceive the miscarriage as a blessing. Having served as a soldier in World War II, Hecht intimately experienced the atrocities that ethnocentrism could produce. As William Logan explains, Hecht "was present at the liberation of a concentration camp, [and] has been haunted by the longer memory of the Holocaust. The beauty of his language . . . is stilled by the horror of knowledge" (150). In "The Vow," Hecht creates juxtaposition by revealing the painful realities of cultural discrimination in his careful crafting of the imagery of domestic loss, love, and bicultural triumph.

Hecht imbues descriptions of the loss of an unborn child with religious imagery, thus emphasizing the sacredness of any life: "The frail image of God / Lay spilled and formless. Neither girl nor boy, / But yet blood of my blood, nearly my child" (3–5). In words that closely mirror the symbolic language used to describe the marriage of Adam and Eve in *Bereshit* or Genesis, the father ponders the loss of something sacred that was the result of a socially undesirable union. The mother also mourns this tragedy, but finds comfort in the notion that her child is spared the "pain and sorrow" (Hecht 10–12) created by life in general, but also by society's ethnocentric attitudes.

The father, however, moves to reject the narrow prejudice inherent in the following notion: *The best / Is not to have been born*" (Hecht 26). He continues: "And could it be / That Jewish diligence and Irish jest / The consent of flesh and a midwinter storm / Had reconciled, / Was yet too bold a mixture to inform / a simple child?" (Hecht 26–32). The speaker seemingly questions whether cultural prejudice destroyed this child prematurely, as the world was not yet ready for its animation. While the love in the conception is emphasized, the fact that the product would not be similarly embraced is a point of tragic irony—an irony made more apparent by the play on cultural stereotypes that reveals the arbitrary limitations placed on cultural identity. In the final stanza, however, we find a renewed hope for future offspring: "The flames are lit / That shall refine us; they shall not destroy / A living hair. / Your younger brothers shall confirm in joy / This that I swear" (Hecht 36–

40). The narrator repositions hope from the distant to the immediate future, referring to his own future children (plural, not singular) and diverse family rather than indefinitely deferring a world that would accept the union of a Jew and a Gentile.

While the father initially appreciates the fear surrounding the child's birth, he mourns the unexpected loss and learns to find familial value in what hybridity may offer rather than focusing solely on cultural difficulties. As J. D. McClatchy suggests, "The words and images he offers them [his tragic subjects], of course, enable the reader to share both the victims' forlorn aloneness and the poet's speculative freedom, both the baffled suffering of humankind and the consoling wonder of language" (xi). Hecht finds freedom in this poem in that he can explore the horror of this loss and the equal horror of the relief it caused, revealing the yet greater horror in accepted cultural prejudice. The narrator himself overcomes all of these repulsions through expression and deliverance in an open language; he finds hope for a future of stronger convictions regarding a pluralized and diverse American family.

Shirley Geok-lin Lim, like Hecht, maintains a dual identity, not only as a US immigrant, but also as a creative writer and scholarly critic. Lim was born in 1944 in Malaysia and immigrated to the United States in her mid-twenties. Lim finds herself marginalized and privileged in differing ways in these two countries, based on her gender and her national heritage. In "Learning to Love America," the speaker learns to love her adopted country, despite its racism, because of her child. He is American by fact of his birthplace, but ethnically Chinese and biculturally Malaysian and American because of his mother. Lim introduces the idea of hybridity in ironically positive terms in the first line of her poem: "because it has no pure products" (1). While purity is traditionally a desired trait, it is only in a country without purity—with a pluralized history, immigrant founders, and a long tradition of cultural blending and borrowing—that hybrid identities should and can thrive. The mother-speaker unites her past and present in the image of the Pacific Ocean sweeping along the shore—a body that simultaneously separates and unites two land masses. She does this again in a description of produce and flowers available in California, one native to Malaysia and one grown in her adopted home: "because I live in California / I have eaten fresh artichokes / and jacarandas bloom in April and May" (Lim 6–8). By blending multiple cultures in the shared food and smells, both of which are taken into the body, Lim unites the outer culture with the inner sense of self. The narrator reveals her full adoption of this foreign land: "because I say we rather than they" (Lim 5). She also preserves customs from her homeland: "because I walk barefoot in my house" (Lim 12), again emphasizing the blending of cultures. Her very body is infused with both cultural spaces, and she shares this body and instills this blending in her son: "because I have nursed my son at my breast / because he is a strong American boy / because I have seen his eyes redden when he is asked who he is / because he answers I don't know" (Lim 13–16). The narrator identifies her son as American in birth and body, yet acknowledges that others do not immediately recognize this because of his appearance, and he himself does not know how to handle these questions or accusations.

While her son's identity may be in question for others, the mother longs to transcend these narrow categories. She has accepted her hyphenated status as an immigrant; however, her son has difficult challenges ahead because of the choices she has made: "because to have a son is to have a country / because my son will bury me here / because countries are in our blood and we bleed them" (Lim 17–19). Again, the narrator's connection to both cultures is expressed through the body. She will be buried and become part of the American land, and similarly, the land has become a part of her blood as it has her son's—yet not at the cost of dismissing their land of origin. This shared existence with both lands shows the importance of location to the continued development of one's identity, yet it also expresses the personal violation of accusing an immigrant as being "less" of a citizen or a lesser member of the national family.

In the final stanza, the mother recognizes that "it is late and too late to change my mind" (Lim 20) and return to her homeland and thus spare her son the pain of hyphenation; yet she also acknowledges that "it is time" (Lim 20) to face this pain and embrace the liminal space between cultures. As Andrew Ng asserts, "The artist who deliberately conjures spectres in her work must also imaginatively 'bear' the burden of their painful circumstances" (170). While the persona may seem haunted by her choice and her homeland, it is empowering in itself that she has made this choice and has narrated it publicly, as this would not be an option in her land of origin because of her gender. Eddie Tay argues that: "As an Asian American woman, Lim's identity is liminal as she is doubly marginalized by race and gender . . . she often writes of Asian women as being doubly oppressed by patriarchy and by colonialism" (304). Similarly, throughout Lim's poem, there is no mention of a father, indicating both the narrator's purposeful break from the patriarchal Malaysian culture that silences women and her own embracing of—yet not quite assimilating into—a new empowering American culture. In the final line, the author includes the first and only end punctuation in the poem, emphasizing both the finality of her decision and the real living presence of hybridity within American culture and family structures. Yet Lim's ultimate hope—"To transgress the nation-state and to imagine a transnational location of the self" (Schultermandl 40)—has yet to be obtained by the mother who is haunted and the son who is without a secure sense of cultural self. In an America not yet ready to embrace immigrants as equal social and cultural members of the domestic family, these hybridized and hyphenated poetic personas remain disjointed and divided—though they do not exist without aspirations for acceptance and unification. Like Hecht, Lim invokes the need for acceptance on the part of older generations, and similar to Trethewey and Espaillat, she highlights the struggles of the hybrid child to locate a place of cultural and familial belonging.

These poems cross cultural boundaries in terms of ethnicity, race, linguistics, gender, and religion; they present the diverse struggles and celebrations of many versions of complex hybridity in relation to identity development. Eventually, the protagonists in these works, like their authors, make the choice to acknowledge their hyphenated status, to embrace all sides of their identities, and to make a new American family despite cultural pressure, stigmas, or limitations. In considering these works in relation to bicultural identity formation and negotiation, we recognize how the boundaries of American identity are continually expanding—thanks to those who advocate for the inclusion of individuals on the margins and who work to dismantle the margins altogether through their empathy-invoking works of literature.

Works Cited

Alexander, Lindsey. "Dissection and Other Kinds of Love: An Interview with Natasha Trethewey." *Sycamore Review* 24.1 (2012): 31–45.

Bhabha, Homi K. *The Location of Culture*. London: Routledge, 1994.

Du Bois, W. E. B. *The Illustrated Souls of Black Folk*. 1903. Ed. Eugene F. Provenzo, Jr. Boulder, CO: Paradigm, 2005.

Espaillat, Rhina P. *Where Horizons Go*. Kirksville, MO: New Odyssey P, 1998.

Hecht, Anthony. "The Vow." *The Hudson Review* 10.1 (1957): 45–46. *JSTOR*. Web. 14 Jun. 2012.

Lim, Shirley Geok-lin. *What the Fortune Teller Didn't Say*. Albuquerque, NM: West End P, 1998.

Logan, William. *Reputations of the Tongue: On Poets and Poetry*. Gainesville: UP of Florida, 1999.

McClatchy, "Introduction." *Anthony Hecht: Selected Poems*. New York: Alfred A. Knopf, 2011. ix–xiv.

Ng, Andrew. "The Maternal Imagination in the Poetry of Shirley Lim." *Women: A Cultural Review* 18.2 (2007): 162–181. *Academic Search Premier.* Web. 11 Jun. 2012.

Quayam, Mohammed A. "Shirley Geok-lin Lim: An Interview." *MELUS* 28.4 (2003): 83–100. *JSTOR*. Web. 11 June 2012.

Ramsey, William M. "Terrance Hayes and Natasha Trethewey: Contemporary Black Chroniclers of the Imagined South." *Southern Literary Journal* XLIV.2 (2012): 122–135. *Project MUSE*. Web. 12 June 2012.

Scheele, Roy. "A Conversation with Poet Rhina P. Espaillat." *Texas Poetry Journal* 2.1 (2006): 25–47. *Humanities International Complete*. Web. 12 June 2012.

Schultermandl, Silvia. "Theorizing Experience, Locating Identity, Writing Selfhood: Lisa Suhair Majaj's and Shirley Geok-lin Lim's

Transnational Life-Writing." *A Fluid Sense of Self: The Politics of Transnational Identity*. Eds. Silvia Schultermandl & Sebnem Toplu. Berlin-Münster-Wein: LIT Verlag, 2010. 27–43.

Tay, Eddie. "Hegemony, National Allegory, Exile: The Poetry of Shirley Lim." *Textual Practice* 19.3 (2005): 289–308. *Academic Search Premier*. Web. 11 June 2012.

Trethewey, Natasha. "White Lies." *The Seattle Review*. 15.2 (1992): 96–97.

_____. "Why I Write: Poetry, History, and Social Justice." *Waccamaw* 6 (2010): Web. 12 June 2012. <http://archived.waccamawjournal.com/pages.php?x=323>.

Turner, Daniel Cross. "Southern Crossings: An Interview with Natasha Trethewey." *Waccamaw* 6 (2010): Web. 12 June 2012.

CRITICAL
READINGS

Legalized Hearts: Legal Identity in Larry Kramer's *The Normal Heart*

Gad Guterman

...gathered here together...

On June 24, 2011, minutes before midnight on the eve of Gay Pride weekend, New York State legalized same-sex marriage. Less than sixteen hours later, at a matinee performance of Larry Kramer's *The Normal Heart*, openly gay actor Jim Parsons, in the role of Tommy, delivered the following line to thunderous applause: "Maybe if they'd let us get married to begin with none of this would have happened at all" (73). The moment was electric. The Golden Theatre seats just over eight hundred people; it was packed that afternoon (I was in attendance). This revival production of the play about the onset of the AIDS crisis had already generated much buzz. In his *New York Times* review, Ben Brantley stated that the 1985 play "is breathing fire again," that show-stopping monologues garnered "the kind of sustained applause usually reserved for acrobatic tap dancers," and that "even people who think they have no patience for polemical theater may find their resistance has melted into tears" (C1). A week before, *The Normal Heart* had received the 2011 Tony Award for Best Revival of a Play. But the kind of applause that afternoon transcended the celebration of extraordinary performances. Those eight hundred audience members erupted into an intense, communal moment of commemoration. The applause seemed to usher in a new way of being for gay individuals. The history on stage became somewhat ancient, even as the live performance in front of viewers kept it very much alive in the present.

I do not suggest that the history staged in *The Normal Heart*—a true-to-life chronicle of the early days of AIDS in New York City—has ceased to capture ongoing realities of a devastating disease or of lasting homophobia. As a diatribe against the apathy and disdain that exacerbated the epidemic, *The Normal Heart* rightly continues to receive wide attention. Kramer remains a leading advocate for the fight against AIDS, and his establishment of the Gay Men's Health Crisis (GMHC) and later the AIDS Coalition to Unleash Power (ACT UP!) is well known. Yet, in the face of changing legislation surrounding the rights of gay men and lesbians, the play's reception that afternoon merits consideration.

To that end, this essay focuses on what *The Normal Heart* tells us about law. By reading the play with the concept of legal consciousness in mind, this essay proposes connections between legal realities and identity. In particular, the play's staging of a same-sex wedding ceremony offers an opportunity to discuss the role that law plays in establishing a sense of self. Given Kramer's interest in examining what a gay identity might entail, *The Normal Heart* provides fertile opportunity to investigate how such a concept intersects with a legal identity. In other words, let us consider here how "gay" is constructed alongside and often against specific laws. Law's power to forge identities is made all the more palpable when we trace the trajectory of gay rights from the early 1980s, staged by the play, to 2011 and the legalization of same-sex marriage in New York State.

...in the presence of this witness...

The Normal Heart is set in New York City between 1981 and 1984. It focuses on Ned Weeks' efforts to mobilize a response to a then-unknown, nightmarish virus seemingly targeting gay men. The play is a staged history of Kramer's work with the GMHC, and Ned is a thinly veiled version of the playwright. The autobiographic narrative tracks the infuriating resistance Ned faces, from deaf ears at City Hall and the *New York Times*, from his family and friends, and from a frightened gay community unsure about Ned's tactics. One of the play's major plotlines involves Ned's attempts to gain the support of his older brother, Ben, a senior partner at a premier law firm. Like the other characters in the play, Ben is based on a real-life counterpart: Kramer's own older brother, Arthur Kramer. The playwright insists in an afterword that "everything in *The Normal Heart* happened" (Kramer 94). Therefore, Ben's character easily stands in for Arthur, a well-respected attorney and founding partner of the firm Kramer Levin. But Ben becomes more than an avatar. As a stage figure, Ben represents an entire legal system that very much marginalized homosexuality. At the same time, the lawyer Ben—we could say the entity of law—provides Ned with a viable strategy for fashioning a new position in a changing culture. Ben witnesses and helps effectuate Ned's shifting legal identity.

Before focusing on Ned and Ben's relationship, let us consider the legal and cultural context for the New York portrayed by Kramer. Most historians agree that the modern gay rights movement began on June 28, 1969. When policemen raided the Stonewall Inn in the city's Greenwich Village, members of the gay community revolted. Raids on so-called gay establishments were common; 1950s McCarthyism had galvanized homophobia and cast governmental suspicion on homosexual activity. But on the heels of the Civil Rights Movement, the war against such oppression was imminent. Stonewall shepherded a movement in the 1970s focused on overturning current structures, with sexual freedom at the forefront. The push for gay liberation, drawing from the civil rights campaigns of the 1960s, aimed less directly for integration and equality and more for a radical reimagining of US society (S. Engel 387). Institutions such as marriage and monogamy—social traditions that arguably perpetuated the so-called normalcy of heterosexuality and patriarchy—became the target of people seeking to redefine sexual relationships. As the character of Mickey describes in the play, "the battle against the police at Stonewall was won by transvestites. We all fought like hell" (Kramer 33). The comment is telling, as it challenges the "Brooks Brothers guys," whom Mickey is addressing, to remember a now apparently faraway history (Kramer 33). In Mickey's view, the fights initiated by the emerging AIDS crisis in the early 1980s are undermining the movement he had helped build just a few years before.

Ned surfaces as a new kind of activist. His opinion of past struggles betrays a suspicion of Stonewall tactics, and importantly, it indicates a desire to utilize, rather than combat, the current legal regime. Ned is hesitant even to participate in "gay politics," an arena he feels is "filled with the great unwashed radicals of any counterculture" (Kramer 18). Instead, Ned believes that gay men will gain acceptance and respect by claiming sameness. We could say that Ned seeks to carve a place at the table, while the earlier movement wanted to dismantle the table altogether. In the face of a sexually transmitted epidemic, Ned's ideas challenge the newfound liberation that Stonewall had emboldened. Especially in the early days of the outbreak, when the causes of AIDS were largely misunderstood, Ned's calls for abstinence, safe sex, and monogamy are met with vocal resistance. "I've spent fifteen years of my life fighting for our right to be free and make love whenever, wherever. . . . And you're telling me that all those years of what being gay stood for is wrong . . . and I'm a murderer," Mickey charges (Kramer 75). Yet, Ned is adamant that "the gay leaders who created this sexual-liberation philosophy in the first place have been the death of us" (Kramer 60). Through this conflict, Kramer stages more than the realities of containing the HIV virus. Ned's position speaks to a desire for defining gayness outside the context of sex.

Indeed, while *The Normal Heart*'s major concern is to recount and broadcast the severe obstacles faced by victims of AIDS in a homophobic society, Kramer's play also chronicles Ned's endeavors to redefine "gay." Ned thinks it imperative to move beyond a conception of homosexuality rooted predominantly in sexual behavior and/or desire, a trend made more pronounced after Stonewall. Ned urges those around him, as well as the play's audiences, to consider instead the productive role that gay men play in society. He stresses the contributions of notable gay thinkers, artists, and scientists to our culture: "all through history we've been there" (86). Moreover, Ned underscores the potential power of a significant political and consumer group. Increased visibility and cohesion could lead to votes and boycotts that will change the status of gay men. "Don't you have any vision of what we could become?" asks Ned, "A powerful national organization effecting change!" (Kramer 58).

The change that Ned hopes for is intricately linked to issues of law. His sense of what "gay" could mean depends on legal recognition. For this reason, the character of Ben becomes a mirror through which Ned can consider his own legal identity. In the second of three scenes that take place in Ben's law office, Ned begs his brother to join the board of directors for the new activist organization. Ned is adamant that the support of a prominent, heterosexual family man will garner the necessary attention and support the gay community has been unable to find. Ben, described by theatre scholar James Fisher as "a father figure [serving] as society's disapproving voice on the 'gay lifestyle'" (19), refuses to lend his name to the cause. Ned's frustrations come to a boil:

> **NED.** You've got to say it. I'm the same as you. Just say it. Say it!
>
> **BEN.** No, you're not. I can't say it.... My agreeing you were born just like I was born is not going to help save your dying friends.
>
> **NED.** Funny—that's exactly what I think will help save my dying friends.... You can only find room to call yourself normal.
>
> **BEN.** You make me sound like I'm the enemy.
>
> **NED.** I'm beginning to think that you and your straight world are our enemy.... You still think I'm sick, and I simply cannot allow that any longer. I will not speak to you again until you accept me as your equal. Your healthy equal. Your brother! (Kramer 46–47)

When we consider Ben not only as a voice for "straight society" (Sinfield 321), but more specifically as a symbol for US law, Ned's call for equality illuminates a vital connection between law and identity.

...the authority vested by the laws of the state...

What might constitute a legal identity? David Engel and Frank Munger, leading participants in a conversation about the role that law plays in shaping our everyday lives, explore productive connections between identity and law in *Rights of Inclusion*. Rather than considering "law" a special sphere reserved for statutes, court proceedings, and complicated legalese, scholars like Engel

to view himself through the categorical exclusion to which he is subject" (Strong 179).

The characters in Kramer's play grasp the real consequences associated with homosexual activity, even in a relatively more liberated, post-Stonewall period. There is awareness among them that the law specifically leaves them unprotected. When Bruce suggests that Ned's push to demand abstinence from gay men violates their civil rights, Mickey quickly interjects. The very idea that same-sex sex would be considered a civil right seems unimaginable to him. "Don't we just wish," he laments (Kramer 36). Likewise, Mickey is the first to point out that "it is not illegal to discriminate against homosexuals" when Bruce complains that no one in the city wants to rent office space to their organization (Kramer 61). This latter interchange occurs in the mayor's office, "in some basement room that hasn't been used in years" (Kramer 57). Quite literally, the gay men find themselves in the shadows, deprived of legal protections afforded to others.

Within this context, the pressures of closeting oneself become clear. The closet—an active concealment of one's homosexuality in one or more meaningful aspects of one's life (Seidman 25)—provides means for securing certain legal protections. Even as Ned openly criticizes closeted gay men and especially closeted activists, Kramer stages the blunt realities that sustain the need to hide. During the course of the play, for instance, Mickey faces threats of losing his job, and we understand that he is without legal recourse to prevent abuse (Kramer 64, 72). In a harrowing monologue, Bruce describes the utter, but then-commonplace and legally sanctioned, dehumanization of his lover at the hands of the Phoenix police and an airline, a hospital, and a morgue—all highly legislated industries (Kramer 77–78). Of course, the strategy of the closet comes with dark consequences. To avoid falling outside the protections of the law, men concealing their sexuality easily fall into traps of self-erasure and perhaps self-hatred. As exemplified by Bruce, the fear of losing a livelihood and a career he loves prompts attempts to fit into rather than combat a homophobic culture. "My boss doesn't know [about me] and he hates gays. He keeps telling me fag jokes and I keep laughing at them," Bruce confesses (Kramer 41). His legal identity emerges from knowing that a part of him is marked illegal and must remain hidden in some contexts.

Critic Alan Sinfield describes Kramer's characters as "outlaws in that they are gay." But Sinfield reminds us that these "white, male, affluent, professional, metropolitan" individuals enjoy certain privileges as well (323). Ned, especially, begins to use law in meaningful ways. For instance, he recognizes that his activist organization needs first to be legally established. He uses Ben's firm to incorporate the organization and to apply for tax-exempt status (Kramer 25). Similarly, it is in Ben's law office that Felix manages to turn his dying wish—making Ned the sole beneficiary of his will—into a "quite legal" reality (Kramer 91). In this way, Ben's office operates as a productive space within the world of the play in which change effectively happens, albeit in the face of other insurmountable obstacles. And in that office, Ned's plea for equality to his brother is, more broadly, a plea for repositioning within the US legal system. Not yet awarded the kinds of rights that will transform his sense of belonging, as Engel and Munger might predict, Ned is nevertheless aware of the power of rights. He, therefore, exemplifies a legal consciousness in transition. His perceived lack of legal rights, which arguably has an adverse effect on his identity, fuels a passionate entreaty for new rights in the wake of the AIDS crisis.

Through his interactions with Ben, Ned demonstrates a changing stance in relationship to the law. In the face of a health catastrophe, Ned maintains that the gay community in New York City is not really dealing with civil rights issues but rather with "a contagion issue" (Kramer 73). Nevertheless, it is clear that in order to deal with the contagion, Ned and those around him need to fight for alternate ways of being recognized. Ned has told his friends that he "do[es not] want to be considered different" (Kramer 36). It is from his attorney brother that Ned most forcefully demands equality and full, unconditional acceptance. These demands, voiced chiefly in the second scene in the law office and quoted above, follow Ned's initial visit with Ben. In that first interaction, Ned professes his profound love for Ben. "I think my world would come to an end without you," Ned admits (Kramer 26). This sentiment is echoed in the second scene between the brothers. Ned confesses, "Ben, you know you mean more to me than anyone else in the world; you always have" (Kramer 46). On a symbolic level, Ned's appeals to Ben reveal a desire to be embraced by an already existing and powerful legal system. The problem, as Ned identifies, is that Ben— the law personified—refuses to see past gross stereotypes or let go of long-held prejudices. Confronted by Ben's misguided notion that gay men somehow "don't seem to understand why there are rules, and regulations, guidelines, responsibilities," Ned pins the problem back on his brother. It is the "single-minded determination of all you people to forever see us as sick" that needs to change (Kramer 45).

...let them speak now...

Visibility surfaces as Ned's main strategy to fight for change and acceptance. The under-reported, under-funded, under-researched health crisis in the gay community bespeaks broader invisibility and marginalization. Ned despairs:

> We're all going crazy, living this epidemic every minute, while the rest of the world goes on out there, all around us, as if nothing is happening, going on with their own lives and not knowing what it's like, what we're going through. We're living through war, but where they're living it's peacetime, and we're all in the same country. (Kramer 76)

His ally, Dr. Emma Brookner, insists that the one immediate cure for what is happening might be a "big mouth" (Kramer 15). Kramer proceeds to showcase Ned's tireless efforts to shine a spotlight on a pandemic already in motion.

The play's build-up allows Kramer to address more than the health catastrophe. We could say that visibility offers a remedy for the crisis at hand, but that legal matrimony serves in the mid-1980s as a utopian goal to reimagine gay identity in the United States. After all, the play's final scene is a bedside wedding and, it follows, an assertion of a new legal identity. Ned and his beloved Felix are married by Emma "in the sight of God" in *her* church, the hospital (Kramer 93). The only other witness is Ben, who returns apologetically to Ned despite a previous falling out. Representing law, Ben legitimizes the wedding. He witnesses and affirms the union, so that it is literally, albeit not legally, under the law. Once Felix passes away seconds after saying "I do," Ben and Ned "*kiss and embrace and hold on to each other*" for the play's final image (Kramer 93). Monica Pearl proposes that the play's resolution is inconclusive:

> The wedding at the end and the death suggest closure, but a very uncertain and, indeed, genre bending closure: with a (real) death and a (faux) wedding. Is this a comedy or a tragedy? It is the answer to this question that renders it so heartbreaking: it appears to wish fervently to be a comedy, but under the dire circumstances can only unfold as tragedy. (113)

She adds, "That the play ends in a gesture toward marriage suggests that marriage is the aspirational conclusion, the goal: not necessarily the cure for AIDS, but nevertheless its panacea—the antidote" (113). Such antidote is imagined as a legal act, through which yet-to-be achieved rights are exercised. So, by play's end, there is at least one certain conclusion: law embraces Ned.

According to law professor Michael Klarman, the push for legalizing same-sex marriage did not gain traction until the early 1990s: "Marriage had not been on the gay rights agenda at all in the first half of the 1980s" (48). Just as Ned seems prophetic about the catastrophic effects that the HIV virus will have, Kramer's protagonist envisages a formidable strategy for demanding a new place in US society for gay men. Today, the right to marry is considered by many to be a critical indicator of equitable human rights for lesbians and gay men (Harding 59). In her studies of legal consciousness and homosexuality, Rosie Harding finds that the campaign for attaining same-sex marriage has allowed gay men and lesbians, as well as their allies, to impact meaningfully "the ways that law develops over time" (23). This impact both confirms and promotes the kinds of changes Ned so desperately fights for in *The Normal Heart*. Harding explains that legal change, seen by many in the gay rights movement as the necessary "foundation for greater acceptance of lesbians and gay men in society," also becomes the "evidence *of* social acceptance" (66). As such, the right to legally wed manages to offset continued discrimination.

The scope of this essay does not allow for a comprehensive critique of Ned's strategies. Certainly in the early 1980s and still today, many believe that the gay community should not strive for a historically heteronormative and patriarchal institution like marriage. For some, the push for legalized same-sex marriage reinforces the authority of the legal system in the first place. Tommy's line in the play about having the right to marry—the line that brought the audience at the 2011 performance to rousing applause—attests to suspicion of Ned's position. "Ned doesn't like sex very much" is how Mickey and others begin to understand Ned's stance against sexual liberation and promiscuity (Kramer 71). In tying rights and acceptance to marriage, Ned promotes the idea that there are "good relationships" characterized by "monogamy, commitment, and coupledom" and, therefore, also "bad relationships" (Richardson and Seidman 10). Ned becomes, in this way, a legal-like voice, furthering the very logic that underpins all law. Boundaries, after all, are inherent to law (Amsterdam and Bruner 8–9). Ned and Felix's union at play's end promises a potential new normal, which simultaneously rejects alternatives.

However, what is imperative to note is that the play's final union highlights Kramer's engagement with legal consciousness as a critical factor in identity formation. In an April 2011 interview (two months before New York State would legalize same-sex marriage and two years before the Supreme Court would effectively require federal recognition of same-sex marriages), Kramer plainly protests that the move toward making gay marriage legal has "taken forever." He contends that the issue must "go to the Supreme Court as fast as possible" and that, until all legalized inequality is abolished, we must remain galvanized (Rogers). Indeed, in the play, Ned achieves his "new definition of what it means to be gay" (Kramer 86) by partaking in the quasi-legal event. Although audiences understand that Emma and Ben do not have the legal authority to pronounce

Ned and Felix married, Kramer's ending points to the need for legally recognized gay relationships. At least in the immediacy of the moment, Felix and Ned's will remains "quite legal" (Kramer 91), making the couple something new.

...now pronounce...

Theatre critics and historians are fairly unanimous when they assess the significance of *The Normal Heart*. Kramer's work not only heralded the explosion of so-called gay theatre that was to come after the 1980s, it also meaningfully brought attention to the AIDS crisis and helped to change attitudes about the disease. Jacob Juntunen persuasively explores how even for people who did not see the original production at the Public Theater in New York City, reviews, advertisements, and other commentaries on Kramer's work "made a difference" (45). For instance, Juntunen points out how the *Christian Science Monitor* did not even publish the term "AIDS" until it reviewed *The Normal Heart* and acknowledged the disease as "a tragic health disaster" in the article (43). This review appeared in 1985, nearly five years after the initial deaths. *The Normal Heart* continues to be staged worldwide and was deemed one of the "One Hundred Plays of the Twentieth Century" by the Royal National Theatre in England. A 2014 film adaptation, penned by Kramer and directed by Ryan Murphy, features film and television stars Julia Roberts, Mark Ruffalo, Matt Bomer, and Jim Parsons. The play and now film will advance Kramer's lifelong mission to shed light on, as he states in an acknowledgement in the published script, "a people singularly denied the right to know our history" (10). But it is interesting also to note that *The Normal Heart* has been absorbed by the legal field itself. Legal scholars, on occasion, cite the play specifically as an example of literature that may aid in the training of future lawyers and legal clinicians (Grose; Tovino). This means that, potentially, Kramer's work helps shape the consciousness of legal practitioners and, thus, legal practice itself.

This final thought emphasizes the mutual relationship that exists among law, culture, and identity. The lines that seemingly divide the legal sphere from, say, the field of theatre and film are porous. *The*

Normal Heart reflects the power of law to mold identities. In turn, cultural texts, like *The Normal Heart*, urge their audiences to think about and engage with legal realities. Such engagement can alter a legal landscape as well as a sense of belonging that very much participates in the process of identity formation. It is difficult to argue that the recent legal victories for gay men and lesbians in the United States stem directly from the appearance of a play like Kramer's. But without critical works, such as *The Normal Heart*, it is also difficult to imagine the reality of an openly gay Jim Parsons delivering a line advocating gay marriage—to thunderous applause—in front of a packed Broadway house during Pride weekend, just hours after one more state made the union of same-sex hearts legal.

The author thanks Alan Florendo and Emily Scharf for their invaluable assistance.

Works Cited

Amsterdam, Anthony G., & Jerome Bruner. *Minding the Law*. Cambridge, MA: Harvard UP, 2000.

Bowers v. Hardwick. 478 US 186–220. Supreme Court of the US. 1986. *Supreme Court Collection*. Legal Information Inst., Cornell U Law School, n.d. Web. 28 Feb. 2014.

Brantley, Ben. "Raw Anguish of the Plague Years." *New York Times* 28 Apr. 2011, C1.

Engel, David M., & Frank W. Munger. *Rights of Inclusion: Law and Identity in the Life Stories of Americans with Disabilities*. Chicago: U of Chicago P, 2003.

Engel, Stephen. "Making a Minority: Understanding the Formation of the Gay and Lesbian Movement in the United States." *Handbook of Lesbian and Gay Studies*. Eds. Diane Richardson & Steven Seidman. London: SAGE, 2002. 377–402.

Ewick, Patricia, & Susan S. Silbey. *The Common Place of Law: Stories from Everyday Life*. Chicago: U of Chicago P, 1998.

Fisher, James. "From Tolerance to Liberation: Gay Drama in the Mainstream from *Torch Song Trilogy* and *The Normal Heart* to *Angels in America, Love! Valour! Compassion!* and *Take Me Out*."

"We Will Be Citizens": New Essays on Gay and Lesbian Theatre. Ed. James Fisher. Jefferson, NC: McFarland, 2008. 7–31.

_____, ed. *"We Will Be Citizens": New Essays on Gay and Lesbian Theatre*.

Grose, Carolyn. "A Field Trip to Benetton . . . and Beyond: Some Thoughts on 'Outsider Narrative' in a Law School Clinic." *Clinical Law Review* 4 (1997): 109–7.

Harding, Rosie. *Regulating Sexuality: Legal Consciousness in Lesbian and Gay Lives*. New York: Routledge, 2011.

Human Rights Campaign. "Maps of State Laws & Policies." Human Rights Campaign, n.d. Web. 24 Feb. 2014.

Juntunen, Jacob. "Mainstream Theatre, Mass Media, and the 1985 Premiere of *The Normal Heart*: Negotiating Forces Between Emergent and Dominant Ideologies." *"We Will Be Citizens": New Essays on Gay and Lesbian Theatre*. Ed. James Fisher. Jefferson, NC: McFarland, 2008. 32–55.

Klarman, Michael J. *From the Closet to the Altar: Courts, Backlash, and the Struggle for Same-Sex Marriage*. New York: Oxford UP, 2013.

Kramer, Larry. *The Normal Heart*. New York: Samuel French, 2011.

Moran, Leslie J. "Lesbian and Gay Bodies of Law." *Handbook of Lesbian and Gay Studies*. Eds. Diane Richardson & Steven Seidman. London: SAGE, 2002. 291–311.

"NT2000 One Hundred Plays of the Century." National Theatre, n.d. Web. 24 Feb. 2014. <http://www.nationaltheatre.org.uk/discover-more/platforms/nt2000-one-hundred-plays-of-the-century>.

Pearl, Monica B. *AIDS Literature and Gay Identity: The Literature of Loss*. New York: Routledge, 2013.

Richardson, Diane, & Steven Seidman. Introduction. *Handbook of Lesbian and Gay Studies*. Eds. Diane Richardson & Steven Seidman. London: SAGE, 2002. 1–12.

_____, eds. *Handbook of Lesbian and Gay Studies*. London: SAGE, 2002.

Rogers, Thomas. "The Problem with Gay Men Today: Interview with Larry Kramer." *Salon*. Salon.com. 23 Apr. 2011. Web. 24 Feb. 2014.

Seidman, Steven. *Beyond the Closet: The Transformation of Gay and Lesbian Life*. New York: Routledge, 2002.

Sinfield, Alan. *Out on Stage: Lesbian and Gay Theatre in the Twentieth Century.* New Haven: Yale UP, 1999.

Strong, Thomas. "Vital Publics of Pure Blood." *Body & Society* 15.2 (2009): 169–91.

Tovino, Stacey A. "Incorporating Literature into a Health Law Curriculum." *Michigan State Journal of Medicine and Law* 9 (2005): 213–55.

Wainberg, Mark A., Talia Shuldiner, Karine Dahl, & Norbert Gilmore. "Reconsidering the Lifetime Deferral of Blood Donation by Men Who Have Sex with Men." *Canadian Medical Association Journal* 182 (2010): 1321–24.

Unspoken Histories and One-Man Museums: Lingering Trauma and Disappearing Dads in the Work of Chang-rae Lee_____

Michael Gorman

Family Trauma and Meaningful Silences

In a 2004 interview, Chang-rae Lee claimed, "Most people don't think about race as much as I do" (Bradbury). Race, vis-à-vis questions of identity, features as a prominent motif in Lee's fiction as well as in the day-to-day awareness of the narrator-protagonists in *Native Speaker* (1995) and *A Gesture Life* (1999). Race and ethnicity conspicuously influence how the protagonists see themselves and relate to family and place. The main characters in both novels are Korean-Americans dealing with the challenge of assimilation. Though it may not always be acknowledged, racial/ethnic concerns are ever-present elements in the lives of these men—one of several factors shaping their individual and collective identities. In fashioning these male characters, Lee carefully alloys gender concerns, traumatic histories, and racial considerations to consider how past experiences impact their behavior as sons, lovers/husbands, and fathers.

"A crucial issue with respect to traumatic historical events," according to cultural historian Dominick LaCapra, "is whether attempts to work through problems, including rituals of mourning, can viably come to terms with . . . the divided legacies, open wounds, and unspeakable losses of a dire past" ("Trauma, Absence, Loss" 697–98). In these texts, Lee attempts to reconcile the "unspeakable losses" and "open wounds" troubling multicultural American families. Paradoxically, the ineffability of the losses suffered lends voice to the narratives as Lee relies upon tropes of absence and silence to depict the toxic effects of trauma upon families and personal identity.

The traumatic experiences haunting the narrators of these novels determine how they present themselves to others, as well as the personal details they decline to share. Narrative omissions abound. Lee employs gaps and silences in the narrative to reflect the lingering influence of trauma upon the protagonists. The narrators profess transparency in the first chapter of each work. In *Native Speaker*, Henry Park contends, "you may know me. I am an amiable man" (Lee, *NS* 7), and Franklin Hata in *A Gesture Life* insists, "People know me here" (Lee, *AGL* 1). The identities reflected in these declarations are one-dimensional, impassive, and unambiguous performances—wish fulfillment, in other words. In the hope of distancing themselves from their traumatic pasts, the narrators in each text have fabricated uncomplicated, uncontroversial, and incomplete fantasy selves. Neither is as simple as he claims.

Grieving and Silence in *Native Speaker*

Critics have most often read *Native Speaker* in connection to issues of race and identity, culture and language—concerns which Lee cleverly addresses through the eyes of Henry Park, an adult child of Korean immigrants. It contains episodes detailing immigrants' struggles to assimilate and passages of flagrant racism and xenophobia. The novel features the struggles of a bi-racial couple—Byong-ho "Henry" and Leila (Boswell) Park—coping with the death of a child. Although they confront bigotry and intolerance as they strive to make sense of this tragedy, *Native Speaker* is less about race, ethnicity, and difference than about family, grieving, and love.

Henry is a spook. A spy. A double agent—emphasis on "double." As a Glimmer & Company operative, he observes and records the activities of Asian and Asian-American subjects for "multinational corporations, bureaus of foreign governments, individuals of resource and connection" (Lee, *NS* 18). Each mission consists of two antithetical tasks. The first part of each assignment is "entirely personal": Glimmer employees are assigned a stranger and must become as close to that person as "a brother or sister or wife" (Lee, *NS* 6). The second part of each job is impersonal; it involves describing "the subject in question," while avoiding "anything that smacks of theme or moral" (Lee, *NS* 203). Glimmer agents must shift from being intimate associates to detached scribes for every assignment. For a time, Henry excels at his bipolar trade and describes it as "the perfect vocation for the person I was" (Lee, *NS* 127). But, as the novel progresses, Lee compels readers to reconsider Henry's suitability for such a schizoid occupation.

By Henry's own admission, "a good spook has no brothers, no sisters, no father or mother" and "seems to have emerged from nowhere. He's brought himself forth, self-cesarean" (Lee, *NS* 173). When the novel opens, Henry's parents are both deceased, and he and Leila are separated. With no siblings, no parents, and no plans to reunite with his wife, he would seem to be an ideal candidate for a Glimmer & Company operative. However, Henry does not—and cannot—pass muster as "a good spook." He meets only the most superficial requirements for the post, for despite his best efforts to extricate himself from the "encumbering remnants of blood and flesh and . . . memory," Henry remains haunted by the specter and reality of family.

Henry Park is American-born, but only by the narrowest margin: "My citizenship," Henry realizes, "is an accident of birth, my mother delivering me on this end of a long plane ride from Seoul" (Lee, *NS* 334). According to Lori Jirousek in "'A New Book of the Land': Ethnography, Espionage, and Immigrants in *Native Speaker*," Henry (like Chang-rae Lee) is a member of "what anthropologist Kyeyoung Park calls the '1.5 generation' of Korean immigrants, those who fall or feel somewhere between the first and second generation and 'practice aspects of . . . Korean and American cultures'" (11). As a child of first generation immigrants, Henry Park is expected to adapt to the conditions in the family's new home as well as to inherit traditions, customs, and practices of the ancestral homeland.

Born and raised in New York, Henry struggled in childhood to comprehend the actions and affectations of his immigrant parents. Confused by their perplexing timidity, he wonders, "what could be so bad that we had . . . to mince delicately about in pained feet through our immaculate neighborhood . . . in our great sham of propriety, as if nothing could touch us or wreak anger or sadness upon us [?]" (Lee, *NS* 52). With incomplete understanding of Korean traditions, Henry judges his parents' behavior by American codes of conduct, ridiculing them for their anxiety and reserve. Even as Henry resented his parents' restraint and their imposition of Korean customs upon him in high school, their beliefs and practices left an indelible stamp upon him. From his parents, for instance, he learns that life's offerings—good or bad—are met with equanimity. His mother teaches him "that suffering is the noblest art, the quieter the better. If you bit your lip . . . you will perhaps persist and endure" (Lee, *NS* 333), and she demonstrates this art when dying from liver cancer. Henry's parents shielded him so completely from her illness that he thinks of it "more a disappearance than a death" (Lee, *NS* 77). Even after losing his wife, Henry's father grieved without betraying any emotion. Henry closely observed his father's stolidity in the months following his mother's death. Despite wondering if his father "was suffering inside, whether he sometimes cried," Henry never asks (Lee, *NS* 59). Instead of sharing his sadness about his mother's death, Henry adopts the gestures of his father. Holding his "chin as rigid and unquivering as any of his [father's] displays," Henry is determined to betray "no shadowy wounds or scars of the heart" (Lee, *NS* 59). This lesson in grief management is something Henry carries with him into adulthood.

Lee makes sure readers understand that Henry's poker face and desire to disappear are not cues of "Asianness." Other Asian American characters in the novel prevent any such stereotypical reading. Neither the Filipino psychiatrist Emile Luzan nor the New York City Councilman John Kwang share Henry's penchant for secrecy. Henry's propensity for silence and disappearance is, therefore, a reflection of his personality and unique experiences rather than racial or ethnic markers. His desire to escape is a learned behavior with roots in traumatic experiences he suffered as a child, such as being taken to his father's Madison Avenue grocery and being pressured to "casually recite 'some Shakespeare words' to 'blue haired matrons'" (Lee, *NS* 53).

Silence and inconspicuousness are hallmarks of a good son in the Park family, but also the features of an effective Glimmer &

Company mole. Henry's upbringing prepared him for a career in espionage:

> I wasn't employing a technique so much as my own instant live burial. It's the prerogative of moles, after all, which only certain American lifetimes can teach. I am the obedient, soft-spoken son. What other talent can Hoagland so prize? I will duly retreat to the position of the good volunteer, the invisible underling. I have always known that moment of disappearance, and the even uglier truth is that I have long treasured it. That always honorable-seeming absence. (Lee, *NS* 202)

At work, Henry is prized for his invisibility. These talents are less appreciated by Henry's wife, Lelia.

Henry's placid demeanor threatens his marriage. Whereas Henry has been taught to sublimate his emotions and finds comfort behind the camouflage of silence, Lelia is "the worst actor on earth," completely unable to hide her feelings (Lee, *NS* 158). Yet Henry appreciates her artlessness: "I loved . . . how she can't hide a single thing, that she looks hurt when she is hurt, seems happy when happy. That I know at every moment the precise place where she stands" (Lee, *NS* 158–59). Leila is a person of action who regards silence as a form of passivity, another trait Lee ascribes to Henry. "When real trouble hits," Henry confesses, "I lock up. I can't work the trusty calculus. I can't speak. I sit there, unmoved. For a person like Lelia, who grew up with hollerers and criers, mine is the worst response. It must look as if I'm not even trying" (Lee, *NS* 158). Lelia is unaccustomed to and uncomfortable with silence of any type and has difficulty comprehending the cultural and individual differences that sculpt her husband's character. Her unease with silence is, at least partly, culturally inscribed. In *Articulate Silences* (1993), King-Kok Cheung explains that the restraint displayed by Asian and Asian Americans has been traditionally condemned in the West. While East Asians see silence as a complement to speech, Westerners view the concepts in opposition, judging speech favorably, but dismissing silence as unfavorable or passive (Cheung 2, 127).

Several passages in the novel highlight the couple's different sensitivities to silences. Three years into their marriage, Lelia is surprised to learn that Henry does not know the name of the Korean "houselady" employed by his father. Lelia cannot fathom how Henry could not know the real name of the woman "who practically raised" him, and she incorrectly views this fact as evidence of misogyny or maltreatment. In astonishment, Leila exclaims, "'This woman has given twenty years of her life to you and your father and it still seems like she could be anyone to you. Right? If your father switched her now with someone else, probably nothing would be different'"(Lee, *NS* 69–70). From Leila's perspective, names help bridge class and generational differences—they are a nod toward equality. Not addressing servants by name strikes her as a denial of their significance or a demonstration of their inferiority.

As an American, Henry understands Lelia's point, but as a Korean-American he also recognizes that Korean standards of respect demand using titles of address in place of names.

> She didn't understand that there weren't moments in our language . . . when the woman's name could have naturally come out. Or why it wasn't important. At breakfast and lunch and dinner my father and I called her "Ah-juh-ma," literally aunt, but more akin to "ma'am," the customary address to an unrelated Korean woman. (Lee, *NS* 69)

Leila's discomfort with silence combines with her ignorance of Korean culture and leads her to misinterpret custom as an omission or a slight—a hurtful silence. However surprising to Leila, the absence of a name in this case is culturally dictated.

In a cruel turn, Lelia and Henry lose their son Mitt on his seventh birthday when he suffocates at the bottom of a "*dog pile*" (Lee, *NS* 105). Henry's father resorts to a familiar mode in the aftermath of this horrible loss. He clears Mitt's bedroom of the toys, clothes, furniture, and wall hangings and proceeds to paint the room a "barren, optic white" (Lee, *NS* 217). Unable to express his grief or bear being reminded of his grandson's death, Henry's father clears and paints the room in a futile attempt to eliminate evidence of the family's terrible loss.

Leila and Henry react to Mitt's death in different ways, and both grieve individually. Mitt died during horseplay turned tragic that few parents could have foreseen or prevented, yet Lelia refuses to acknowledge the tragedy as an accident and probes it for meaning (Lee, *NS* 129). Lelia resorts to listening to tape-recorded conversations with Mitt, and Henry throws himself into his work (Lee, *NS* 116). Lelia feels abandoned by Henry, but when he tries to explain how devastated he was by Mitt's death, Lelia responds incredulously:

> I'm sorry, Henry, I don't want to be no fun but I'm not going to let you step into the middle of my night and start revising our history. . . . The bowing, the white-glove bit. . . . . You're the one who calmly explained to everyone how well we were doing. Of course I was the mad and stupid one. The crazy white lady in the attic. (Lee, *NS* 117)

Despite Lelia's allusion to racial difference in her self-description as "white," there is nothing inherently "Asian" about Henry's "solemn and dignified" response to Mitt's death or, for that matter, his father's phlegmatic reaction to the death of Henry's mother years earlier. In fact, the actions of Henry and his father reflect a common pattern in the West, where men bear the burden of family tragedy in silence.

According to J. M. Anastasi with the National SUID/SIDS Resource Center at Georgetown University:

> Mothers and fathers grieve differently. Traditionally, fathers are expected to be strong and to carry on. They are usually expected to attend to the practical but not the emotional aspects of their child's death. Fathers tend to feel that they must handle all the decisions at this time, but these decisions can have lasting effects on the family. ("The Death of a Child")

Leila's method of mourning differs so radically from her husband's that she cannot recognize his suffering; she considers Henry too detached. Her characterization of Henry's silence as incomprehensible evokes the prejudicial notions of Asian inscrutability. Nevertheless, Henry's silence and withdrawal after Mitt's death cannot be attributed to race. What Lelia construes as detachment is actually socially-conditioned gender behavior, corresponding to an expectation for men to be emotionally strong in response to death and trauma. Henry's subdued bearing after losing his son is as American an expression of grief as Lelia's "crazy white lady in the attic" response. In sorrow, Henry is a native speaker.

Traumatic Memory and Exile in *A Gesture Life*

Like *Native Speaker*, Chang-rae Lee's *A Gesture Life* relies heavily on tropes of silence and withdrawal and their relation to the narrator's traumatic past. In this case, the trauma springs from two sources: atrocities committed during World War II and family strain. The silences in *A Gesture Life* camouflage the lingering effects of the Imperial Japanese military's sexual enslavement of up to two-hundred-thousand women, eighty percent of whom were taken from Korea (Hicks 19, Soh 1227). The protagonist's complicity in this crime haunts him after the war and determines major life choices. To obliterate unsavory past events from his memory, he adopts a new country, new name, and new child.

A Gesture Life views trauma from a transnational perspective, depicting the suffering witnessed, experienced, and inflicted by Franklin "Doc" Hata, an aging immigrant who served as a medical officer with the Imperial Japanese Army during World War II. Though he passes as Japanese, Hata is actually *zainichi kankokujin* (在日韓国人), a Korean citizen born and raised in Japan. In 1963, after traveling briefly in the United States, Hata moved to the suburbs outside of New York City (Lee, *AGL* 3). This decision leads Hamilton Carroll to attribute Hata's immigration to his desire to escape his "liminal status" in Japan ("Traumatic Patriarchy" 599). But why would Lee's narrator deny his Korean heritage after immigrating to the United States? Hata could more easily have moved to South Korea and lived in anonymity as a member of the ethnic majority. His decision to live under an assumed name and false ethnic identity suggests Hata suffers from cognitive dissonance, or a desire to avoid thinking about his complex personal history and culpability in the Second World War.

Hata is both victim of and accomplice to Japanese imperialism. On one hand, he is a Korean citizen whose family is obliged by economic circumstances to live in Japan during Imperial Japan's Occupation of Korea (1910–1945). While living in Japan, he learns self-hate; in addition to facing severe discrimination, he is compelled to leave his family and abandon his family name (Oh) to improve his long-term economic and educational prospects. On the other hand, Hata abets Japan's exploitation of Asia during the war by serving with the Imperial Army. In his capacity as a medical officer, charged with maintaining the health of "comfort women," he is also complicit in the systematized rape of Korean women forced to work as prostitutes for the Japanese military. His decision to move to the United States and pass as Japanese appears to be an attempt to forget a convoluted and contradictory past.

Despite his efforts to forget and start afresh, trauma lingers in a way that mirrors Dominick LaCapra's description in *Writing History, Writing Trauma*:

> . . . the historical past is the scene of losses that may be narrated as well as of specific possibilities that may be conceivably reactivated, reconfigured, and transformed in the present or future. The past is misperceived in terms of sheer absence or utter annihilation. Something of the past always remains, if only as a haunting presence or revenant. (49)

Lee's *A Gesture Life* reflects the truth of LaCapra's statement. Absences, elisions, and intervals in the novel do not supplant loss. Instead, they subtly indicate the presence of trauma and loss.

A Gesture Life is a frustratingly indirect narrative. Lee suggestively locates the 'drama' of the novel in the gap between narration and content and seems more interested in narrating *around* an event rather than depicting it outright (Lee, *AGL* 101). He fills Hata's story with vacuoles, including decades-long gaps in time. These absences speak volumes.

Several omissions in *A Gesture Life* relate to the central character's ethnicity and the processes of migration and exile. Hata's silence about his origins is one of the most suggestive of the many gaps in the novel. Lee introduces the narrator as "Franklin Hata," a retired proprietor of a medical supply store, living comfortably in Bedley Run, an upscale suburban community outside New York City. Hata asserts confidently, "everyone here knows perfectly who I am. It's a simple determination," and adds, shortly thereafter, "my name, after all, is Japanese" (Lee, *AGL* 1–2). Franklin? Japanese? Hata's identity is not as simple as he insists.

The personal history of this venerable Japanese American retiree is more complex and secretive than he initially concedes. Franklin Hata is known in the community of Bedley Run as "Doc," though he has never worked as a physician in the United States. He was raised in Japan, yet is not Japanese. He was born into a Korean family (the Ohs) working as resident aliens in Kobe, Japan (Lee, *AGL* 238, 243–44, 255, 257) and was sent to live with a Japanese couple when he was a middle school student. From them, he took the name Jiro Kurohata. Although he forever abandoned his Korean name, he found it more difficult to distance himself from his Korean identity.

Major erasures revolve around Hata's experiences during the Second World War, memories of which he carefully represses and avoids sharing with his adopted Korean daughter, Sunny (Lee, *AGL* 146). While stationed in Burma as a junior medical officer with the Imperial Japanese Army, Hata was charged with "maintaining the readiness" of the "comfort women" (Lee, *AGL* 166). "Military comfort women" is a literal translation of *juugun ianfu* (従軍慰安婦) the Japanese euphemism for the sex slaves abducted (or recruited under false pretenses) by the Japanese military from conquered territory throughout Asia, particularly Korea. While attending to the medical needs of "female volunteers" (Lee, *AGL* 161) attached to his outfit, Hata falls in love with Kkutaeh, a woman whose Korean parents offered her and her sister to the Japanese military to save her brother from conscription (Lee, *AGL* 250). Kkutaeh repeatedly asks Hata to kill her to spare her from being forced to "receive" soldiers. As a medical officer, Hata knows the horrible fate awaiting her (Lee, *AGL* 226), yet he refuses her pleas (238, 254, 300–301).

Hata moves to the United States, in order to shelve his traumatic memories from Burma and especially to suppress his guilt for failing to prevent Kkutaeh's brutal murder (Lee, *AGL* 303–05). To aid him in forgetting, he searches for an empty and foreign landscape. He chooses the new suburban development of Bedley Run for his home because of its perceived capacity to help him erase the troubled part of his past: "It looked sterile and desolate, like fresh blast ground, not in the least hopeful, and yet I felt strangely drawn to the town" (Lee, *AGL* 2–3). The narrator's attraction to the barren site is no mystery; it symbolizes his desire to annihilate his past. Regrettably, the sterility of his new environment does not prevent the periodic resurfacing of traumatic memories and associated feelings of guilt that prompt him to adopt Sunny, an abandoned child from Korea, to atone for failing to protect Kkutaeh.

Sunny's adoption is another traumatic element in the story. Adoption is a process tinged with anguish on all sides: a sense of loss distresses parents who relinquish children, children may feel abandoned, and adoptive parents may be "compelled to imagine primal scenes they missed" (Homans 7). For Sunny, additionally, the sense of loss and dislocation would have been especially disturbing, since she was removed from an orphanage in Pusan not as an infant, but as a "skinny, jointy young girl with thick, wavy black hair and dark-hued skin" (Lee, *AGL* 74, 204). Being sent overseas for adoption at seven must certainly have been traumatic for Sunny, but the novel does not consider it from her perspective. Lee presents it, instead, via Hata's warped viewpoint and motivations.

"Adoptive parents," according to Margaret Homans, "often describe their feelings about meeting their children as falling in love" (Lee, *AGL* 7). Hata's reaction to meeting his daughter could hardly be more different. Before Sunny's arrival from Korea, he had imagined that his acquaintances would have no trouble imagining the girl as his child. "But," Hata explains, "when I saw her for the first time I realized there could be no such conceit for us. . . . Her hair, her skin, were there to see . . . and it was obvious how some other color (or colors) ran deep within her. And perhaps it was right from that moment, the very start, that the young girl sensed my hesitance, the blighted hope in my eyes" (Lee, *AGL* 204). As the child of a Korean mother and an African American serviceman,

Sunny's racial hybridity did not fit Hata's essentialist notions about respectable families.

Hata's reasons for adopting were not about providing for the child's happiness. Rather than a new start for Sunny, the adoption was to mark "the recommencement of [his] days" (Lee, *AGL* 74), his chance to put his guilty memories from the war to rest and move on with his life. Unfortunately for father and daughter, the adoption accomplishes just the opposite of Hata's intentions. Sunny serves as reminder of Kkutaeh, whom Hata refers to posthumously as K. In "Recognizing the Transracial Adoptee," Mark Jerng posits that Hata projects his history with K onto Sunny, essentially trapping her "in an earlier, guilt-ridden relationship that involves the Japanese occupation of Korea" (56). The result is a dysfunctional father-daughter bond.

Hata's final conversation with K shapes his treatment of Sunny. Just before her brutal murder, K asks to be left alone and implores, "Please, Lieutenant. Don't touch me" (Lee, *AGL* 300). Decades later, K's words are fresh in Hata's mind and prevent him from providing the attention, comfort, and discipline a child needs. Hata resisted openly communicating with or expressing affection for Sunny from the day she stepped into his life: "I remember first walking Sunny into the foyer . . . and she actually began to titter and cry. I didn't know what to do for her, as she seemed not to want me to touch her, and . . . I stood apart from her while she wept, this shivering little girl of seven" (Lee, *AGL* 26). With K's last words in mind, Hata hesitates to comfort a frightened child. His ability to comfort Sunny does not improve with time. When Sunny is eighteen, she reveals that she was sexually assaulted and declares, "Nothing like that is ever going to happen to me again. I'll kill myself before it does" (Lee, *AGL* 150). Hata is paralyzed by Sunny's words and the memories they awoke:

> I would have suggested something then . . . but she spoke those last words with such a finality and resolve. . . . I was simply shocked . . . but even more . . . I felt the drug of fear course through me, and with it the revisitation of a long-stored memory of another young woman who once spoke nearly the same words. (Lee, *AGL* 150)

Recollecting K prevents Hata from acting on his fatherly instincts and helping his daughter cope with traumatic ordeals. He has internalized the memory of his failure to protect K as well as her rejection of his affections, and he fears that any attempt to love or protect Sunny may result in a similar catastrophe.

Hata uses his constructed identity as Japanese to maintain a distance from Sunny that he was unable to do with K. After inviting her into his home, Hata becomes a virtual non-presence in her life, fading unnaturally into the background. "My wish," Hata explains, "was that she study hard and practice her piano and read as many books as she could bear, and of course, when there was free time, play with her friends from school. A child's days are too short, and my sense then was that I should let her focus on activities that would most directly benefit her" (Lee, *AGL* 27). Ironically, Hata fails to provide Sunny with a more caring environment than he had after being "adopted" into a Japanese family. Hata not only removes himself from Sunny's daily routine, he literally deletes himself from conversations with her. Even when encouraging her to practice for a piano recital, he eschews the first-person: "Why don't *you* play some more? *Your* teacher wishes that *you* practice more than *you* do. *You* must push yourself" (Lee, *AGL* 28). In talks with Sunny, Hata becomes a non-presence, like the silences he finds so "magical and haunting" in her recital piece: Chopin's Opus 32, No. 1. The pauses and elisions in this composition suggest the presence of unstated trauma in the novel. The intervals between the "lyrical, impassioned musings" of Chopin's arrangement signify losses that Hata and Sunny have endured, but decline to share with each other.

Hata provides Sunny all the accoutrements of a good home, but he does not act like her father when it counts. Evidence of his parental failings abounds. Most obvious is his refusal to handle Sunny like a child. He endeavors to treat her "with respect" (Lee, *AGL* 60) rather than as his daughter. In general, he avoids disciplining her (despite urges to do so) and defers to her judgment in a highly unfatherly fashion. Hata attributes his hands-off style of parenting to a cultural fantasy. Neither he nor Sunny are Japanese, yet he insists that his conduct is normal for Japanese fathers, whom he claims are "extremely permissive and obliging with their little ones" (Lee, *AGL* 71). In reality, his parental failings derive from a pathological lack of conviction: the "the germ of infirmity" Captain Ono witnessed in Burma (Lee, *AGL* 266). Instead of taking the proper course of action and breaking the malignant silences, he performs superficial gestures of fatherhood, leaving his family's survival and his daughter's development in the hands of fate.

Hata's Bedley Run home stands as a monument to his dual failure to sustain a family and assert himself. Despite having lived there for decades, he has left little imprint on the property. The house remains a "darkened museum of a one-man civilization, whose latent history . . . would be left always unspoken" (Lee, *AGL* 7). Hata has chosen silence over coming to terms with trauma. To this end, when Sunny moves away, Hata works to "clear the room completely" of anything that would remind him of her: "furnishings," "bric-a-brac," and "mars in the plaster" (Lee, *AGL* 14–15). The painstaking process of working "in half-foot squares" to fill hundreds of tiny "tack holes" in Sunny's room aptly serves as a metaphor for the difficulty involved in willfully forgetting. Hata attempts to lock his traumatic experiences away like the flag from the war that he keeps hidden in his closet or the photographs of Sunny he left in his former place of business.

In the end, Hata has to admit the entire foundation of his American life is fraudulent: he has never been Japanese; he is no longer a business owner; he has not been a successful and loving father. He fears that he has lived silent as his ghosts: "I have not been living anywhere or anytime, not for the future and not in the past and not at all of-the-moment, but rather in the lonely dream of an oblivion, the nothing-of-nothing drift from one pulse beat to the next . . . automatic and involuntary" (Lee, *AGL* 321). By refusing to address the trauma and contradictions of his past, Hata denies much of his own existence. Without acknowledging his role in history and the disturbing elements of that history, he forfeits his own identity and has nothing substantial to contribute to his community or family.

Conclusion

In "This Way Up: A Profile of Chang-rae Lee," Amy Rosenberg views *Native Speaker* and *A Gesture Life* as "meditation[s] on location and identity, on what it means to belong to any group that has come here from elsewhere and struggled to create . . . wealth, stability, and the illusion of living out the American dream" (35–36). But these works involve more than musings on ethnicity, community, and prosperity. They consider the influence past trauma exerts on identity and upon families in crisis.

The narrators in each book are emotional escape artists who, in the words of Michiko Kakutani, "work hard at avoiding emotional engagement and risk" ("Flying Instead of Feeling"). The difficulty Lee's male protagonists have communicating makes them better suited for the Blue Man Group than for fatherhood or family. Speaking in an interview about Henry Park from *Native Speaker*, Lee asserted, "there is something absolutely dramatic about someone who wants to feel and does, but somehow can't do the things that allows himself to communicate" (Foley). The weight of his past experiences makes it difficult to share his feelings with others. The same thing could be said about Franklin Hata. In these books, Lee maps the confluence of trauma, fatherhood, and silence; deconstructs racialized and gendered notions about taciturnity; and explores the impact of latent trauma, the perils of isolation, and the process of grief and recovery.

Works Cited

Anastasi, J. M., ed. *The Death of a Child, The Grief of the Parents: A Lifetime Journey*. 3rd ed. Washington, DC: National Sudden and Unexpected Infant/Child Death and Pregnancy Loss Resource Center at Georgetown University. Mar. 2011. Web. 17 Aug. 2014.

Bradbury, Lorna. "Chang-rae Lee: Lorna Bradbury Meets a Korean-American Novelist Who's Obsessed with the Suburbs." *Telegraph* 20 June 2004. Web. 17. Aug. 2014.

Carroll, Hamilton. "Traumatic Patriarchy: Reading Gendered Nationalisms in Chang-rae Lee's *A Gesture Life*." *Modern Fiction Studies* 51.3 (2005): 592–616.

Cheung, King-Kok. *Articulate Silences: Hisaye Yamamoto, Maxine Hong Kingston, and Joy Kogawa*. Ithaca, NY: Cornell UP, 1993.

Foley, Dylan. "Chang-rae Lee Skewers American Overconsumption in 'Aloft.'" *Dylan Foley's BookPush*. 25 Nov. 2011. Web. 17 Aug. 2014. <http://dylanmfoley.blogspot.com/2011_11_01_archive.html>.

Hicks, George. *The Comfort Women: Japan's Brutal Regime of Enforced Prostitution in the Second World War*. 1994. New York: Norton, 1997.

Homans, Margaret. "Adoption Narratives, Trauma, and Origins." *Narrative* 14.1 (2006): 4–26.

Jerng, Mark C. "Recognizing the Transracial Adoptee: Adoption Life Stories and Chang-rae Lee's *A Gesture Life*." *MELUS* [Varieties of Ethnic Experience] 31.2 (2006): 41–67.

Jirousek, Lori. "'A New Book of the Land': Ethnography, Espionage, and Immigrants in Native Speaker." *Modern Language Studies* 36.1 (2006): 8–23.

Kakutani, Michiko. "Books of the Times; Flying Instead of Feeling, But the Fantasy of Motion Is Also Risky." *New York Times* 9 Mar 2004. Web. 17 Aug. 2014.

LaCapra, Dominick. "Absence, Trauma, Loss." *Critical Inquiry* 25.4 (1999): 696–727.

_____. *Writing History, Writing Trauma*. 2000. Johns Hopkins UP, 2011.

Lee, Chang-rae. *A Gesture Life*. 1999. New York: Riverhead, 2000.

_____. *Native Speaker*. 1995. New York: Riverhead, 1996.

Lee, Christopher. "Form-giving and the Remains of Identity in *A Gesture Life*." *Journal of Asian American Studies* 14.1 (2011): 95–116.

McGrath, Charles. "Heading Home to Adultery and Angst; A New Generation of Authors Discovers the Suburbs." *New York Times* 1 April 2004. Web. 17 Aug. 2014.

Rosenberg, Amy. "This Way Up: A Profile of Chang-rae Lee." *Poets & Writers* (Mar./Apr. 2004): 32–39.

Soh, Chunghee Sarah. "The Korean 'Comfort Women': Movement for Redress." *Asian Survey* 36.12 (Dec. 1996): 1226–40.

"She's left me her legacy nonetheless": Boundaries and Female Connection in Cuban American Women's Literature_____

Jessica Labbé

The problematic, yet powerful bonds between female characters in Cuban American women's literature deserve deeper investigation because these bonds influence the women's communicative self-actualization. Just as importantly, they symbolize the experiences faced by those who cross psychological, physical, geographical, and political boundaries. In the fiction of celebrated Cuban American authors Cristina García, Achy Obejas, and Alisa Valdes-Rodriguez, female identity highlights relationships: mother, daughter, granddaughter, sister, cousin, and friend. The characters' experiences range from loss, violence, and telepathic communication to nurturing and social bonding. Taken together, the works illustrate that female self-realization is rooted in these relationships, for better or for worse. The connections between women in these texts are often broken, stunted, and it is the boundaries between these women that constitute the rocky terrain of this literary tour.

The characters' interactions operate as microcosms of the identity struggles experienced by Cuban American women. These bonds between women represent larger issues of self versus communal identity, gender roles and expectations, generational conflicts, multicultural life, hybridity, and cultural fluidity. Moreover, the young protagonists featured in these works reveal that walking the line between multiple identities and cultures can be trying, and yet the experience is filled with potential. As a new hybrid generation, these young women must honor their past, yet remain open to the creative possibilities of "life on the hyphen," to borrow Gustavo Pérez-Firmat's now-famous phrase. Mirroring the "New Mestiza" figure Gloria Anzaldúa imagines in her ground-breaking work *Borderlands/La Frontera*, each young female character becomes "a creature that questions the definitions of light and dark and gives them new meanings" (103). As this study reveals, more often than not, the gatekeepers to such power are fellow women.

Within the larger context of women's studies and the struggle for women's rights, female fellowship and cooperation is a highly politicized and prickly issue. As we have seen throughout the evolution of feminism, women's groups are sometimes at odds with each other, especially with regard to race and class. Therefore, some women have experienced a double exile: from male culture and from each other. Though women's formal and familial bonding can be traced to times well before the turning point of women's rights in America—the Seneca Falls Convention (1848)—it was not until Nancy Friday's *My Mother/My Self* (1977) that an in-depth study of the complex psycho-social bond between mothers and daughters became available to mass audiences. The feminist movement of the 1960s and 1970s unleashed a critical interest in the bonds between women. From a feminist activist perspective, women needed to recognize what comprised these connections and how they influenced women in terms of race, class, generation, sexuality, and politics. "Consciousness-raising," activities that highlight the connections between the personal and the political, increased women's collective and individual awareness of internal and external environments, conditions, and thoughts. The women who participated in "consciousness-raising" sessions discovered that the ties that bind women—to their family members, friends, and lovers—are far more complicated than popular media represents them as being.

It is important to note that the tensions between the women characters analyzed here are rooted in the Cuban American diaspora, which is central to the Cuban American exile experience. For Cuban Americans, diaspora is the site of a psychological wound grounded in the forced flight from Cuba. The contemporary Cuban American diaspora began in the 1960s in response to the Cuban Revolution, the result of which was Fidel Castro's appointment as premier and his transformation of Cuba's economy from capitalist to socialist. One of the first steps taken by Castro's government was the seizure and redistribution of the land and assets of upper-class Cuban citizens. This was an often violent and terrifying event for those affected and is frequently dramatized in Cuban American women's literature. In response to being stripped of their possessions and often fearing for their lives, many Cubans fled their homeland for the United States, drawn by its seemingly happy marriage of proximity to the homeland and the promise of the American Dream. These novels, however, reveal that proximity would be more haunting than comforting and that the dream could remain in the realm of promise, rather than reality. Therefore, Anzaldúa's concept of the Borderlands (*La Frontera*) is applicable here as well. Anzaldúa explains that "the Borderlands are physically present wherever two or more cultures edge each other, where people of different races occupy the same territory, where under, lower, middle and upper classes touch, where the space between two individuals shrinks with intimacy" (19). The female characters created by Cuban American women inhabit the borderlands in physical, geographical, and psycho-social ways.

As a result of this destabilizing combination of experiences and after almost fifty years of exile, literary representations of the Cuban American diaspora have molded into their own unique shape. Virgil Suarez and Delia Poey vividly describe the characteristics of this representation: "a longing for roots, a sense of displacement, the persistence of memory, a need to replay history and an idealization of Cuba itself" (11). Though all novels analyzed in this study show evidence of these themes, they also demonstrate the particular experience of "Pérez-Firmat's demarcation of a distinct 1.5 generation" that "separates those who mourn the Cuba they knew firsthand from their North American grandchildren who can only acquire it through stories or memories" (Socolovsky 236). The young female characters featured in these narratives are a "generation of North American Cubans who move between the two cultures and who have . . . a double perspective and attachment that allows them to feel an affective and intense connection both to the land of their past (or their parents' past) and to that of their present and future" (Socolovsky 236)—in other words, embodiments of Anzaldúa's New Mestiza.

These insights into the shaping of literary representations of Cuban American diaspora provide context for the diverse portraits of Cuban-Americanhood in the lives of Obejas, García, and Valdes-Rodriguez and, in turn, the characters and relationships they bring to life in their fiction. While Obejas and García were born in Cuba and came to America as young children, Valdes-Rodriguez was born in the United States to Cuban parents. Obejas, who grew up in the Midwest, explains, "I was born in Havana and that single event has pretty much defined the rest of my life. In the U.S., I'm Cuban, Cuban-American, Latina by virtue of being Cuban . . . always and endlessly Cuban. I'm more Cuban here than I am in Cuba" (Shapiro). Cristina García likewise has "always thought of [her]self as Cuban" (Lopez 104) even though she was not raised in a Latino/a or Cuban community. Influencing García's sense of self was her parents' sense of loss, which infused her childhood: "I grew up in the wake of my parents' displacement and nostalgia. . . . It's a part of me" (Murphy). For Valdes-Rodriquez, who was born in New Mexico to a Cuban-émigré father and a New Mexican mother, her father's status shaped her worldview. She explains, "the . . . driving force in my life has been justice . . . fairness for all kinds of people," which derives from "being the daughter of an immigrant who was grossly underestimated for most of his career and life, and the sort of despair you feel watching that happen" (Queirós). Based on their unique experiences of life on the hyphen, these authors would likely agree with García that "there is no one Cuban exile" (Kevane & Heredia 75), a concept explored here through the boundaries faced, overcome, and surrendered to by female characters.

The popular and award-winning works featured in this study— García's *Dreaming in Cuban*, Obejas' *Memory Mambo*, and Valdes-Rodriguez's *The Dirty Girls Social Club*—address issues of family related to exile and the cultural hybrid experience. As Jacqueline Stefanko observes, works like these seek to "heal the fractures and ruptures resulting from exile and dispersal" (50). Stefanko connects these seemingly personal fictions to historical events: "Colonization, revolution, and threatened invasion entwine around the personal issue of family separation and exile" (56).

Mothers, Daughters, and Granddaughters

In contemporary culture, the mother-daughter relationship is recognized as one of the most important influences in the development of identity and history. Lara Walker explains that mothers and daughters "attempt to establish their own identity in contradistinction to each other, yet in connection to the matrilineal family as a whole" (67). Rocío G. Davis witnesses this trend in American multiethnic literature and adds that, "the place of the mother . . . directs, modifies, and influences the daughters' responses to both individual and cultural demands" (60). Therefore, "understanding and bonding between mothers and daughters" is "a fundamental step toward self-awareness and mastery of the culture" (Davis 60). In García's narrative, the daughter must "take on and continue" the mother's stories while transforming those stories through her own experiences (Davis 60).

The Revolution plays a central role in the breakdown of bonds between women in *Dreaming in Cuban*. The novel begins and ends with the Cuban grandmother/mother, Celia, and tells the story of her two daughters—Lourdes and Felicia—and their daughters, Pilar and "the twins," Luz and Milagro. Walker accurately observes that all of the mother-daughter bonds in the novel are problematic (69). Though the diaspora adds to the tension in these relationships, the play reveals the prerevolution roots of Celia's problematic relationship with her daughters. When Celia is sent by her mother to live with her Aunt Alicia, she "lost her mother's face, the lies that had complicated her mouth" (García 92). The gentle, yet strong aunt, operating as Celia's adoptive mother, positively influences Celia by exposing her to museums, symphonies, long walks, and the piano. After marriage, Celia leaves this encouraging home space for the dysfunctional, cruel home of her husband, Jorge, who abandons Celia for extended periods of time with his abusive mother and sister. Celia's mother and sister-in-law, aided by her husband, drive her insane. Severe postpartum depression compounds her situation, leading Celia to reject Lourdes after the child's birth.

This rejection understandably infuses Lourdes' perception of her mother throughout her life. Even when her father returns as a ghost and requests that she express his apology to Celia, Lourdes will not give her mother that small bit of solace: "The words refuse to form in her mouth" (García 238). Despite the personal nature of Lourdes' psychological wound, the tension between mother and daughter takes political shape as a result of the Revolution: Celia supports it, Lourdes does not. Lourdes' distrust of the Revolution is reinforced by a violent rape at the hands of the Revolution's henchmen, a rape that coincides, symbolically, with her personal property being appropriated by the government. Celia, however, never knows the reason for her daughter's hatred of the Revolution because Lourdes never tells anyone.

Lourdes, who becomes a successful capitalist in the United States, bears a daughter more alike in nature to Celia than to herself: "Pilar is like her grandmother, disdainful of rules, of religion, of everything meaningful. Neither of them shows respect for anyone, least of all themselves" (García 168). Though this similarity frustrates Lourdes, it buttresses both Celia and Pilar. This connection begins in Cuba; when Pilar is a baby, Celia notes that the child "seemed to understand her very thoughts" (García 119). Despite being removed to the United States, Pilar connects telepathically to her grandmother in Cuba. Celia says, "I hear her speaking to me at night just before I fall asleep" (García 29). As Davis notes "Celia provides for Pilar the connection that Lourdes has severed" (64). Pilar underscores the importance of this connection to her grandmother when she notes, "[m]ost of what I've learned that's important I've learned on my own, or from my grandmother" (García 28). The telepathic connection ends as mysteriously as it began, yet "she left me her legacy nonetheless . . . . Even in silence, she gives me the confidence to do what I believe is right, to trust my own perceptions" (García 176). Stefanko supports the reading that Pilar's connection to her grandmother empowers and enables the young woman: "Celia and Pilar share knowledges that have the power to imagine community in alternative, transnational ways, thus permeating boundaries and allowing us to question the construction of borders as pure and inflexible" (57). Like most of the young protagonists featured in this study, Pilar struggles to determine where she "belongs"—in the United States or Cuba. Undoubtedly due to her connection with her grandmother, Pilar believes, "If I could only see Abuela Celia again, I'd know where I belonged" (García 58). Pilar fulfills this prophecy when she visits her grandmother in Cuba, for it is this trip that cements her American identity: "I know it's where I belong— not *instead* of here, but *more* than here" (García 236).

The constructive grandmother-granddaughter relationship strongly contrasts the negative mother-daughter dyads: Lourdes and Pilar, Felicia and Luz/Milagro. Lourdes labels Pilar "irresponsible, self-centered, a bad seed" (García 168) and "is convinced it is something pathological, something her daughter inherited from Abuela Celia" (García 172). Pilar's impression of her mother is equally unflattering: "Mom is arbitrary and inconsistent and always believes she's right" (García 140). Pilar identifies "one thing I have in common with my mother," noting: "If I don't like someone, I show it" (García 135). To complicate matters, the singular moment of love that Pilar feels toward her mother derives from a misunderstanding of her mother's actions. This occurs when Lourdes defends Pilar's punk painting of the Statue of Liberty at its unveiling (García 144). The reader later discovers that Lourdes did not protect the painting out of love or respect for her daughter, but because she "wouldn't tolerate people telling her what to do on her own property" (García 171). In the midst of their visit to Cuba, mother and daughter conspire to help a young cousin escape Cuba, suggesting that their antagonism may be overcome by a shared goal—or at least a shared revelation about the hopelessness of life in Cuba.

Though Felicia enjoys a more positive relationship with Celia, she is even more estranged from her daughters than Lourdes is from Pilar. Luz and Milagro (meaning 'Light' and 'Miracle,' respectively) "are always alone with one another, speaking in symbols only they understand" (García 38). The twins formalize their reproach for Felicia by calling her "not-Mama" (García 121); they make a pact to ignore and "to stay as far away from her as possible" (García 121). The twins' solidarity grows from their special connection as explained by Luz: "Milagro and I have each other. We're a double helix, tight and impervious. That's why Mama can't penetrate us"

(García 120). The boundary devised by the twins is simultaneously protective and destructive; it protects them from their mother's madness, yet it deprives them of any connection to her.

The troubled mother-daughter relationships in these texts serves as a poignant reminder of the difficulties inherent in an experience of hybridity that grows out of violence and separation. As Celia darkly prophesizes about her daughters, "There is no solace among them, only a past infected with disillusion" (García 117). Pilar, too, feels that, "Something got horribly scrambled along the way" (García 178). Nonetheless, promise does arise from pain experienced by these characters. Echoing Anzaldúa's vision of the New Mestiza, García proposes that power lies in a hybrid new generation, symbolized by Pilar. According to Anzaldúa, the mix of races (in this case, cultures) "provides hybrid progeny, a mutable, more malleable species" that is gifted with "a new *mestiza* consciousness" (99), and, so, "The new mestiza copes by developing a tolerance for contradictions, a tolerance for ambiguity" (79). An empowered figure, like the one Anzaldúa imagines, is who Celia has in mind when she asserts that granddaughters can "save" their grandmothers and "guard their knowledge like the first fire" (García 222). Because Pilar is a writer and inherits her grandmother's letters, she is poised to claim her past and continue the story for future generations. In light of this reading, it is interesting to note that all the young, hybrid protagonists in this study take up writing in some form, thereby symbolically seizing the tools of self-expression necessary for writing a new narrative, a new self, a new culture.

Sisters

The existence of a closeness between sisters is sometimes taken for granted, but sisterhood is a complex relationship. To elucidate the dynamics of this bond, Helena Michie developed the concept of "sororophobia," which "is about negotiation; it attempts to describe the negotiation of sameness and difference, identity and separation, between women of the same generation, and is meant to encompass both the desire for and the recoil from identification with other women" (10). Moreover, this concept "is a matrix against and through which women work out—or fail to work out—their differences" (10). This matrix is in operation within the stories of García and Obejas.

Lourdes and Felicia, the sisters in *Dreaming in Cuban,* have differing relationships with their mother, which then influence their interactions with each other. As a child Felicia adored Lourdes, but the women are not close as adults. Celia observes that, in adulthood, her daughters are "desolate, deaf and blind to the world, to each other, to her" (García 117). Here, García sandwiches their inability to see and hear each other between their inability to do so with the world they inhabit and with their mother. It also reinforces the extent to which a lack of connection between the sisters originates from their lack of connections with the mother, and, perhaps by extension, the "motherland." As noted above, Lourdes collapses her contempt for her mother with her disdain for the Cuban Revolution. In response to this, Lourdes becomes an über-capitalist in the United States and focuses more on her business than on her family. Felicia, eternally ambivalent about the Revolution, escapes through madness, hysteria, and *Santería*. Through their choices, which are influenced by their political and social experiences, Lourdes and Felicia sacrifice their own relationship with each other and alienate their daughters.

The sisterly bond is at risk in Obejas' *Memory Mambo*, as well. Juani, the youngest daughter in a tightly knit Chicago Cuban family, struggles with hyphenated identity in much the way Pilar does in *Dreaming in Cuban*. Juani feels herself to be "comfortably part of the family portrait," but "also a stranger in [her] family" (Obejas 79). Juani links this estrangement to her sexuality: "My lesbianism is not the cause of my alienation, but it's a part of it" (Obejas 79). This tension is important to Obejas, as she explains, "culturally we're defined by our families . . . Juani doesn't just function in the world as a lesbian. Mostly she functions in the world of her family. Her community is her family" (Kleindienst 14). The idea that Juani does not "fit" anywhere underscores her liminality and feeds her desire to know the "truth" about her family's history. Juani claims that "in this house of nostalgia and fear, of time warps and trivias, I'm the only one I know for sure" (Obejas 79), but Obejas reveals that in this context the "self" is just as elusive as the "truth" about one's family. The effects of this tension between reality and fabrication on one's identity is the focal predicament of Obejas' novel.

To highlight the obstacles erected by the geographically distant state of their relationship, Obejas stages one of the most important conversations in the novel between the sisters, a conversation that gives the book its title. Juani's sister, Nena, is conspicuously absent from the Chicago-centered action of the novel and for good reason: Nena has escaped to Miami. Though extremely close in Chicago, the distance between their hometown and Miami takes its toll on the sisters' relationship. In this conversation, Juani and Nena discuss their family's preoccupation with storytelling. Juani says to Nena, "*everybody* in our family's a liar" (Obejas 194). Nena, however, does not perceive this as "lying." Nena likens her family's storytelling "to singing 'Guantanamera'—everybody gets a chance to make up their own verse" (Obejas 194). Juani joins in the impromptu "signifying" by adding that the process is like "Memory Mambo": "one step forward, two steps back" (Obejas 194). Despite the playfulness of this conversation, a significant dissimilarity arises between the sisters: to Nena, the family's storytelling is communal, creative, and fun; moreover, it allows everyone to participate. Juani, however, sees the process as regressive, constantly preventing the 'dancer' from moving forward. It also is unclear if Juani means the original Cuban mambo of the 1930s, which was free of breaking and basic steps, or the Americanized version of the dance formulated in the 1970s by Puerto Rican immigrants. In either case, both versions reveal another layer of meaning: in a world characterized by hybridity and the dissolution of boundaries, how can one distinguish between "adaptation" and "original"?

Cousins

The bond between cousins is equally complicated as that between sisters and is just as important in Cuban American exile and literature. Hispanic literature scholar Nicolás Kanellos identifies Celedonio Gonzonio's 1971 novel entitled *Los Primos* (*The Cousins*) as the first Cuban American novel to turn attention away from Cuba and

---

toward "the development of Cuban culture in America" (57). The hybrid cousins "create a new syntax," Juani proposes, thus creating a figuration of the empowered potential of Anzaldúa's New Mestiza, who can use her liminal status to produce and facilitate new, inclusive hybrid cultures. The cousins also illustrate how the family is reshaped and redefined in exile. They enable a connection to the lost homeland and help to perpetuate its culture in a new space.

In *Memory Mambo*, cousins play a vital role in the narrative. Juani identifies the cousins' unusual liminal status by explaining that they are "part of the family and yet they're not" (Obejas 12). This bond springs from what Juani calls an "unmistakable stamp of kinship. It's all in the eyes—something tragic, perhaps" (Obejas 12). This "stamp" and the related "tragedy" are rooted in a shared disconnect from the homeland. Juani proposes that their unique form of communication binds them: "We have an affinity, a way of speaking that's neither Cuban nor American . . . We communicate, I suspect, like deaf people—not so much compensating for the lost sense, but creating a new syntax from the pieces of our displaced lives" (Obejas 13).

Due to the large family represented in the novel, this discussion focuses only on two cousin characters—Caridad, and Titi—and how they influence Juani's self-development. Caridad, whom Juani takes care of each time she is beaten by her husband, is a symbolic tether that, like a yo-yo, continually pulls Juani into dysfunctional cycles, mirrored in the cycle of domestic violence. Juani's passive role in this relationship should be noted, as it serves as a microcosm for her passiveness overall. Juani's inaction occurs in speech, either words not spoken or conversations avoided. For instance, when Caridad asks Juani if the bruises on her breasts might have more serious repercussions, Juani distracts the conversation with a joke (Obejas 48–9). Though Juani believes she is helping, her actions garner Caridad's contempt. In a revelatory moment in the text, Caridad challenges Juani's role in the family: "Just 'cause I call you—just 'cause anybody calls you—doesn't mean you gotta run" (Obejas 198). In saying this, Caridad deconstructs Juani's sole purpose—to be of service to her family—thereby forcing Juani to question her identity and further alienating her from her family.

Juani's psychic mirror and Cuban doppelgänger is Titi, the cousin who cannot escape Cuba, no matter how hard she tries. Her presence turns the identity lens to sexuality. Paul Allatson highlights Titi's importance to the narrative: "As lesbians separated by exile . . . Titi's and Juani's experiences of sexualized boundaries provide yet more bodily parallels to broader familial and national divergences and reconvergences" (Allatson). Juani projects onto Titi her own inner pain: "I . . . know that the damage in Titi's soul . . . is connected to how she loves, or more precisely, how she's not allowed to love" (Obejas 75). In Juani's opinion, Titi's has the "need to be loved in the daylight" (Obejas 76). Juani connects Titi's desire to escape Cuba to her desire to be openly gay: "once here, she might be free to be queer" (Obejas 76). However, Juani and her closeted girlfriend, Gina, are proof that living in the United States does not lead to loving openly. Though Juani imagines that she and Titi would share a unique bond based on sexual orientation, she cannot even write a letter to Titi: "What, after all, do you say to a person you've never met?" (Obejas 176). Juani's lack of ability to express herself to her cousin contrasts with the characters in *Dreaming in Cuban* who write and thus find powerful outlets of self-expression. Through the dramatization of Juani's inability to communicate, Obejas demonstrates how exile can prevent connections that could prove beneficial to those on either side of the ninety-mile oceanic divide, and on the borders of more than one culture.

Friends

Though the heroines of Valdes-Rodriguez's *New York Times* bestselling novel *The Dirty Girls Social Club* experience challenges in their friendships, the novel sends a strong message in support of women's social bonding. The description "dirty girl" is translated from the Spanish slang "*buena sucia*" and is used ironically by the women in the group. The irony derives from the fact that none of the women are "dirty" or "naughty" in actuality, though society may perceive them as such. The story centers on six diverse Latina friends, who form a bond in college and make a formal commitment to continue their friendship into adulthood.

The main Cuban American character in the text is Lauren, a self-described "crazy paranoid" who feels "pathetic" (Valdes-Rodriguez 35) in comparison to her friends. Similar to Obejas' character Juani, Lauren—from whose perspective the book begins and ends—illustrates how one's ethnically liminal status can lead one to feel "homeless" in professional, personal, and romantic relationships. She openly blames her low self-esteem on her Cuban American identity, especially her father's rampant nostalgia for a Cuba, for which exiles can find "no country more fascinating and important" (Valdes-Rodriguez 3). Lauren reveals the psychological price young women must pay for familial exile when she admits, "When your whole family lives with a lie that big, living with men who lie is easy" (Valdes-Rodriguez 4). As a result of this, her therapist suggests she get a "cubadectomy" (4), since "Cuba is the oozing recurrent tumor we inherit from our fathers" (4).

Most of Lauren's growth is a product of her friendships. Though Lauren hates herself "because no one else has ever bothered to love [her]" (Valdes-Rodriguez 7), she is precious to her fellow "dirty girls," who counter Lauren's low self-esteem. One friend counsels her, "you've got a real self-destructive streak. You must protect yourself more" (Valdes-Rodriguez 37). Then, they encourage Lauren to end her engagement with a cheating, unappreciative fiancé. Lauren finally accepts their support when she realizes how much her friends value and love her, unlike her fiancé. This revelation causes her to ask the group, "Why can't there be one single guy out there as committed as all of us?" (Valdes-Rodriguez 40). This quotation shows how women's bonding can facilitate the restructuring of negative relationship patterns; Lauren's next boyfriend cherishes and respects her and, in doing so, helps her to begin accepting herself and the complexities inherent in the New Mestiza identity.

Conclusion

In addition to their contributions to the literary canon, these narratives provide essential insight into the lives of an immigrant population that has, yet again, reshaped American identity. The political restrictions that circumscribe this group's lives—trade embargoes, strict visitation procedures, and tense political relations between their "homelands"—remain hotly debated more than fifty years after the Cuban Revolution. Therefore, if "narrative is the vehicle by which the ruptures of exile can be healed and that the gesture of traveling/ dwelling can be negotiated via the text" (Stefanko 66), writing is a personal and cultural necessity for these authors. After all, it is through the act of writing that these writers ensure for themselves and other women what Celia longs to teach her granddaughter, Pilar: "to understand the morphology of survival" and to "outlast the hard flames" (García 42). In the act of entwining their own voices with those that came before and with them, García, Obejas, and Valdes-Rodriguez teach us that despite loss, nostalgia, and the pain inherent in beginning anew, the female ancestor "left [them] her legacy nonetheless—a love for the sea and the smoothness of pearls, an appreciation of music and words, sympathy for the underdog, and a disregard for boundaries" (García 176).

In the larger context of creating new identities, Cuban American women's fiction reflects Edward Said's belief that "exile, immigration and the crossing of boundaries can . . . provide us with new narrative forms" (255) in that it reimagines the boundaries of genre, storytelling, and identity. In terms of immigrant literature as a tradition, these authors also reflect David Cowart's point that, "the emotions and experiences of new immigrants constitute a bracing corrective to narrowly policiticized theories of ethnic identity" (8). As such, these authors problematize Ambrosio Fornet's enduring question: "When we speak of frontiers, diaspora, identity, periphery, multiculturalism, where are we speaking from? Are we on the inside, on the outside, or on the fence?" (99). These authors and their texts prove that the concepts of "where-ness" and "location" are just as slippery as the notions that inside/ outside, problem/ solution are *de facto* separate conditions. If asked 'where are you speaking from' and 'where are you,' García, Obejas, and Valdes-Rodriguez would likely answer, "everywhere." Their work recognizes the complex relationship between problem and solution, without which hybridity and innovation would be impossible.

Works Cited

Allatson, Paul. "Memory Mambo: Cuban Memory, 'American' Mobility, and Achy Obejas' Lesbian Way." *Ciberletras* 7 (2002): n.p. *MLA International Bibliography*. Web. 13 Apr. 2012.

Anzaldúa, Gloria. *Borderlands/La Frontera: The New Mestiza*. 2nd ed. San Francisco: Aunt Lute, 1999.

Cowart, David. *Trailing Clouds: Immigrant Fiction in Contemporary America*. Ithaca, NY: Cornell UP, 2006.

Davis, Rocío G. "Back to the Future: Mothers, Languages, and Homes in Cristina García's *Dreaming in Cuban*." *World Literature Today* 74.1 (2000): 60–68. *MLA International Bibliography*. Web. 13 Apr. 2012.

Fornet, Ambrosio. "The Cuban Literary Diaspora and Its Contexts: A Glossary." *Boundary 2* 29.3 (2002): 91–103. *MLA International Bibliography*. Web. 13 Apr. 2012.

García, Cristina. *Dreaming in Cuban*. New York: Ballantine, 1992.

Kanellos, Nicolás. *Hispanic Literature of the United States: A Comprehensive Reference*. Westport, CT: Greenwood, 2003.

Kevane, Bridgit, & Juanita Heredia. "At Home on the Page: An Interview with Christina García." *Latina Self-Portraits: Interviews with Contemporary Women Writers*. Albuquerque: U of New Mexico P, 2000. 69–82.

Lopez, Iraida H. ". . . And There Is Only My Imagination Where Our History Should Be: An Interview with Cristina García ." *Bridges to Cuba/Puentes a Cuba*. Ed. Ruth Behar. Ann Arbor: U of Michigan P, 1995. 102–114.

Michie, Helena. *Sororophobia: Differences Among Women in Literature and Culture*. New York: Oxford UP, 1992.

Murphy, Jessica. "The Nature of Inheritance (Interview)." *The Atlantic*. April 2003. Web. 1 Aug. 2012.

Obejas, Achy. *Memory Mambo*. Pittsburgh: Cleis, 1996.

Pérez-Firmat, Gustavo. *Life on the Hyphen: The Cuban-American Way*. Austin: U of Texas P, 2012.

Queirós, Carlos J. "From Dirty Girls to Enlightened Ladies: Chica Lit Writer Alisa Valdes-Rodriguez Challenges Genre Expectations with Her Novel *The Three Kings*." *AARP VIVA*. Winter 2010. Web. 1 Aug. 2012.

Said, Edward. "Representing the Colonized: Anthropology's Interlocutors." *Critical Inquiry* 15 (1989): 225.

Shapiro, Greg. "In 'AWE': Achy Obejas on Her New Work." *Windy City Times*. 8 Aug. 2001. Web. 1 Aug. 2012.

Socolovsky, Maya. "Cube Interrupted: The Loss of Center and Story in Ana Menémdez's Collection *In Cuba I Was a German Shepherd.*" *Critique: Studies in New Fiction* 46.3 (Spring 2005): 235-51.

Stefanko, Jacqueline. "New Ways of Telling: Latinas' Narratives of Exile and Return."

Frontiers 17.2 (1996): 50–69. *MLA International Bibliography*. Web. 13 Apr. 2012.

Suarez, Virgil, & Delia Poey, Eds. *Little Havana Blues: A Cuban-American Anthology*. Houston: Arte Publico, 1996.

Valdes-Rodriguez, Alisa. *The Dirty Girls Social Club*. New York: St. Martin's Griffin, 2003.

Walker, Lara A. "Persistent Tensions and Powerful Bonds: Mothers and Daughters in Cristina García's *Dreaming in Cuban*." *Osamayor* 5.11–12 (1999): 67–74. *MLA International Bibliography*. Web. 13 Apr. 2012.

Race, Ethnicity, and National Identity in Paule Marshall's *Brown Girl, Brownstones*, or How the Barbadian Becomes American

Joanna Davis-McElligatt

As Selina Boyce, the young protagonist of Paule Marshall's *Brown Girl, Brownstones* (1959), stands on the small veranda of her Brooklyn apartment surveying her neighborhood, she bears witness to the influence of the previous generations of immigrants who built the community. Selina recalcitrantly raises her arm in weak protest against her strict mother, who has forbidden her to leave the confines of the porch, when her attention is drawn to the "two heavy silver bangles which had come from 'home' and which every Barbadian-American girl wore from birth" (Marshall 5). Though the "bangles sounded her defiance" (Marshall 5), she knows she has also been forbidden to remove the jewelry, which keeps her own attention trained always on her Barbadian "home," however foreign a place it might be. The buildings lining her street reinforce her sense of confinement; they are "all one uniform red-brown stone," so similar they appear to be "one house reflected through a train of mirrors" (Marshall 3). Yet for all their "same brown monotony," Selina notes that:

> each house had something distinctively its own. . . . Here, Ionic columns framed the windows while next door gargoyles scowled up at the sun. There, the cornices were hung with carved foliage while Gorgon heads decorated others. Many houses had bay windows or Gothic stonework; a few boasted turrets high above the other roofs. (Marshall 3)

These idiosyncratic embellishments typically found on castles and manors are historical inscriptions of nineteenth-century immigrants, the "Dutch-English and Scotch-Irish who had built the houses" (Marshall 3). By constructing, in the New World, abodes that mimicked old European finery, these immigrants wanted to make it clear that, in America, they could be anything they wanted—as rich as a burgher, as propertied as a lord, and as cultured as a king. Though the neighborhood had been populated by whites for generations, in 1939, the year the novel opens, a large migrant influx of West Indians arrived. These new West Indian immigrants, not unlike the Europeans who came before, wanted to acquire certain things that had been more or less denied them in the colonies: home, land, and business ownership, relief from an inflexible caste system, and improved opportunities and living conditions for their children. The brownstones rented by West Indian immigrants served a symbolic function, then, not only because so little of the land in the colonies was available to be bought and sold by peoples of African descent, but also because their new homes could prove that certain modes of class suppression and racial oppression practiced on the islands could be avoided in the States.

Selina's mother and father, Silla and Deighton Boyce, are among those immigrants who hope to make their fortunes in America, though in very different ways. Silla, a naturalized citizen, ardently works cleaning homes and, later, on the line in a munitions factory. She squirrels away every penny she earns so that her family can purchase their rented brownstone—which Silla eventually does, but only with the help of a loan shark. Silla earns extra cash by renting spare rooms and hopes to make enough to see to it that Selina and her sister Ina have a fine education. Deighton, on the other hand, wants to get rich, and invests in various schemes he believes will help him rise quickly through the ranks of American capitalist enterprise. Deighton plans to return to Barbados a wealthy man, where he will construct an elaborate mansion, grow fruit and sugar cane, and generally live as the white colonialists do. Deighton enters the country illegally, refuses to go through the naturalization process, and works hard to keep his daughters emotionally and mentally attached to the island neither has ever seen. Though Selina accepts that her parents are immigrants, she nevertheless thinks of them as being fundamentally different from former immigrant inhabitants of her community, the Dutch-English and Scotch-Irish. The West Indian, unlike the decorous European of Selina's imagination, maintains unusual social customs, and speaks Bajan Creole, a patois of West African languages and English. Selina is well enough aware that the incursion of West Indian immigrants to Brooklyn is the impetus for white flight and seems also to understand why whites would rather abandon their history, homes, and neighborhoods than commune so closely with their "dark[er]" brothers and sisters. Selina is not only coming of age in racist wartime America, but in a community of people desperately working to escape the rigid colonial structure of English imperialism. As such, the complex formations of global white supremacy, nativism, and racism become painfully clear to her.

Selina's fantasies of European tranquility and sophistication stand in direct contradistinction to the hullabaloo that surrounds her at home. Selina's family occupies the first floor of the brownstone. Suggie, a recent Barbadian immigrant rents one room upstairs and Miss Mary and her daughter Martize, the former white maid of the brownstone's owners, occupy the remainder of the second floor. As the youngest child in the crowded building, Selina wanders freely throughout the house and has, therefore, the best opportunity to imagine what the original inhabitants' lives were like, especially considering that her family's rooms came opulently furnished in assorted fixtures and fittings left behind by the owners. Selina's flat is impressive, with its: entrance hall, "a room in itself with its carpet, wallpaper, and hushed dimness"; parlor "full of ponderous furniture and potted ferns which the whites had left"; and sun parlor, a room that made them "very proud" because "not many of the old brownstones had them" (Marshall 8). When alone, Selina often pretends to be one of the white owners, and as she swirls around the parlor in a make-believe gown, "she was no longer a dark girl alone . . . but one of them, invested with their beauty and gentility" (Marshall 5). Yet as soon as she sees herself, small and dark, in the ostentatious floor-to-ceiling mirror, "[t]he illusory figure fled and she was only herself again. . . . She did not belong here. She was something vulgar in a holy place" (Marshall 5–6). Selina feels triply alienated: she is black, in a home (and nation-state) built by whites, and ornamented in an aesthetic suiting their own tastes. As a young black girl, she is incapable of achieving American standards of beauty, always coded as white and feminine. In addition, as both a first-generation Barbadian American and natural-born citizen, she knows very little of Barbados, but is not free to be completely American, either.

Selina is "unhomed" in the sense described by Homi K. Bhabha: "to be unhomed is not to be homeless"; rather, the term "captures something of the estranging sense of the relocation of the home and the world—the unhomeliness—that is the condition of extra-territorial and cross-cultural initiations" (Bhabha 13). As we have seen, despite Selina's attachments to those various spaces and places, she never feels settled in any one of them, torn as she is between nations symbolized by her parents' opposing ambitions. Selina exists, then, in a liminal, in-between space where she is neither Barbadian nor American, girl nor woman, citizen nor immigrant, neither African American nor West Indian. Bhabha has described this position as "a place of hybridity, figuratively speaking . . . *neither one nor the other*" (37, his emphasis). Selina and her family occupy a liminal space that is always mitigated by the complex of outside forces acting on them at any given moment. In contrast to Silla and Deighton, Selina struggles to assert an identity that is essentially transnational and fluid. She fluctuates between Barbados and America, between Barbadianness and Americanness, between Barbadian Americanness and African Americanness, between whiteness and blackness, and between girlhood and womanhood. The novel is an attempt to explore and recover in-betweenness as a point of identification all its own. Indeed, by the novel's end, Selina comes to accept the fact of her transnational blackness by leaving New York for Barbados as a worker on a cruise ship.

Race, Class, Desire, and the Migration of Deighton Boyce

Unlike the other Barbadian immigrants Selina knows, her mother included, who work several jobs and keep long, erratic hours, Deighton spends his days lazing about the sun parlor, half-heartedly pursuing a correspondence course in accounting. Deighton regales

Selina with stories from his Barbadian childhood, when he and his friends spent their days playing cricket and football, or "down Christ Church where the rich white people live" swimming in the ocean: "I not like yuh mother. . . . 'Pon a Sat'day I would walk 'bout town like I was a full-full man. All up Broad Street and Swan Street like I did own the damn place" (Marshall 10). In his casual dismissal of his wife and other working class Barbadians, Deighton paints a picture of a hierarchy both race- and class-based: "rich whites" at the top, the blacks who live near them in "town" in the middle, and the blacks who live "down some gully or up some hill" at the bottom. Deighton's refusal to work, then, is not only an extension of the advantages of his childhood, but also a desperate struggle to avoid the degradations attendant to being a Barbadian colonial subject *and* an assimilating immigrant.

Deighton's egregious sense of entitlement is directly linked to his mother's early treatment of him. Shortly after Deighton's birth, his father left his family to find work in Cuba and never returned. His mother, Ianthe, left alone with three children, became a seamstress. Though terribly poor, Ianthe insisted on keeping her son dressed in new shoes and fine white shirts—or as Virgie, a friend of Silla's who grew up with Deighton, remembers: "He was always dressing up like white people" (Marshall 32). Ianthe scraped together payment for Deighton and both of his sisters to attend college, hopeful that their positions as schoolmasters might rescue them from poverty—even though her heart's desire had been to send Deighton to England to train as a physician. Eager to protect her son from the indignities of being black and poor, Ianthe so shielded Deighton that he cannot understand why he can never seem to find jobs with "big white people in town" (Marshall 33), and quickly comes to resent that the only employment option available to him is to teach poor, black children in rural Barbados. Deighton, raised to mimic and emulate the whites, continually strives to make himself a man in the image of the white colonial master, not only to replace the void left by his own father, but also to displace the shame that acceptance of his station would bring. After migrating to America and meeting Silla, Deighton makes plans to return to Barbados where he might show up the whites who shunned him, the blacks who mocked him, and live the life of leisure he believes is his birthright.

Deighton's refusal to see himself as a permanent US resident contrasts with the efforts of Seifert Yearwood, a Barbadian small-business owner and loan shark. Seifert is exclusively interested in getting ahead in America. Though Seifert is acutely aware that Jim Crow applies to West Indians, he recognizes that his immigrant status enables him to evade some of the restrictions that hinder the progress of native-born blacks, such as voter suppression, and lack of access to loans for homes and businesses. Seifert explains that purchasing property in neighborhoods populated by white ethnics is the only way "a man your color gon get ahead" (Marshall 39). It is, therefore, almost impossible for Seifert to understand Deighton's refusal to make a move on the family's brownstone, or his insistence on holding out for an accounting position at a bank. No matter how talented you might be, Seifert explain to Deighton, whites will never "have you up in their fancy office and pulling down the same money as them" (Marshall 39). Deighton recoils from Seifert, for he "recalled things thrust deep into forgottenness: those white English faces . . . and himself as a young man . . . asking them for a job as a clerk—the incredulity, the disdain and indignation that flushed their faces as they said no" (Marshall 39). Deighton's desire to become like the whites and return to Barbados is a neurotic response to his having been spurned as a young man, coupled with his inability to see himself for what he truly is—neither white, nor inferior to whites. Whereas Seifert is willing to work long hours, purchase property slowly, and suffer injustices, Deighton refuses to engage with the system at all. Deighton's refusal to work is, in its own way, a form of resistance. By rejecting the strictures Jim Crow laws place on him and his livelihood, Deighton is attempting to preserve his dignity. However, his repudiation of Jim Crow does not dismantle the system of oppression that prevents him from earning a living in his chosen profession; rather, his refusal to work further alienates him from the support and structures constructed by West Indians to circumvent the limits of Jim Crow. In other words, Deighton's mode of repudiation only serves to alienate him from his wife, his children, and his fellow Barbadians, rather than dismantling the complex of systems which oppresses all of them alike.

Deighton's plan to become wealthy is suddenly achievable after he inherits nearly two acres of land from his sister in Barbados, which, he explains to Selina, "is a lot in a place that's only one-hundred-sixty-six square miles—and a lot for a colored man to own in a place where the white man own everything" (Marshall 25). Deighton recognizes, however, that the acquisition of land is not enough and that he will now need money to maintain a well-heeled lifestyle and to build a house "just like the white people own. A house to end all house!" (Marshall 12). Silla urges him to sell the land and use the money to put a down payment on their brownstone, but she has no legal right to it, and she understands that his greatest desire is to become white and rich. Despite Seifert's warning, Deighton applies for an accountant's position at, he tells Silla proudly, one of "the three places offering the best salary" (Marshall 81) in New York, and is promptly rebutted. Rather than take Seifert's suggestion that he get a service job, he instead decides to purchase a trumpet and become a musician. Unlike working at an all-white accounting firm or taking a job as a porter or hotel bellman, playing music was work that black men, in particular, could do on their own terms, without recourse to the white world. In other words, playing the trumpet would relieve Deighton of the burden of white supremacy, while also allowing him to participate within the capitalist democracy. As a musician, Deighton believes that he will become fabulously wealthy, while also earning "respect" for his craft, not only from those whites who spurned him, but also from the other Bajan, whom he believes will be forced to recognize his worth "as a man" once he "makes good money and lives good . . . [and] wear the best of clothes . . . [and] eat the finest" (Marshall 85). To that end, his determination to become a trumpeter is also intended to solidify his status as an upstanding member of the Barbadian American community, even as his sights are set on his homeland. Of course, Deighton does not become a famous musician because he, "only half-learn a thing," and also because Silla destroys his instrument in a fit of rage.

to buy books), a fur coat for Silla, and an expensive new trumpet for himself: "When I went in these store the first thing I did was to lif muh head and not act like I coming asking for a job sweeping the floor or cleaning out their toilet. . . . But all I did was to start counting muh money . . . and I tell yuh they almost break their neck running to wait 'pon muh" (Marshall 125). Silla, Selina, and Ina are horrified that Deighton would sacrifice the family's future for the brief fulfillment of his fantasy of wealth and white power, but he evinces not one iota of regret. Unable to receive a divorce without her husband's consent, Silla borrows money from a loan shark for a down payment on the brownstone, forces Deighton out of the house, and proceeds to act as if he has died.

Deighton's exclusion from the family is mirrored by a larger one by the Barbadian immigrant community. At a wedding attended by several members of the Association of Barbadian Homeowners and Businessmen, a group Silla has recently joined, Deighton arrives during a rousing chorus of a Barbadian folk song, "Small Island," in which an immigrant comes to America and does well for himself, much to the chagrin of the white man. In a gesture both symbolic and literal, the guests turn their backs to Deighton, effectively closing him out of their circle. By refusing to become an American citizen, purchase the brownstone, and work on building the Bajan community, Deighton unwittingly forfeited his connection to the group. Selina finds the community's rejection of her father nearly unbearable, not only because she is prevented from going to his side by her mother, but also because she still loves him deeply. In her father's absence, Silla becomes increasingly obsessed with the education of her daughters, and Selina begins to feel stifled by the pressure to be Barbadian American in her mother's image. Though Selina exclusively keeps the company of Barbadians, as she enters adulthood she finds that she still knows nothing more concrete about her parents' homeland than she did as a small girl. Selina resents that her academic successes are inevitably lumped in with Silla's obsession with assimilation, in particular because, given her sister Ina's feebleness, it will be Selina's exclusive responsibility to make good by becoming a successful doctor.

No matter how fantastical and ludicrous her father's ambitions might have been, they at the very least offered Selina an opportunity to escape the burdens of success as defined by Silla. Selina knows that she is expected to marry a Barbadian American man and to be as limited by the restrictions of marriage and childrearing as her mother had been. For the first time in her life, while spending time with other first-generation Barbadian Americans like herself, Selina begins to feel "a sharp sense of alienation," as though "there was no place for her here" (Marshall 141)—just as she'd felt as a child while pretending to be white in the parlor of her family's home. Selina's internal struggle is more fundamentally an expression of a deep desire to find a place for herself on her own terms, external to her parents' marital conflict and the larger conflicts they represent— between the assimilated citizen and the migrant desperate to return. Silla will eventually end Selina's relationship with Deighton by spitefully arranging for his deportation to Barbados. Shortly after his departure, the Boyce women receive news that he drowned, after having likely jumped overboard to avoid an uncertain and unhappy return, and was interred at sea within sight of the island. Without Deighton to worry over, Silla is free to pursue her dream of social mobility and home ownership as ruthlessly as she pleases, and she immediately evicts Suggie and Maritze in order to make room for more tenants. Though Silla is finally making money from renters, many of the brownstones in her Crown Heights neighborhood are in the process of being razed and rapidly replaced by city-owned project housing. In fact, most of her West Indian neighbors have sold their properties to the city, recouped enormous profits, and moved on. For all of Silla's allegiance to the Barbadian community, she ends up relatively isolated and utterly alone.

The Homecoming of Selina Boyce: A Conclusion
Determined not to succumb to foolish desire, like her father, and unwilling to sublimate desire in order to do as her mother wishes, Selina sees that she must accept her liminality and learn to live within that space. Selina's awakening comprises two particular aspects: her self-identification as African American and her decision

to investigate her roots in Barbados. The former is inspired by her relationship with Clive, an older and significantly disaffected first-generation Barbadian immigrant. Selina keeps her relationship a secret, not only because she is having a sexual relationship with Clive, but also because her mother disapproves of his Bohemian lifestyle. Clive, a failed artist and war veteran suffering from post-traumatic stress disorder, is similarly disaffected and alienated by the Barbadian community and its obsession with upward mobility. Clive also helps Selina to see that blackness is an identity that is inclusive of Barbadianness, though decidedly broader than it. Selina explains to Clive that, in the presence of whites, she has often felt veiled, "like I didn't exist but was only the projection of someone or something else in their mind's eye" (Marshall 253)—the invisibility of blackness, she explains, makes her feel as though she has no identity at all, as though she's not even a person. Clive explains to Selina that "at some point you have to break through to the larger ring which encompasses us all—our humanity. To understand that much about us can be simply explained by the fact that we're men, caught with all men within the common ring" (Marshall 252). Though Selina quickly comes to resent Clive's insistence on maleness as universal, he helps her understand that to be black is to be human. Clive's refusal to allow his Barbadianness to eclipse his black Americanness, or to overdetermine his humanity, profoundly impacts Selina. Though she will eventually end the relationship, before she does, Selina finds that she is able to, at long last, assert herself and explains that, although she loves her parents, she "won't be cut out of the same piece of cloth" (Marshall 264). This means, of course, that she will refuse to pursue the path of assimilation outlined by her mother, even if it costs her a relationship with her mother and sister, a scholarship from the Barbadian Association to pay for her schooling, and the Bajan community's support.

Selina's close friendship with Rachel, a young Jewish woman, leads her to investigate her Barbadian roots. Rachel appreciates as well as Selina the demands of upwardly-mobile immigrant parents and likewise understands just how difficult it can be to balance one's individual desires against those of the community. Encouraged by

Rachel, Selina joins her as a worker on a cruise ship bound for the West Indies. Selina understands that until she reconciles her parents' past by visiting their homeland, she will never be able to move on with her own life. In the final scene of the novel, Selina stands on the veranda of her mother's home and examines her block where the brownstones are being replaced by a long, oppressive line of apartment complexes and with them "all the familiar voices that had ever sounded in those high-ceilinged rooms shattered" (Marshall 310). Overcome by a need to leave something of hers behind, "she remembered the two silver bangles she had always worn. She pushed up her coat sleeve and stretched one until it passed over her wrist, and, without turning, hurled it high over her shoulder" (Marshall 310). Selina no longer needs the bangles as a reminder of "home," but keeps one as a symbol of her Barbadian American roots. One thing that remains abundantly clear to Selina in the end is that the dreams of her immigrant mother and father had been, in many ways, an abject failure. Her father is dead, and her mother's home will, soon enough, be reduced to rubble—and with it, decades of her mother's effort. The looming housing projects have "shattered" the uniqueness of each brownstone and the memories of generations of immigrants, as an extension of the broader nationalizing project, one that has the potential to destroy as well as create.

In an afterword to the novel, Mary Helen Washington explains that *Brown Girl, Brownstones* is about the "next generation" (323) of Caribbean immigrant women, who were not prepared to accept the fates their countries, their cultures, and their men foisted upon them. Women like Selina Boyce are representative of a new generation of black feminists, who wanted to humanize the American landscape for their immigrant brothers, sisters, mothers, and fathers, but who were unwilling to be subjected to the injustice and indignities of racism and sexism, and who will not swallow whole the myth of American social uplift. Selina's journey, in the end, is "a kind of reverse Middle Passage, taking them, and us, from the United States to the West Indies, to Africa, and back to the States again" (Washington 324). Yet Selina's journey is also an exploration of her liminality and hybridity. By taking to the sea, midway between one world and the next, Selina hopes not only to recover her past, but accept her present. In other words, by accepting her own subject position as in-between and by making the literal journey between nations, Selina locates *herself* as fluid and transnational. By giving voice to Deighton and Silla Boyce, immigrants who struggled with imperialism, capitalism, nativism, and racism and who were both vanquished and triumphant, and their extraordinary daughter, Selina, who never wavers in her determination to find herself, Marshall's novel requires readers to confront and acknowledge histories and experiences, which have been ignored for too long.

Works Cited

Bhabha, Homi K. *The Location of Culture.* New York: Routledge, 1994.

Marshall, Paule. *Brown Girl, Brownstones*. New York: Feminist P, 2006.

Washington, Mary Helen. Afterword. *Brown Girl, Brownstones*. By Paule Marshall. New York: Feminist P, 2006.

"A Pizza Hut, A Pizza Hut": Junk Food and *Bildungsroman* in Bich Minh Nguyen's *Stealing Buddha's Dinner*

Tina Powell

In 2003, an obscure British pop band named Fast Food Rockers released "The Fast Food Song," a studio version of a song that American children had been singing on the playground since at least the 1980s. "The Fast Food Song" and the version that preceded it are celebrations of corporate branding; the lyrics identify several fast food brands, including Pizza Hut, Kentucky Fried Chicken, and McDonald's, and certain hand motions accompany each brand name. Children and adults perform the song en masse and upload their videos to YouTube, the Boy Scout Council lists it as a trail song, and elementary schools across the United States have, at one point, included it in their curriculum. Knowing songs like "The Fast Food Song," certain advertising jingles, and, as Morgan Spurlock demonstrated when he spoke to children in *Super Size Me* (2004), corporate iconography, are integral to the American cultural lexicon. This corporate marketing is so pervasive and successful that, at least on the surface, it ties disparate groups to each other. An African American child from a poor urban background is just as likely to know this lexicon as the white grandchildren of Pizza Hut's founders, Dan and Frank Carney.

However, integration through American consumer culture extolled by songs like "The Fast Food Song" is deceptive, as Bich Minh Nguyen illustrates in her memoir, *Stealing Buddha's Dinner* (2003). "The Fast Food Song" and other similar jingles can work as badges of inclusion. In particular, Nguyen recalls a popular song in the same vein as "The Fast Food Song" that she hears on the school playground. The song lists popular food items familiar to the American palate—"Hamburger, filet-o-fish, cheeseburger, french fries, icy Coke, thick shakes, sundaes, and apple pies" (Nguyen 56)— and familiarity with these items provides an open invitation to join the chorus. While "The Fast Food Song" and the variation Nguyen remembers from her childhood detail the gastronomical pleasures of American junk food, they also gesture towards assimilation and loss of ethnic identity. Joining the chorus of American consumer culture requires familiarity with its foods and brands, which is achieved through participation in the marketplace. In the case of the song Bich recalls, fluency with American English is necessary because an incorrect pronunciation or heavy accent can ruin the rhythm of the song.[1] Although Bich is familiar with the items, she is excluded from the activity and called "chop suey" a slur directed at her racial difference. Although ironically, chop suey is a dish that originated in the United States as an early kind of "fast" food, its association with foreign peoples excludes it from songs celebrating a homogenous American palate.

Nguyen's memoir is often described as a love letter to consumer culture; as a young Vietnamese refugee, Bich longs to be accepted by the white majority in her new home, Grand Rapids, Michigan. In 1975, when Nguyen is less than a year old, she flees Vietnam with her father, two uncles, her sister Anh, and her grandmother Noi. The family escapes by boat, ends up in a refugee camp in the Philippines, and eventually resettles in Grand Rapids. The Nguyens are one of the first Vietnamese families in Grand Rapids and Nguyen's memoir tracks the family's financial and emotional struggles with resettlement. It also details how the pressures of American society, through assimilation, marginalization, financial hardship, or the resentment Americans felt towards the Vietnam era, begin to unravel the promise of the Nguyens' new life. The Nguyens' first years begin with promise; Bich's father marries Rosa, a Mexican American woman he meets at a party, and with their marriage, Bich gains an older stepsister, Crissy, and eventually a half brother, Vinh. However, as outside pressures mount, the family frays and Bich is left with the impression that the promising future offered by the United States was a façade.

As a Vietnamese refugee, Bich is faced with negotiating a complex web of US national narratives, national symbols, and cultural landscapes—what Lisa Lowe calls national culture—that work to create the American subject. For Nguyen, national culture is represented by junk food, and she uses junk food as her *Bildung*—the process that develops subjecthood. In this way, *Stealing Buddha's Dinner* falls within a tradition of American *Bildungsroman* and Nguyen's relationship with food tracks its completion. In doing so, Nguyen uses the *Bildungsroman* to show the impossibility of assimilation, resulting in a liminal identity between "Vietnamese-ness" and "American-ness."

The *Bildungsroman*—the novel of development, often referred to as the coming-of-age novel—is traditionally a male-centered literary genre with a basic ideological trajectory built into the narrative. The narrative form follows the growth of a protagonist into maturity, what Marianne Hirsch describes as "a search for a meaningful existence in society" (297) that involves an undeveloped, immature protagonist and his *Bildung*—an initiation process that develops subjecthood. The protagonist is thus formed into an accepted member of society who has assimilated to its norms. In becoming so, he affirms the normative traits of that society.

Assimilation as the means to development is problematic for immigrants who are racial Others. The genre of the *Bildungsroman*, Lowe argues, "[demands] that the immigrant subject 'develop' into an identification with the dominant forms of the nation" (29), often norms that marginalize. Not identifying with these norms is to remain undeveloped and a non-subject. Since the *Bildungsroman* is a genre where a subject "[comes] to terms with [her] identity" (Otano 45), Asian Americans and other racialized people are at a disadvantage because their identity is developed through marginalization of their race (Otano 45). This marginalization is exacerbated in the *Bildungsroman* because, Patricia Chu argues, subjectivity can only occur through assimilation, where the protagonist becomes a "good citizen" by relinquishing his or her difference and accepting white normativity (12). In essence, the traditional *Bildungsroman* is the narrative of assimilation; it narrates the integration of difference into a homogeneous identity.

The ideological impetus towards assimilation can easily describe US immigration policy. In particular, Vietnamese refugees, whose immigration differs greatly from traditional patterns, were accepted under US resettlement and immigration policies that tried to force integration of racial Others. This policy worked as a type of *Bildung* where refugees in particular were expected to accept the way they are represented in the American national narrative and ignore US imperialism in Vietnam. In fact, rather than emphasize their refugee-ness, which Catherine Minyee Fung argues would "[open] up the possibility of considering the utility of alienage and displacement in arguing for civic and political inclusion" (25), Vietnamese refugees made concerted efforts to be placed within American narratives about successful immigrants.

In some ways, Nguyen's narrative does this as well. Although Nguyen was an infant when she fled Vietnam, she retells the story of flight in a way that "normalizes" her family for American readers. By focusing on the things the family lost, like Noi's pet chicken, rather than point out or allude to the US government's role in their flight, Nguyen de-emphasizes her "refugee-ness." The US military appears only on the periphery, primarily as naval ships in the distance that act as "guides" to the Philippines (Nguyen 6). Nguyen even notes how her family had connections to the United States before they became refugees; one uncle had his military training in the United States and Nguyen recalls "a photograph of him confident and grinning in hip-slung bell-bottoms . . . [with] the Statue of Liberty . . . behind him" (5). Although Nguyen does everything possible to show her family in line with traditional immigration stories, she is still reminded frequently that she is dependent on US paternalism as a "refugee." Whites marginalize and reject her difference, therefore reminding Bich of her immigration status; she must simultaneously accept that label and forget the very reasons why her family fled. Even Rosa, her Mexican American stepmother who "[knows] what it was to live in this pale city" (Nguyen 20), reminds Bich of her foreignness by emphasizing her difference. Rosa repeats the phrases, "It's the way Vietnamese do things" (Nguyen 21) and "*You* were a refugee" (Nguyen 120). Although Rosa's intentions are to celebrate difference, these statements only fuel Bich's feelings of inadequacy and shame at not being white.

Nguyen's use of American junk food as symbolic of America suggests that assimilation is achieved through the simple process of consumption. However, Bich repeatedly conflates American culture with being white, and as such, she can never "melt" into the monoculture by internalizing, digesting, incorporating, and integrating it into herself. Nguyen's choice of junk food as symbolic of a homogenous (white) American culture is appropriate. Food has been used in many ways to identify and define groups of people and Nguyen chooses a food that is mass-produced, readily available, and nutritionally deficient. Food choices, as Jennifer Ann Ho, Deborah Lupton, and Wenying Xu argue, reflect a person's place in the social order; what someone chooses to eat demonstrates her class, culture, region, and, often by extension, gender, race, and religion. These choices help form community identification, as Xu argues, because they "[induce] an imaginary solidarity among members of a community" (4). In choosing junk food, Nguyen comments on the empty promises of integration for racial Others, much like the empty nutritive promises of the foods themselves.

Bich attaches immense power to "white food" because she feels marginalized. She writes: "all I wanted was to sit at a dinner table and eat pork chops the way my friends did. Because I could not, because our household did not, I invested such foods with power and allure" (Nguyen 53). Food has this power, Lupton argues, because it is "central to our subjectivity or sense of self, and our experience of embodiment, or the ways that we live in and through our bodies, which itself is inextricably linked with subjectivity" (1). In this way, food works as a *Bildung*; through its consumption, the consumer defines herself and develops into a subject. Ingestion is also connected to speech because both are facilitated by the mouth which is, according to Lupton, "a potent symbol of both consumption and its control, combining in the one site [eating and taste] with [speech]" (18). Therefore, eating and speech are inextricably linked, as both work to form one's subjecthood.

Even though American junk food is attached to whiteness, the consumer narrative sells a particular image that appeals to a broad base of people. The food is often inexpensive and readily available, therefore, it is easily accessible to all consumers. In this way, a wide range of people can be united through their consumption. By tying her *Bildung* to that food, Bich believes eating "white food" will make her a "real person" and she hopes to be granted membership to white American culture that would otherwise be denied to Asian Americans. As Jennifer Ann Ho argues, "relationships to food represent [Asian Americans'] struggle to embrace an American identity, forcing them to acknowledge bi-cultural or multi-cultural status as hyphenated peoples" (3). Therefore, in her effort to become American, Bich becomes a glutton, coveting "cookies, . . . candy and cake, popsicles, ice cream, endless kinds of dinner" (Nguyen 71). Her consumption is excessive, which, Ho argues, "leads to an erasure of racial identity" (143). In gorging herself on "white food," Bich is trying to become the only acceptable type of American: white.

For Bich, American junk food is more important for its identification with Americanness than for taste. Nguyen rarely describes the taste of the food she ingests and consumes it for its symbolic value, not alimentary pleasure. As Nguyen writes:

> At home, I kept opening the refrigerator and cupboards, wishing for American foods to magically appear. I wanted what other kids had: Bundt cakes and casseroles, Chee*tos and Doritos. My secret dream was to bite off just the tip of every slice of pizza in the two-for-one deal we got at Little Caesar's. The more American foods I ate, the more my desires multiplied, outpacing any interest in Vietnamese food. (50)

In order to "melt," she is expected to excise racial and cultural difference. Junk food symbolizes what being American means to Bich, and it is at the expense of Vietnamese-ness.

Being invited to participate in the performance of Americanness, like joining the chorus in playground songs, is symbolically "the price of admission to a long-desired home" (Nguyen 71). However, that "home" is hostile to Bich. Her impressions of her new home are filled with anxiety over whether she belongs. To Nguyen, the very fabric of Grand Rapids is "a reminder of what and whom the town represents, as if the sea of blonde . . . could let a foreigner forget" (11). To her, America becomes "a world of cold snow and people leaning down, saying, *What? What did you say?*" (Nguyen 71). It is a place where Americans give her "funny looks, [and] polite no-thank-yous that signify, *You're different. You're strange. You people*" (Nguyen 70). The comments directed at Bich clearly signal her foreignness, a manifestation of resentment towards Asians for the seismic changes of the 1960s and 1970s. Vietnamese, in particular, were reminders of the Vietnam War and the rising civil strife in the United States. This resentment illustrates the barriers Bich faces in trying to assimilate. American racism and xenophobia make melting into the monoculture impossible. Bich cannot become a blonde girl in a white dress, yet because she so desperately wants integration, she longs for "white food."

Food and foodways have played an important role in Asian immigration to the United States and, as such, hold a significant place in the expression of Asian American experience and identity. Xu notes how food and foodways have been used to stereotype and fetishize Asian Americans as Other in white America, while Ho has discussed how food is used as a medium to mark compliance or resistance of Asian Americans to an American identity that does not account for ethnic and racial complexities (3). Historically, as Ronald Takaki points out, Asian Americans and Asian immigrants were driven out of the general labor market and into service industries by racism and exclusion laws in the early twentieth century. This movement into the service industry, particularly in the laundry and restaurant business, kept Asians a voiceless, invisible class that relied on catering to white sensibilities and palates for financial solvency. In some ways, this marginalization is replayed through reactions to Vietnamese food. While Nguyen notes that Asian food was eventually normalized by the American palate, her childhood was "before Thai restaurants became staples in every town" (10). Instead, Vietnamese food is repeatedly rejected and deemed inedible. Her neighbor, Jennifer Vander Wal, is "afraid" of Noi's food (Nguyen 63) and Crissy screams "NASTY" at Bich and Anh's dried squid (Nguyen 45). This rejection is particularly apparent when Bich and Anh bring Noi's food to school. As part of the school's attempt at multicultural inclusion, the principal decides to celebrate Tet, linking it to an assembly about Vietnamese immigration and culture. As part of the celebration, Bich and Anh are expected to perform their Vietnameseness; they wear *ao dai*s and share the prized treat of Tet, Noi's *banh chung* (green sticky rice cakes) with their classmates. The girls try to preserve the savory cakes as part of their private celebration, eating them out of sight. However, a teacher tells them that they must share with the rest of the school. Their enjoyment of eating the cakes, secluded from prying and judging eyes, becomes a moment of public spectacle, of "white people looking and declining. The cakes would grow crusty and stale under the recoiling gaze of our classmates. They would be ruined by the staring" (Nguyen 102). Through this rejection of food, white people are also rejecting Bich as unappealing and offensive to their sensibilities. For the girls to eat the cakes publicly, then, would be to complete a disgusting act, thereby performing their difference under the gaze of white society. It would also reinforce the belief that she and her sister are foreigners and not assimilable. Bich internalizes that disgust and feels shame at being labeled a "refugee," a position that she associates with poverty, hunger, and difference. She "dare[s] not take another" *banh chung* (Nguyen 104) and tries to excise her difference by rejecting "ethnic food"; she "wrinkles" her face at Rosa's *sopa* and "scowls" at "Noi's *pho*, shrimp stews, and curries" (Nguyen 52).

Despite the hostility she encounters, Bich strives to become a white American, to be like the blonde kids at school and the prim white girls pictured on the packages of baked goods. When "white food" is withheld or inaccessible, Bich feels like she is being "prevent[ed] from fitting in and being like everyone else" (Nguyen 52). Being denied access to "white food" creates "shame and resentment" and Bich is "convinced [she] was falling far behind on becoming American" (Nguyen 52). She feels the pressures of assimilation, "the push and pull" of immigrant life that tell her: *Come on in. Now transform. And if you cannot, then disappear*" (Nguyen 11). However, that transformation is not as simple as adopting and taking in the cultural rituals and traditions of the United States that the mere consumption of junk food suggests. Rather, transformation requires being white; she is expected to become what the dominant culture is, but that dominant culture is made up of "blond heads [gliding]" through school hallways (Nguyen 11).

Although Bich cannot assimilate into white America, she can approximate integration by performing the model-minority. The model-minority paradigm offers the racial Other a chance to "melt" into the monoculture, but that privilege is conditional on the minority's acceptance of white superiority. The model-minority is used to pit racial Others against each other in an effort to receive better access to education, jobs, and other privileges leading to upward mobility. In this competition for resources, the majority typically rewards the group passive to white supremacy; frequently, this status is attributed to Asian Americans, who are compelled to erase any trace of "Asianness," except for their racial features, in order to gain white privilege.

Bich, in particular, tries to exemplify the well-behaved version of the model-minority; she strives for academic success, and she is passive to criticism. To her, "being good meant freedom from watchfulness" (Nguyen 74), so innocuous to the white majority that she might simply "melt" in. At school, Bich is granted gold stars (for good behavior and studiousness), independent studies, and minimal teacher oversight. But, no matter how many "good student privileges" she receives, she is never granted the privilege that white students, like Holly Jansen, receive. Although Bich is tied with Holly for gold stars, Holly receives the prized stuffed lion every month. Despite Bich's academic success and English proficiency, her teacher chastises her reading and language skills. When Bich wins a spelling bee, proof of her language prowess, she is awarded a Mr. Goodbar and a certificate of achievement, two symbols of inclusion. But, when teachers think she is out of earshot, they remark "Can you believe it? . . . . A foreigner winning our spelling bee!" (Nguyen 82). Although she asserts subjectivity with her voice, the Americans she is asserting it to either refuse to hear her or reject that voice outright. So, despite her performance of the model minority, she is denied privilege because of her Otherness. The expectations of the model-minority are not just pushed by whites; even Rosa falls into the trap and dreams of Bich becoming "a classical violinist like the graceful Asian prodigies she saw on T.V." (Nguyen 74), despite Bich showing absolutely no musical aptitude.

Performing the model-minority has limited benefits. The reality of that "white world" and its tokens of inclusion are false. Like the food Bich covets, it is empty of nutritive value or nourishment, gloppy, and distasteful:

> Most provocative were listings that mentioned choice, the word itself conjuring possibility: 'choice of hamburger or cheeseburger'; 'choice of whole milk or chocolate milk.' In reality, hot lunch meant soggy cheese sandwiches encased in steamed-up plastic pouches; perforated boxes of greasy, chewy fried chicken; elastic potatoes; canned fruit in heavy syrup. (Nguyen 77)

Her disappointment with the lunch food expresses her frustration with her struggle. She still longs for those promises, "the potatoes churned into clouds," but begins to realize those promises are false and merely hide something distasteful.

Despite all of her attempts to "melt" in, it is made abundantly clear that there is an unequal distribution of power between whites and racial Others who are immigrants. She observes this inequality in her daily life, noting that her Otherness meant she was "not allowed to just walk in [to her neighbor Jennifer's house], the way [Jennifer] did in [Bich's] house" (Nguyen 66). This simple acknowledgement of her relationship with Jennifer also illustrates the complex intersections of race, nativity, and class that dictate belonging in her neighborhood. Jennifer moves easily around the neighborhood, clearly claiming any space she wants, whereas Bich is an unwelcome guest, invader, or "squatter," who is claiming space that belongs to someone else. This inequality, what Nguyen labels a "paradigm unspoken," eventually leads to conflict. At one point, Bich's father and Jennifer's get into a disagreement that quickly escalates. Nguyen describes her father "lunging," but he stops short of striking Cal Vander Wal. The fight itself is minor, but Bich and

Anh secretly wish to see "fist against face, Cal falling into his prized green lawn. [We] wanted something to be smashed and broken—the paradigm unspoken that ran between us [the Nguyens and Vander Wals] like the chain-link fence in the backyard" (Nguyen 68). This imagery, of destroying the barriers that kept her from Jennifer's world, illustrates Bich's frustration at trying to achieve something that is impossible. However, like her father, she has to show great restraint in order to maintain access, albeit severely limited, to Jennifer's world. Instead, Bich opts for small rebellions, like stuffing "tufts of grass through the chain-link fence" onto the Vander Wals' immaculate lawn, "littering" that goes unnoticed (Nguyen 62). She also insults "white food," describing Jennifer's Kool-Aid pops as bland, although in Jennifer's presence, she treats them like "the only delicacy I would ever have" (Nguyen 66). These transgressions are Bich's way of rejecting her marginalization, yet they are nearly invisible because she still desires assimilation.

Her transgressions are not merely acts of frustration from someone who does not fit in; they are also framed in the language of immigration. Bich covets being Jennifer, whom she holds as the model of American-ness, racially and socioeconomically. The Vander Wals never make Bich feel welcome in their home or in the neighborhood, and the only way Bich can enter that home is through invitation (which the Vander Wals rarely extend) or invasion. Bich and Anh, in an effort to gain access to the Vander Wals' home, break in one night while the family is away. They vandalize Jennifer's room, balling up her papers and dousing her clothes in baby powder. The two "moved in swift silence" and Bich feels "the thrill of trespass" (Nguyen 69). Nguyen's description playfully echoes anti-immigration rhetoric that invokes the nation as a home under invasion. The girls are caught and forced to apologize for their trespass; however, Bich is able to steal a Tollhouse cookie without the Vander Wals noticing. Part of Bich and Anh's invasion, stealing the cookie, is invisible; Bich is able to deprive Jennifer of that resource, but it is such an innocuous theft that it goes unnoticed.

Despite her efforts, Bich's development is stunted, and instead, Nguyen develops a liminal space between the promise of integration created by consumption—what Nguyen calls a "myth of endlessness"—and the reality of the violence of flight and racial struggle in the United States. This liminal space, what Nguyen calls "missingness," results in Bich becoming a racial melancholic, which illustrates the impossibility of a completed *Bildung* under the conditions of assimilation. A racial melancholic, according to Anne Anlin Cheng, is a racial Other "who has been placed in a suspended position. . . . whereby [her] racial identity is imaginatively reinforced through the introjection of a lost, never-possible perfection, an inarticulable loss that comes to inform the individual's sense of [her] subjectivity" (xi). Bich associates becoming American against a racial identity she can never be, and failure to become white results in her mourning for something she never had. That "missingness," or "inarticulable loss," increases as Bich's attempt to integrate through junk food repeatedly fails.

Bich expresses the "inarticulable loss" that comes with trying to assimilate with a catalogue of the things she rejects in that pursuit. She has to leave the comfort of the "cocoon" of Noi's kitchen (Nguyen 84), regrets not learning the words to the Vietnamese songs her father sings (Nguyen 63), and feels left out of a vibrant community where she could embrace her difference. Bich foregoes friendships with Vietnamese kids for ones with white girls, and as she gets older, she regrets her choice when she realizes she has become an outcast at the Vietnamese parties her father and Noi love to attend. Nguyen writes, "The fact was clear: the other Vietnamese kids had been united all that time we had stayed at home. They had shared holidays and birthdays and board games. They knew each other, had grown up together, and had no need for us. They sat in a group, laughing and speaking a flurry of mixed Vietnamese and English" (Nguyen 114). The other Vietnamese American kids laugh at Anh and Bich and call them "Twinkies" (Nguyen 115), leaving Bich to wonder: "Was that what I had longed to achieve, after all?" (Nguyen 115). Bich wants, most of all, to find a space of belonging. The other kids are able to achieve some type of middle ground between their American social lives and Vietnamese private lives, a version of what Renny Christopher calls "biculturality." They are able to become "American [while] insist[ing] on remaining Vietnamese" (Christopher 30); they dress, act, and appear to be like Americans, but they still honor the rituals and relationships that tie them to Vietnam. More importantly, they have the economic power to purchase that image (Christopher 48).

Bich, however, is embarrassed and afraid to let her friends know about that Vietnamese life. Keeping a dual life like the other Vietnamese kids was "exhausting." Although she finds comfort in Noi's food and Noi's ritual of placing fruit at her altar, the significance of those ties to the homeland are too much to bear: "I could shed tears for the Joads [poor family of tenant farmers featured in John Steinbeck's *Grapes of Wrath*], but I did not wish to imagine other Nguyens working for food in Vietnam. I knew the dragon shape of the country, its gauntness and curves, but I couldn't imagine where my actual mother could be in it" (Nguyen 129). Bich relates only to Americans and, in doing so, cannot process what was lost when the family flees Vietnam. In particular, when Bich and Anh's mother appears back in their lives years after they arrive in the United States, Bich finds her existence disruptive to the identity she has worked hard to cultivate.

Both of the primary models for Bich's identity formation as a Vietnamese American fail; she cannot become white, like the Vander Wals, and living a dual life is an invitation for further marginalization. In many ways, she looks to Rosa for an alternative model of identity. Rosa refuses to assimilate; growing up in a migrant family where home was mobile and unstable, Rosa rebels against her parents and the white America that marginalized them. She actively celebrates her difference and fights for the disenfranchised. She teaches English to immigrants, does outreach work, and tries to incorporate the Vietnamese world into her own. Her rejection of whiteness is apparent in her palate; Mexican food is a rejection of whiteness that "oppresse[s], suffocate[s] and isolate[s]" her (Nguyen 53). In contrast to the "bland," artificially-flavored white food that "was as repugnant . . . as tulips and the Dutchness and conservatism they represented," Rosa's cooking "was different—richer, she insisted, with *real* flavor" (Nguyen 52–53).

Although Rosa offers a model critical of assimilation and aligned with the disenfranchised, it is at the expense of Bich's growth. Rosa fails to teach Bich important cultural norms, particularly surrounding eating. Teaching Bich simple things, like how to use silverware, are pushed aside for teaching Bich the importance of labor unions and cultural pride. While those lessons are undoubtedly important, what Rosa teaches, and fails to teach, becomes for Bich more fodder for her marginalization. Her unfamiliarity with using a fork and knife while eating dinner at her friend Holly Jansen's house produces the same feelings that anti-Asian slurs produce. She feels like an "imposter" and expresses anxiety about her inability to "melt" in at the dinner. Bich struggles to cut into the pork chop she has been served: "when the knife pushed through the final barrier or flesh and hit the plate, it made the sound that ice skates make when a skater slices into a jump. The stub of meat, cleaved free of its chop, sailed through the air and dropped onto the carpet near Mr. Jansen's chair" (Nguyen 92). Bich's fear, that she will fail to be innocuous and, therefore, fail to "melt," is on display at meal time. Her inability to use the silverware creates a noticeable sound and a stain on the Jansens' carpet. Her presence is marked by its disruptiveness. While Rosa expresses sympathy for Bich's embarrassing dinner and teaches her how to use a fork and knife after the fact, she prefers to teach her the European way and to emphasize an appropriate type of difference.

In the end, Bich concludes that her identity is fluid and unstable. She prefers to be innocuous, picking and choosing pieces to integrate into herself. As her struggle to integrate into a white world threatens to "fall down, smother and erase [her]" (Nguyen 81), she rejects the artificiality of American junk food for items like Noi's *cha gio* and Rosa's tamales. As Nguyen notes, there is no "white" equivalent of these two food items; making them is labor intensive, a contrast to the prepackaged Jiffy muffins and cookie mixes that Bich once equated with maternal love. Her rejection of junk food illustrates her acknowledgement that she has been marginalized. So, although Bich struggles towards assimilation, she eventually dismantles the myth of assimilation.

Bich Minh Nguyen's memoir, *Stealing Buddha's Dinner* (2007), challenges the notion that it is easy to develop bicultural identity. She demonstrates how a smooth incorporation into mainstream American society is an ahistorical myth because in practice, xenophobia, racism, nativism, and classism are obstructions for many newly arrived groups. Because of these obstructions, Nguyen illustrates how hard it is to become "American" as a racial Other when the norm is white, while also trying to maintain connections to her Vietnamese family and its traditions. In order to sustain the quest for assimilation, Bich has to break off the things that make her different. Eventually, Nguyen notes, Vietnameseness is accepted when there are "white people in the Vietnamese market, white people eating bean curd and *banh bao*" (250). Bich becomes part of the community; when white Americans seek out the food they once rejected, her ethnicity, through food, becomes a desired consumable. However, this acceptance comes at a steep price—the severance of "Vietnameseness" that Bich cannot reconcile. She even returns to Vietnam as an adult to find her roots, but she only feels regret and exhaustion (Nguyen 245). In the end, Bich's *Bildung* remains unfinished, and she still hungers for a space where she belongs.

Note

1. In this essay, Nguyen's first name, Bich (pronounced 'Bic'), is used when referencing her activities as the memoir's protagonist. Her surname (the popular, anglicized pronunciation of which is 'Winn') is used when referring to her authorial strategies.

Works Cited

Aguilar-San Juan, Karin. *Little Saigons: Staying Vietnamese in America.* Minneapolis: U of Minnesota P, 2009.

Cheng, Anne Anlin. *The Melancholy of Race.* New York: Oxford UP, 2000.

Christopher, Renny. *The Viet Nam War/The American War: Images and Representations in Euro-American and Vietnamese Exile Narratives.* Amherst: U of Massachusetts P, 1995.

Chu, Patricia. *Assimilating Asians: Gendered Strategies of Authorship in America.* Durham, NC: Duke UP, 2000.

Fung, Catherine. "A History of Absences: The Problem of Reference in Monique Truong's *Book of Salt*." *Novel* 45.1 (2012): 94–110.

Hirsch, Marianne. "The Novel of Formation as Genre: Between *Great Expectations* and *Lost Illusion*." *Genre* 12.3 (Autumn 1979): 293–311.

Ho, Jennifer Ann. *Consumption and Identity in Asian American Coming-of-Age Novels*. New York: Routledge, 2005.

Lowe, Lisa. *Immigrant Acts: On Asian American Cultural Politics*. Durham, NC: Duke UP, 1996.

Lupton, Deborah. *Food, the Body and the Self*. Thousand Oaks, CA: Sage, 1996.

Nguyen, Bich Minh. *Stealing Buddha's Dinner*. New York: Penguin, 2007.

Otano, Alicia. *Speaking the Past: Child Perspective in the Asian American Bildungsroman*. New Brunswick, NJ: Rutgers UP, 2004.

Spurlock, Morgan. *Super Size Me*. Sony, 2004. Film.

Takaki, Ronald. *Strangers From a Different Shore*. 1989. Boston: Little, Brown, 1998. Print.

Xu, Wenying. *Eating Identities: Reading Food in Asian American Literature*. Honolulu: U of Hawai`i P, 2008.

Neither Insider nor Outsider but Both: Multicultural Identity in Edith Eaton's "Mrs. Spring Fragrance" and "The Inferior Woman"

Linda Trinh Moser

In "Mrs. Spring Fragrance" and its companion story, "The Inferior Woman" [1] (hereafter, "Mrs." and "Inferior"), Edith Eaton, writing under the pseudonym Sui Sin Far, creates an idealized world in which Jade Spring Fragrance reigns. Her Chinese immigrant characters live harmoniously with their Anglo American counterparts in an integrated Seattle neighborhood where there was "social good feeling between the American and Chinese families" (Sui Sin Far, "Inferior" 38). The lack of tension is the result of each group's deference to and appreciation for different cultures. Mrs. Carman, the Spring Fragrances' widowed next-door neighbor, had lived in China, and her "prejudices did not extend to the Chinese" (Sui Sin Far, "Inferior" 38). Her son Will is "interested in Chinese literature" (Sui Sin, "Inferior" 29) and attends "smoking parties" given by a very Westernized Mr. Spring Fragrance. Jade's cultural cross-over is even more extensive than that of her husband or her neighbors, although this had not always been the case. Upon her arrival in the United States, she had refused to wear Western-style clothing and had been "unacquainted with even one word of the American language" (Sui Sin Far, "Mrs." 17). And yet after a mere five years in the United States, she has undergone a complete transformation. She "adore[s] the American dress" (Sui Sin Far, "Inferior" 30) and, "[t]here are no more American words for her learning" (Sui Sin Far, "Mrs." 17).

Underlying the idyllic environment Jade believes she inhabits, however, are cultural misunderstandings, gender bias, and class discrimination, which are played out in the efforts to separate two sets of young lovers. In "Mrs.," an arranged marriage between Tsen

Hing and Mai Gwi Far, known as Laura, prevents the latter from marrying her "sweetheart" Kai Tzu. In "Inferior," Mrs. Carman blocks the romantic relationship between her son, Will, and Alice Winthrop. In the depiction of arranged marriages in Chinese culture in the first story, Eaton provides a critique of gender inequity. In the second, she adds the dimension of class in the depiction of Mrs. Carman's resistance to her son's romantic interest; her opinion of Alice as "inferior" is based on a bias against working-class women. In her role as matchmaker in both stories, Jade undermines the status quo. In "Mrs.," Jade secretly encourages Tsen Hing to fall in love with and marry Ai Oi, thus leaving Laura and Kai Tzu free to marry. In "Inferior," Jade overcomes Mrs. Carman's objections by pointing out the inherent gender inequities in them. Although Mrs. Carman overlooks Mr. Spring Fragrance's humble origins in her praise for him, she is unwilling to see Alice in parallel terms as "a woman who has made herself" (Sui Sin Far, "Inferior" 39). As Jade brings the young couples together, the imaginary aspects of her integrated world become exposed. By discussing gender and class equity in the context of immigrant Chinese characters, the stories also expose the racial bias of mainstream America. They map a complicated terrain of identity issues, with race, gender, and class concerns interweaving in, out, and around one another.

Although Eaton's depiction of rapid assimilation and make-believe community of racial harmony may only be a fantasy, they serve as an example of cultural hybridity. Jade's role as a "trickster" figure (White-Parks 168), who transforms and manipulates Chinese and American cultures, is a reflection of Eaton's multicultural identity. Eaton identified herself as Eurasian. Her English father, Edward Eaton (1839–1915) and Chinese mother, Grace A. Trefusis (1846–1922), met and married in China during the early 1860s. The couple had sixteen children, fourteen of whom survived infancy. Edith, who was the second-oldest child and eldest daughter, was born in Edward's hometown, Macclesfield, England, where the family would stay until she was about seven years old. In the early 1870s, the Eatons relocated to Hudson City, New York, and then to Montreal where they would eventually settle. Edward never earned enough to support his ever-growing family. At various times, the older Eaton children were taken out of school to help support themselves and their younger siblings. Eaton left Montreal to pursue a writing career, going first to Kingston, Jamaica, where she was employed as a newspaper writer and reporter. She later traveled to the West Coast, living first in San Francisco, then Seattle, where she remained for about ten years, and then to Boston. Throughout her residence in the United States, Eaton continued to work as a stenographer, which allowed her to support her parents and younger siblings still living at home. Writing under the pseudonym Sui Sin Far, Eaton's essays and fiction appeared in the papers of the various cities in which she lived: the *Boston Globe*; *Montreal Daily Star*; *Los Angeles Express*; and *San Francisco Call*. Her stories appeared in a variety of magazines, including *Overland Monthly*, *Land of Sunshine*, *Independent*, and *Good Housekeeping*. In 1912, her collected stories, including "Mrs." and "Inferior," were published as *Mrs. Spring Fragrance*. The *New York Times Book Review* praised the book as well as its author:

> Miss Eaton has struck a new note in American fiction. The thing she has tried to do is to portray for readers of the white race the lives, feelings, sentiments of the Americanized Chinese of the Pacific Coast, of those who have intermarried with them and of the children who have sprung from such unions. ("New Note" 405)

Eaton's sympathetic portrayals of Chinese immigrants attempted to expose American racial bias. Rather than focusing on Chinatown "bachelors" and laborers, the topic of mainstream publications, her work depicts immigrant families of all classes. By placing the Spring Fragrances, a Chinese immigrant couple, at the center of the stories, Eaton challenges the invisibility of sympathetic Asian characters in popular American literature. As Annette White-Parks notes, Eaton presents a "direct counter-perspective to conventional portrayals" by foregrounding Chinese immigrant life ("Reversal" 17). Both the Spring Fragrance stories present obvious examples of the "reversal" strategy. In "Mrs.," the reference to Tennyson as an "American" rather than an English poet mirrors a common inability, on the part of Anglo Americans, to distinguish the ethnic backgrounds of Asian immigrants. Another reversal occurs in "Inferior" in the description of Jade's plans to write a book about Americans. Using words associated with Chinese immigrants in the popular press, Jade describes white characters as "mysterious, inscrutable, incomprehensible" (Sui Sin Far, "Inferior" 33). By making Anglo Americans the "inscrutable" Other, the story reverses reader expectations and exposes the stereotypes inherent in Western literary depictions. While they offer readers a glimpse into the concerns related to early Chinese immigration, "Mrs." and "Inferior" also often pander to the West's fascination with the exoticism of Asian cultures. Like a tour guide, Jade leads readers through the Chinese communities of San Francisco and San Jose, California, revealing details about Chinese festivals, food, and customs. The narrator emphasizes the exotic nature of the surroundings and characters by using phrases supposedly (but not actually) translated from the Chinese. San Francisco, for example, is called "the city of the Golden Gate" and a month is "a moon" (Sui Sin Far, "Mrs." 20). The narrator also includes explanations for those uninitiated into Chinese culture. A footnote to the words "plum blossom," Jade's nickname, explains: "The plum blossom is the Chinese flower of virtue. It has been adopted by the Japanese, just in the same way as they have adopted the Chinese national flower, the chrysanthemum" (Sui Sin Far, "Mrs." 21). These exotic touches entertain the reader, while the stories deliver arguments against race, class, and gender discrimination.

In her positive assessment of Eaton's oeuvre, Annette White-Parks nonetheless describes Jade's amelioration of societal divisions as "glib" (205) and finds that "Mrs." and "Inferior" "violate the readers' sense of believability" (165). Dominika Ferens, too, views the setting of the Spring Fragrance home, situated "next door to the Chin Yuens, a traditional Chinese family, on one side and the Anglo-American Carmans on the other" as "probably allegorical rather than factual" (102). Behind these observations is the notion that Eaton's work must be historically accurate. The familiarity with which the Spring Fragrances negotiate their dual cultures and Chin Yuen's willingness to forego tradition and accept his daughter Laura's romantic choice, for example, preclude attention to generational conflicts and loss of Chinese culture associated with American assimilation. Mrs. Carman's radical change of heart regarding the reputation of a working woman also seems unrealistic because it occurs without an examination of the way in which class affects gender solidarity. While Sean McCann invokes neither authenticity nor insider status in his discussion of Eaton's stories, he finds her "political thinking," to be similarly "sketchy and undeveloped" because she "displace[s] political concerns with personal fables":

> Thus, in . . . "Mrs. Spring Fragrance," the protagonist's husband complains briefly to a neighbor that his emigrant brother has been imprisoned in an American 'Detention Pen' (23). But having subtly noted the tension between democratic rhetoric and the unjust actions of the state, the story passes on to its real concern, a tale of courtship and marriage that thematizes more indirectly [Eaton]'s concern with the effects of American democracy. (78–9)

This negative assessment of Eaton's social commentary is countered by literary critics who commend Eaton's work according to the historical and cultural "authenticity" of her representations. Implicit in their praise is the notion that Eaton's work reflects an "insider" or authentic Chinese immigrant identity. Amy Ling, for example, asserts: "No one before her had written so sympathetically and so extensively about the Chinese in America, and never before from this far inside" ("Edith" 292). S. E. Solberg, likewise, describes her writing as "outside the boundaries of any of the main currents of American writing" (32). The promotion of Eaton's authenticity and insider status also finds its way into a discussion of her life. Critics argue that her chosen pseudonym, Sui Sin Far, underscores Eaton's personal and literary authenticity because it reveals her Chinese ancestry. This appraisal, however, is related just as much to her stance against racism as to the historical accuracy of her portrayals of Chinese immigrants. The editors of *Aiiieeeee! An Anthology of Asian American Writers* place her work in opposition to the "White tradition of Chinese novelty literature (F. Chin, et al. vii) and describe her as "one of the first to speak for an Asian-American sensibility that was neither Asian nor white American" (F. Chin, et al. xxi–xxii). In the introduction to her stories in their follow-up anthology, *The Big Aiiieeeee!*, they insist she was "writing from reality instead of prejudice" and place Eaton in opposition to "Christian missionary cant and social Darwinist scientific rhetoric, the racist science fiction, and the low racist humor that molded the image of the Chinese" (Chan, et al. 111).

The emphasis on tracing authenticity and a literary tradition separate from mainstream Western letters challenges the historical invisibility of Asians in the United States. While making Asian American experience visible is an important project, the emphasis on authenticity and separation obscures the experiences of Asians of diverse backgrounds because it relies on "[t]he premise that a definitive version of the life of an ethnic group exists" (Wong 4). Both Eaton's life and writing challenge the notion of a monolithic Chinese American identity and indeed demonstrate the extent of Western influence. As a Eurasian, who immigrated to the United States from Canada (after a childhood in England), not China, her experiences were significantly different from those of most Chinese immigrants in North America at the turn of the twentieth century. The Chinese American characters she created likewise represent an array of backgrounds ranging from poverty-stricken immigrant laborers to American-born entertainers to wealthy China-born merchants. Furthermore, racism in the United States is far from monolithic. Taking many forms, American racism is always snared in a web of contradictions. While the US government enacted legislation prohibiting Chinese immigrants from entering the country and becoming citizens, Americans were fascinated and charmed by Chinese and Chinese immigrant culture. Eaton herself noted the increasing popularity of Chinese culture. In a letter to her editor Charles Lummis, dated September 16, 1900, she wrote: "Everything Chinese seems to be taking now" (White-Parks, *Sui* 111). Eaton took advantage of the growing interest. After she began writing about Chinese immigrant communities and signing her work with a Chinese name, she found more occasions to publish.

The emphasis on separation and "authenticity" also reinforces, rather than overthrows, ethnocentric thinking. By not examining the limitations of Eaton's "reversal" strategies and foregrounding what they believe to be "authentic" representations of "Asian" culture, critics repeat racial hierarchies, albeit in reverse. In their reverse images, white American cultures become subordinate to Asian cultures. Even critics who recognize the limitations of Eaton's views on race have tended to dismiss, excuse, or overlook them in order to construct her as an "insider" to Chinese American culture. Amy Ling, for example, dismisses an obvious racist assumption in Eaton's autobiographical essay: "Edith slips unwittingly into the assumption that her 'white body' is the stronger, more martial half" (*Between* 35). The editors of *The Big Aiiieeeee!* overlook textual evidence of Eaton's training in Western literature and Christianity when they differentiate her work from "fake" texts, which derive from "sources in Christian dogma and in Western philosophy, history, and literature" (Chin, et al. xv). While Eaton tries to depict Chinese immigrants in a sympathetic and realistic light, her efforts do not abandon the Western literary traditions with which she was most familiar. Consequently, her work is imbued with the racism of that tradition, yet also reveals what King-Kok Cheung describes as "one of the most defining characteristics of Asian American literature . . . hybridity" (19).

Eaton's reliance on the works of mainstream Western writers for her sympathetic portrayals of Chinese immigrants has been noted. Xiao-Huang Yin, for example, connects her to British and American writers: "Cheerful, energetic, and persistent, [Mrs. Spring Fragrance] is reminiscent of Elizabeth in *Pride and Prejudice* or, perhaps more appropriately, a type of Louisa May Alcott's 'Little Women'" (94). In addition to character similarities, Eaton's stories also mirror the thematic concerns of these novels. Elizabeth Bennett and Jo March resist society-approved marriages to men with whom they are not in love; Mrs. Spring Fragrance encourages Laura and Ethel Evebrook to do the same. Similar class concerns appear as well. The mostly female households created by Austen and Alcott are hampered by their genteel poverty, as is Alice Winthrop in "Inferior." While Jo is a prototype of the working-woman Alice becomes, Elizabeth precedes Jade, who undermines Mrs. Carman's prejudice against working-class women. Eaton's connection to another American writer, Sara Payson Willis Parton—better known as Fanny Fern—is investigated by Ning Yu who argues "that Eaton deliberately emulated Parton" (46). Ling likewise notes that the title of Eaton's autobiographical essay, "Leaves from the Mental Portfolio of an Eurasian," is "reminiscent of Parton's popular book *Fern Leaves from Fanny's Portfolio*" (32).

Eaton's stories emphasize the human dignity of racial Others while attempting to depict and alleviate their suffering. Thus, as a writer, Eaton seems indebted to the work of another well-known nineteenth-century writer: Harriet Beecher Stowe. As with Stowe's *Uncle Tom's Cabin* (1852), Eaton focuses on domestic situations, particularly the relationships between husbands and wives, parents and children, and siblings. Many of Eaton's stories demonstrate a certain amount of social reality in this regard. The seemingly authentic descriptions of early Chinese immigrant clothing, furniture, food, and customs, however, appear within a decidedly Western framework, which makes it difficult to separate her work from a mainstream literary tradition. Taking Jane Tompkins' analysis of Stowe's *Uncle Tom's Cabin* as a model, readings of "Mrs." and "Inferior" should consider the ways Eaton uses the conventions of sentimental fiction, in particular domestic ideology, as a starting point to criticize and reform racism in American society. Like Stowe, Eaton plays with the notion of separate spheres, with women wielding their influence in the private domestic sphere of home and family, while men rule the public sphere of politics, law, and economics. As mothers and wives, women can extend their influence by helping to shape the character of men. In *Uncle Tom's Cabin*, Stowe protests slavery on the grounds that it eliminates the distinction between spheres. For a slave, there is no distinction between private and public spheres. The novel's subtitle, "The Man Who Was a Thing," reinforces the problem of turning individuals into products used for economic profit. Although the characters in Eaton's stories are not slaves, their domestic lives are intimately connected to and adversely affected by economic and political concerns.

Far from supporting the image of Eaton as an insider to Chinese culture, her similarity to Stowe suggests familiarity with a Western tradition. But her stance is not necessarily monocultural. In her depictions of Jade Spring Fragrance, Eaton aspires to construct an identity that "draws on both cultures," as Charlotte Rich notes. Rich argues that "Mrs. Spring Fragrance's hybrid, syncretic identity is an empowered location from which she speaks to evaluate the benefits and detriments of Chinese and American culture" (133). In this way, "Mrs." and "Inferior" underscore the limitations of "authenticity" models, which elide the experiences of Asians of diverse origins. Eaton's stories offer a range of options between "insider" and "outsider." As Noreen Lape argues, Eaton provides "alternatives" to "the extreme responses to culture contact . . . to preserve the culture and follow orthodox Chinese ways or to assimilate and observe orthodox Anglo customs" (88). Instead, Eaton's characters enjoy multiple possibilities, while resisting notions of an authentic cultural identity.

The identity of Eaton's characters invoke gender and class. Feminist scholars have questioned the focus on race to the exclusion of gender and class. Cheung, for example, notes that those concerned with authenticity overlook covert feminist strategies against racism and sexism in their tendency "to dismiss Asian (American) traits that are less than 'heroic" (i.e., militant) as resulting from white indoctrination or from Christianity" (17). They also ignore class concerns of many Asians Americans who, like Eaton, felt the constraints of poverty throughout her childhood and early adulthood. In "Mrs.," the discussion of arranged marriages in Chinese culture contains an obvious critique of gender inequality. Like Mr. Chin Yuen, Mr. Spring Fragrance espouses the Asian custom, emphatically disagreeing with his wife's support of romantic love (which she demonstrates by her efforts to thwart a betrothal arranged by Chin Yuen for his daughter Laura). Jade finds her husband's "old-fashioned" belief "strange." Before their own arranged marriage, she notes "he had fallen in love with her picture before *ever* he had seen her, just as she had fallen in love with his!" (Sui Sin Far, "Mrs." 25). After the wedding, their relationship continues to be marked simultaneously by "old-fashioned" and "new" ideas, described as "Chinese" and "American," respectively. Rather than limit his wife, he allows her a great amount of independence. Mr. Spring Fragrance also balks at the suggestion that Jade is becoming a "butterfly" or loose woman, a description proffered by an elder relative who has spied her in the company of "a good-looking youth." Mr. Spring Fragrance's response reveals a sense of cultural relativity. "This is America," he insists, "where a man may speak to a woman, and a woman listen, without any thought of evil" (Sui Sin Far, "Mrs." 22). Despite his trust in "American" customs, however, Mr. Spring Fragrance begins to doubt his wife.

The arranged marriage described at the story's beginning is not the real problem, nor are the supposed cultural and generational differences. Indeed, Mrs. Spring Fragrance overcomes the obstacle of Laura Chin Yuen's unwanted betrothal before even one-third of the story has been told. In doing so, she plays matchmaker, a role that ironically supports the practice of marriage arranging. The conflict over arranged marriages and Jade's resulting inability to confront her husband are symptoms of a social threat posed by an unequal gender system supported by patriarchy and not just Chinese patriarchy. Although the story codes as "Chinese" the practice of arranging marriages and, thus, hindering a woman's freedom, Mr. Spring Fragrance is "Americanized" (Sui Sin Far, "Mrs." 18) especially in his treatment of his wife. More specifically, the amount of freedom he grants Jade is dictated by domestic ideology. While he concerns himself with commerce and political concerns, he grants her autonomy only in the domestic realm. Jade can make extended visits to relatives and is granted privacy when she speaks with her friends, "[n]ot wishing to hear more of the secret talk of women" (Sui Sin Far, "Mrs." 26).

While Eaton invokes domestic ideology, her stories do not demand a return to separate spheres. As the misunderstanding between Jade and her husband develops, Eaton exposes the limitations of domestic ideology to grant women social influence and power even as wives and mothers. Jade's lack of authority in the domestic realm is symbolized by her inability to control her status as a mother. In the only sad note in the story, readers learn that she "had had two [children] herself, but both had been transplanted into the spirit land" (Sui Sin Far, "Mrs." 20). Another lack of control is symbolized by a "jadestone pendant." For Jade, the pendant is a reminder of the only "occasion since their marriage" that her husband had "slighted her wishes." Although "[s]he had signified a desire for a certain jadestone pendant, . . . he had failed to satisfy that desire" (Sui Sin Far, "Mrs." 22). Mr. Spring Fragrance buys the pendant, but his growing mistrust of her prevents him from giving it to her. By withholding it, he emphasizes her lack of control; the wife only receives what a husband wishes to give. Mr. Spring Fragrance, for his part, is not an abusive or domineering husband. He is most often generous, but his pride and desire to appear as if he controls his wife is symptomatic of gender inequity. He conceals the details of his wife's prolonged absence. Instead of telling his neighbor that Jade wanted to stay in San Francisco for an additional week, he makes it seem as if it were his idea. He says: "I have changed my mind about her" and "am bidding her remain a week longer, as I wish to give a smoking party during her absence" (Sui Sin Far, "Mrs." 23). He wants to appear as if he had more control over his wife's movements.

Mrs. Spring Fragrance's actions challenge the limited role she is granted by both her husband and domestic ideology. Unable to use indirect influence, Jade uses immediate action to prevent the arranged marriage. She refuses tradition and disobeys patriarchal authority to help Laura escape a situation in which she is given no choice. Yet, Jade manages to mask her own empowerment in letters she writes to her husband, playing the role of "ever loving and obedient woman." She also elevates her husband as "Great and Honored Man," describes him as the "Sun," and describes herself as "clumsy" and "Stupid Thorn" (Sui Sin Far, "Mrs." 21). The depiction of Jade's writing is, as Mary Chapman notes, "compatible with stereotypes of Asian women's quietness and earlier U.S. models of domestic feminism" (979). Her activities—fudge-making, entertaining, and shopping—are also appropriately domestic, except for one. She attends a "magniloquent lecture" given by Mrs. Samuel Smith:

The subject was "America, the Protector of China!" It was most exhilarating, and the effect of so much expression of benevolence leads me to beg of you to forget to remember that the barber charges you one dollar for a shave while he humbly submits to the American man a bill of fifteen cents. And murmur no more because you honored elder brother, on a visit to this country, is detained under the rood-tree of this great Government instead of under you own jumble roof. Console him with the reflection that he is protected under the wing of the Eagle, the Emblem of Liberty. (Sui Sin Far, "Mrs." 21)

The irony of Jade's letter is obvious. The examples she presents contradict Mrs. Smith's Progressive Era ideas. Far from being the "protector" of China and immigrants from China, America exploits them. In addition, the examples show the ways in which the domestic sphere is contaminated by political and economic concerns. Mr. Spring Fragrance has no control over the fate of family members. "By listening to competing Progressive Era discourses and transcribing them in a way that mirrors their limits," Chapman argues, "Sui Sin Far effects a 'revolution in ink'" (979) that calls attention to racial discrimination.

Jade's invocation of race convinces her husband of the importance of gender equality. She shows him that "racism and sexism are rooted in the same error: the belief that one is innately superior to another" (Ling, *Between* 43). From his experience with racism, he comes to understand the unfairness of sexism, and he changes his opinion regarding arranged marriages. In "Inferior," Jade uses a similar tactic with Mrs. Carman, whose class prejudice keeps her son from marrying Alice Winthrop. Mrs. Carman deems the younger woman "inferior" because "she is not only uneducated in the ordinary sense, but her environment, from childhood up, has been the sordid and demoralizing one of extreme poverty and ignorance" (Sui Sin Far, "Inferior" 35). Jade's comparison of the "inferior" woman with her husband reveals Mrs. Carman's gender bias. She reminds Mrs. Carman of how Mr. Spring Fragrance "[w]orked his way up" and "had made money, saved money, and sent money home. The years had flown, his business had grown" (Sui

Sin Far, "Inferior" 33). Alice, who "entered a law office at the age of fourteen," likewise ascends in the workplace to become the "private secretary to the most influential man in Washington" (Sui Sin Far, "Inferior" 29). Mrs. Carman quickly sees the error of her thinking when Jade tells her:

> You are so good as to admire my husband because he is what the Americans call 'a man who has made himself.' Why then do you not admire the Inferior Woman who is a woman who has made herself. (Sui Sin Far, "Inferior" 39)

Mrs. Carman whose "prejudices did not extend to the Chinese"— nor to men it would seem—is quick to recognize the error of her thinking. Just as Mr. Spring Fragrance extends his desire for racial equality to gender equality, Mrs. Carman extends her admiration for a "self-made" Chinese merchant to a similarly "self-made" working woman. For Mrs. Carman and Mr. Spring Fragrance, the importance of racial equality is a given that helps them overcome their class and gender biases.

Eaton's audience, however, may not have shared her fictional characters' concerns about race. *Hampton's* magazine, which first published the Spring Fragrance stories, "was known for taking on such issues as rights for working women and for attacking monopolies like the Southern Pacific Railroad" (White-Parks, *Sui* 147). While white working women often competed with Chinese for employment, labor parties concerned about unchecked capitalism traditionally conflated the interest of big business with those of Chinese immigrants. Members of the West Coast Workingmen's Party, for example, changed their initial slogan, "Down with the Bloated Monopolists!" to "The Chinese Must Go!" Unlike Mr. Spring Fragrance and Mrs. Carman, *Hampton's* readers would not have to be convinced of the importance of class and gender equality. Quite the opposite, these readers would have to be convinced to embrace the racial equity the characters already value. By appealing to her audience's progressive ideas about class and gender equity, Eaton seeks to transform their ideas about race.

The complexity of Eaton's work and life cannot be described as "authentic" or "exotic," "insider" or "outsider," "real" or "fake." Describing Eaton in either/or terms undercuts her attempt to maneuver between the cultures with which she identified. Educated in British and North American literary traditions, Eaton was influenced by popular images of Asian immigrants despite her identification with Chinese immigrants and her interest in learning about her mother's root culture. Although stereotypical notions about Chinese culture appear in "Mrs." and "Inferior," these stories attempt to break down barriers constructed between Asian and Anglo American communities. By simultaneously conforming to and resisting Western thought and literary traditions, Eaton reveals the complexity of responses to the volatile and variable nature of American racism.

Note

1. Both stories were published in *Hampton's* magazine. Mrs. Spring Fragrance" appeared in the January 1910 issue and "The Inferior Woman" appeared in the May 1910 issue.

Works Cited

Chapman, Mary. "A 'Revolution in Ink': Sui Sin Far and Chinese Reform Discourse." *American Quarterly* 60. 4 (December 2008): 975–1001.

Chan, Jeffery Paul, Frank Chin, Lawson Fusao Inada, & Shawn Wong, eds. *The Big Aiiieeeee! An Anthology of Chinese and Japanese American Literature*. New York: Penguin, 1991.

Chin, Frank, Jeffery Paul Chan, Lawson Fusao Inada, & Shawn Wong, eds. *Aiiieeeee! An Anthology of Asian-American Writers.* 1974. Garden City: Anchor-Doubleday, 1975.

Cheung, King-Kok. *Articulate Silences: Hisaye Yamamoto, Maxine Hong Kingston, Joy Kogawa*. Ithaca: Cornell UP, 1993.

Ling, Amy. *Between Worlds*. New York: Pergamon, 1990.

_____. "Edith Eaton: Pioneer Chinamerican Writer and Feminist." *American Liteary Realism* 16 (1983): 287–98.

Ferens, Dominika. *Edith and Winnifred Eaton: Chinatown Missions and Japanese Romances*. Urbana: U of Illinois P, 2002.

Lape, Noreen Groover. *West of the Border: The Multicultural Literature of the Western American Frontiers*. Athens: Ohio UP, 2000.

McCann, Sean. "Connecting Link: The Anti-Progressivism of Sui Sin Far." *Yale Journal of Criticism* 12 (1999). 73–88.

"New Note." *New York Times Book Review* 7 July 1912: 405. Microfilm.

Rich, Charlotte J. *Transcending the New Woman: Multiethnic Narratives in the Progressive Era.* St. Louis: U of Missouri P, 2009.

Solberg, S. E. "Sui Sin Far/Edith Eaton: First Chinese American Fictionist." *MELUS* 8. 1 (1981): 27–39.

Sui Sin Far [Edith Eaton]. "The Inferior Woman." *Mrs. Spring Fragrance and Other Writings*. Eds. Amy Ling and Annette White-Parks. Urbana: U of Illinois P, 1995. 28–41.

_____. "Mrs. Spring Fragrance." *Mrs. Spring.* 17–28.

White-Parks, Annette. *Sui Sin Far/Edith Maude Eaton: a Literary Biography*. Urbana: U of Illinois P, 1995.

_____. "A Reversal of the Concept of 'Other-ness' in the Fiction of Sui Sin Far" *MELUS* 20 (1995): 17–34.

Wong, Sau-Ling Cynthia. "Necessity and Extravagance in Maxine Hong Kingston's *The Woman Warrior*: Art and the Ethnic Experience." MELUS 15.1 (1988): 4–26.

Yin, Xiao-huang. *Chinese American Literature since the 1850s*. Urbana: U of Illlinois P, 2000.

Yu, Ning. "Fanny Fern and Sui Sin Far: The Beginning of an Asian American Voice." *Women and Language* 19.2 (Fall 1996): 44–47.

Intimate Relations: Land and Love in *The Descendants*

The figuring of Hawai'i as "paradise" has proliferated throughout historical and fictional accounts of the Pacific, since Western contact in the late 1700s. Colonized islands, like Hawai'i, have been constructed according to Western economic and cultural investments. The tourist industry and Hollywood are two of the main disseminators of Hawai'i as a place of fantasy subject to commodification. The illegal annexation of Hawai'i by the United States in 1898 and the Islands' statehood in 1959 often are overlooked in popular portrayals, thus eclipsing the complex relationships among Hawaiians, Asian immigrants, and Americans. Kaui Hart Hemmings' 2007 novel, *The Descendants*, and its 2011 cinematic version offer insights into how America's narrative idealization of "paradise" has influenced Hawai'i's culture and identity. Given the prominence surrounding Alexander Payne's film adaptation of Hemmings' novel, this essay explores how both the novel and film portray protagonist Matt King as a multiracial subject, part-*haole* (Caucasian) and part-*kanaka maoli* (Native Hawaiian), whose relationship to indigenous history and land is intimately connected to his wife's infidelity.

Both the novel and film emphasize the complex formation of multiracial identity through Matt's attitude towards Hawai'i and his family's inheritance as members of an elite class of mixed-race Hawaiians. *The Descendants* offers an alternative figuration of racial identity in Hawai'i that addresses the interracial mixing of Native Hawaiians and Caucasians; this highlights a correlation between marriage and the intimate relationship of *kanaka maoli* to land and also, marital infidelity and the sale of Hawaiian land held in trust. Both the novel and its film adaptation utilize marital infidelity as a way to comment and raise questions about the deeply intimate relationship of *kanaka maoli* to land. Matt's shocking discovery of his wife's affair parallels the impending decision for the sale of his

Critical Insights

family's inherited land that raises larger questions about of Hawai'i's history, tourism, and the complex social relationships at stake in the Islands. The film benefits from the multi-sensory experience; Payne's recurrent use of the song "Hi'ilawe," performed by Gabby Pahinui in crucial scenes, allows for a nuanced reckoning between Matt's marital and land sale dilemmas. Ultimately, Matt's decision to keep his family's land reflects an awareness not only of an ethical responsibility to his *kanaka maoli* past, present, and future, but also suggests a preference for community over individual gain. The personal and economic choices Matt faces are intricately linked to the problematic history and contemporary status of Hawai'i.

The Descendants as both a novel and film opens up Western representations of Hawai'i as an object for possession and as a mysterious destination. Hemmings' and Payne's versions of the Pacific allow for complex representations that attend to indigenous history. Elizabeth DeLoughrey argues that islands with colonial backgrounds, such as Hawai'i, are "simultaneously positioned as isolated yet deeply susceptible to migration and settlement" and have been categorized by Europe and America as "new Eden, a sociopolitical utopia" (9). The trope of the island, described by DeLoughrey, as an ideological system of "islandism" operates "as a reflection of various political, sociological, and colonial practices" in literature (12–13). In other words, Western nations have construed islands as Edenic, virgin territory in order to advance their own imperialistic projects. In particular, the supposedly *terra nullius* of Hawai'i operated as a foundation for American imperial designs and the erasure of *kanaka maoli*. Explaining how America viewed Hawai'i, Vernadette Gonzalez asserts the Islands encompassed "the imperial military and commercial dreams of the United States in the region" (12). From initial contact, the isolation of Hawai'i exemplified a capitalistic opportunity for trade and tourism as well as fortifying military presence. Rob Wilson, in *Reimagining the Pacific*, describes how the contemporary industries of tourism and Hollywood, in conjunction with the global capitalist economy, continue to exploit images of Hawai'i as exotic and available for Western consumption. As a result, *kanaka maoli* culture, identity, and history are often re-imagined and reproduced in service for a tourist economy. Indigenous scholar and activist, Haunani-Kay Trask critiques how the exploitation of Native Hawaiian culture involves "the hotel version of the *hula*, [where] the sacredness of the dance has completely evaporated, while the athleticism and sexual expression have been packaged like ornaments" (144). Trask continues to explain how "the word 'Aloha' is employed as an aid in the constant hawking of things Hawaiian. In truth, this use of *aloha* is so far removed from any Hawaiian cultural context that it is, literally meaningless" (Trask 144). Trask identifies how Hawaiian language and art have been emptied of all cultural context, viewing it as an example of the violence of the tourist economy. Other targets for touristic amnesia include *kanaka maoli* spirituality, history, and the significance of the land—a central focus throughout the novel's representation of inherited land as indigenous legacy.

Hemmings' novel introduces the reader to Matt and his wife, Joanie (called Elizabeth in Payne's adaptation), who is in a coma, to foreground the family drama and Matt's impending decision about keeping her on life support. In this way, Hemmings conveys the contradictory nature of island life: "The sun is shining, mynah birds are chattering, palm trees are swaying, so what. I'm in the hospital and I'm healthy. . . . My wife is on the upright hospital bed" (3). Matt emphasizes the banality of the sun, birds, and palm trees in contrast to his wife's dire condition. The comparison immediately overthrows expectations about life in paradise. Matt's subsequent comments further highlight the limitations of stereotypes: "The tropics make it difficult to mope. I bet in big cities you can walk down the street scowling and no one will ask you what's wrong or encourage you to smile, but everyone here has this attitude that we're lucky to live in Hawaii; paradise reigns supreme. I think paradise can go fuck itself" (Hemmings 5). This suggests a particular mode of existence predicated on the idea of perpetual bliss. Matt's emphatic "paradise can go fuck itself" rejects stereotypical visions of Hawai'i and foregrounds a stance against colonization.

Hemmings' depiction of Matt's cynical perspective is visually conveyed in the film where Matt's opening voiceover is juxtaposed with images of Honolulu not often seen on the Mainland: congested freeway traffic, poverty, homelessness in the city as well as in beach camps, and multiple multiracial crowd shots. Matt in the film narrates: "My friends on the mainland think just because I live in Hawaii, I live in paradise. Like a permanent vacation—we're all just out here sipping mai tais, shaking our hips, and catching waves" (Payne, Faxon, & Rash). Matt's list of stereotypical assumptions combined with selected images of a non-idyllic tropical existence speak to the film's refusal to convey an idealized paradise. Matt continues, "Are they insane? Do they think we are immune to life? . . . paradise? Paradise can go fuck itself" (Payne, Faxon, & Rash). In posing questions, Matt explicitly refuses the Western narrative of an Edenic existence in a place identified as "paradise." The images paired with Matt's interrogation work to resist one-dimensional portrayals of Hawai'i in a more detailed approach than the novel's straightforward statements. In both openings though, it is clear *The Descendants* marks the significance of the wife's coma to Matt's perspective and his refusal to proliferate distorted versions of Hawai'i.

Both versions also highlight the interconnectedness between Matt's impending decision about keeping his wife on artificial life support and one "on who should own the land that has been in my family since the 1840s" (Hemmings 7), land held in trust that is intimately connected to *kanaka maoli* identity. While it might be easy to write off these choices as personal, Hemmings links Matt's struggles to a larger collective crisis. Hemmings conveys Matt's burden of responsibility in the ongoing conversation he has with himself. He says, "maybe I feel a bit guilty, having so much control. Why me? Why does so much depend on me? And what did the people before me do in order for me to have so much. Maybe I subscribe to the idea that behind every great fortune is a great crime" (Hemmings 13). Matt's guilt results in his position as the majority voter; he holds "about 1/8 of the trust, whereas the others get 1/24" (Hemmings 23). The convoluted history of Matt's ancestors is suggested in his description of the relationship between the "fortune" of the land trust with the historical "crime" of acquiring the Hawaiian lands. Matt's questions can also apply to the responsibilities attending him as the sole parent after his wife's accident. He tells us: "I have inheritance issues. I belong to one of those Hawaii families who make money off of luck and dead people. . . . We [the descendants] sit back and watch the past unfurl millions into our laps" (Hemmings 22). Matt's decision will affect his children and all his future descendants who inherit not only land, but the responsibility—for Hawaiian identity and culture—that comes with it.

Matt continues to dwell on his inherited status as he critiques his relatives, who have passively accepted a fortune partially from the Hawaiian monarchy. Hemmings situates the complexity of land issues and racialized familial histories through Matt's guilty conscience. By acknowledging the historical and legal processes around Native Hawaiian and Caucasian intermarriage as well as the particularly fraught constitution of *kanaka maoli* classification, Hemmings calls attention to these often overlooked issues. While interracial marriage was never legally prohibited in Hawai'i, as it was in other states, the status of mixed race individuals became explicitly intertwined with American classifications of citizenship, in terms of claims to land and sovereignty. J. Kēhaulani Kauanui's work on the logics of the blood quantum classification in definitions of Native Hawaiian identity reveals the intersection of quantifiable blood ancestry and legitimate land ownership. In particular, Kauanui discusses the Hawaiian Homes Commission Act of 1920, which required individuals to demonstrate fifty percent Hawaiian ancestry (later amended in 1997 to twenty-five percent) to be eligible for the US Congress' allotment of "200,000 acres of land." Kauanui notes that while this legislation was initially "intended to encourage the revitalization of a particular Hawaiian demographic, the act simultaneously created a class of people who could no longer qualify for the land that constitutes the Hawaiian Home Lands territory" (3). This parsing of definable indigeneity, Kauanui argues, dismisses social epistemologies of kinship and "undermines Kanaka Maoli sovereignty claims—by not only explicitly limiting the number who could lay claim to the land but also reframing the Native connection to land" (9). Kauanui's analysis links the colonial legacies of land dispossession with the creation of "Hawaiianess" through tying proof of blood to land rights. The "imposed state policy of blood" of the Hawaiian Homes Commission Act also disregarded indigenous definitions of family where "blood was understood in terms of performative kinship relations" (Halulani 45). *The Descendants* is embroiled in these tumultuous legal and political struggles over land dispossession, eligibility, and production of indigenous identity. Matt King, as a multiracial inheritor of indigenous land, embodies the friction between American classifications of race and individual ownership of land and *kanaka maoli* genealogy with a communal relationship to land.

Matt's last name, "King," highlights his complicated identity in its evocation of Native Hawaiian royalty, who complied with American colonial divisions of land and Western definitions of property. Hemmings' attention to the historical context of Matt King's position is critical and is further compounded by a continual emphasis on Matt's nagging suspicions about his wife's infidelity (with a real estate broker) and its connection to her sudden interest in the family land sale. As Matt reflects on his dilemma over picking a buyer for the land, he remembers how Joanie "would ask me what was happening with the sale, so uncharacteristically interested, my appreciation would turn into paranoia, and this was before I found the note. I wondered if she was planning to divorce me after I sold my shares" (Hemmings 39–40). In pairing Joanie's unusual interest in the land sale with Matt's ruminations on her possible infidelity, Hemmings aligns their marriage with *kanaka maoli* history and land. Matt's public decision about the economic future of Hawai'i and his descendants' right to land is imbued with his own unstable marriage, his children, their future, and concerns about his wife's fidelity. Joanie's marital betrayal and corresponding interest in selling the land becomes a metaphor for a larger betrayal that would come should Matt decide to sell the land for economic purposes. Matt's growing awareness and acceptance of his wife's infidelity act as a measure of his changing views about the land sale.

Payne's film adaptation amplifies Hemmings' assertive demonstration of the parallel development of Matt's real estate and personal crises with the use "Hi'ilawe," a well-known Hawaiian song. The song accompanies two critical scenes that explicitly deal with the land sale and Joanie's affair. These scenes also highlight Matt's conflicted position as husband, father, and majority voter in the land deal. Composed in the mid- to late 1800s by Mrs. Kuakini, "Hi'ilawe" is a song about a romantic relationship and infidelity that reflects Matt's martial situation. It also suggests Matt's real estate dilemma; "Hi'ilawe" references one of the tallest waterfalls on the Big Island's Waipi'o Valley, a place imbued with historical and cultural value. The song, as described by Elbert and Mahoe, "concerns a girl from Puna who has a love affair at Hi'ilawe waterfall in Waipi'o, Hawai'i. The chattering birds may refer to gossips" (49). Elbert and Mahoe note, "the girl, who is not bashful, calls herself *uhiwai, hiwahiwa* (or *milimili), lei 'a'I* and *'a'I hali 'ia mai*" and by doing so, defines herself as the mist, precious, beloved toy, and as a lei (49). The subtle rendering of objects and categorizations suggest how this girl is not ashamed of her affair, even if the gossips or chattering birds condemn her actions. The song's subtle *kaona* or hidden meaning about the girl's boldness relies upon the imagery of the land, thus highlighting Matt's double dilemma. The cultural importance of the song "Hi'ilawe" also underscores Matt's reckoning with his wife's infidelity along with indigeneity, history, and land. Furthermore, Payne's deliberate selection of Gabby Pahinui's version of "Hi'ilawe" is important. Widely celebrated as the "Father of Modern Slack Guitar," Pahinui's status and contributions to Hawaiian music are legendary. Payne's choice of this Hawaiian song and others on the soundtrack pays tribute to a crucial art form that has its legacy in the revitalization of *kanaka maoli* cultural forms.

The first scene that features "Hi'ilawe" appropriately fits the narrative of the song and melds the music with Matt's awareness of his wife's affair. Here, "Hi'ilawe" lends itself to the twinning of romantic infidelity and a particular relationship between the land and *kanaka maoli* identity. This scene begins in the King's living room when Matt's older daughter Alex reveals her mother's infidelity. In shock and desiring more information from friends, Matt abruptly starts to leave the house. As he clumsily struggles to put on his flip flop sandals, the opening notes of "Hiʻilawe" begin. The music is prominent as Matt runs haphazardly down his driveway into the street lined with lush foliage, evoking the atmosphere of Waipiʻo Valley. Pahinui's voice accompanies the camera as it zooms in on Matt's panicked running face. The opening lines of the song are "*Kūmaka ka ʻikena iā Hiʻilawe*" which translate to "All eyes are on Hiʻilawe" (Elbert and Mahoe 49) and carry resonance as the camera pulls away from Matt's face to show full-body shots of him awkwardly running. Emphasizing the idea of observation and perhaps even surveillance, Payne uses the lyrics of "Hiʻilawe" to echo the sentiments of a cuckolded Matt, while also alluding to the statewide awareness of the sale of the land. Matt is not adulterous in his marriage, but at this point, he may still vote in favor of the land sale and is thus poised to betray his ancestors and descendants. The doubleness of Matt as the betrayed husband and as the prospective betrayer is enhanced by the use of Pahinui's "Hiʻilawe." This moment could also be considered the beginning of Matt's awakening to both elements of his life. The song continues in the background as Matt makes his way to the house of friends, where he proceeds to grill them on the affair. The use of "Hiʻilawe" in this part of the film intensifies Matt's emotional and slightly comical run through the neighborhood as he deals with his wife's infidelity and, perhaps, subconsciously speaks to his probable betrayal.

In the novel, Matt processes Joanie's affair differently; he has already had suspicions and thus, Hemmings focuses on the gravity of Joanie's accident. The novel does not immediately create a parallel between Matt's disintegrating marriage and the land. Hemmings highlights Matt's reaction to the affair with: "It seems that I should feel something right now, like a deep chill . . ., but the only thing I feel is that I've been told something I already know" (94). Matt's numbness illuminates his immobility and the impossible situation of his marriage and family. Unlike the film, Matt breaks down in front of Alex, reluctantly at first, but then, "for the first time, I actually cry, as though I've just now realized what's happening to my wife and to me and to this family. My wife's not coming back, my wife didn't love me, and I'm in charge now" (Hemmings 96). Matt's ability to recognize the situation discloses his complete vulnerability. In building out the metaphor of infidelity, both the film and novel implicitly suggest Matt's suspicions of his wife's affair with the potentially negative consequences of selling the land. The assertive statement of "I'm in charge now," coupled with Matt's emotional run through the neighborhood, speaks to a potential change in his stance on family and the land sale.

Both the novel and the film reflect the inescapable combination of Matt's focus on identifying Joanie's lover, real estate broker Brian Speer, and the deadline to make a decision on a buyer. Matt's search for Brian clinches the familial connections between the economic future of the Islands and Joanie's dalliance. The particularities of this financial impact of the land sale are described as "hotels, shopping centers, condos and golf courses. 3,000 new jobs in the first five years" (Payne, Faxon, & Rash). The economic stakes are obviously an integral part of Matt's decision, but the ones that resonate are more intimate—those related to his wife's affair, to the land betrayals of *kanaka maoli* ancestors, and to indigenous identity. The disclosure that Brian is the brother-in-law of the favored buyer, Don Holitzer, is a detail included in both the novel and film. Hemmings writes: "I finally get it. Brian is basically a Realtor with about three hundred thousand acres of commercial and industrial land, my land. . . . Joanie . . . [would] divorce me for a business partner of Don Holitzer, potential largest landowner in Hawaii" (199). Matt's suspicions about his wife's marital duplicity are confirmed as Matt begins to understand how she would benefit financially. For Hemmings' Matt, Joanie's affair was a complete betrayal of the family and her actions are inseparable from his pending decision. In the film, Payne forgoes a voiceover that would provide insight into Matt's tumultuous thoughts as his cousin explains Brian's familial relationship to Don. Payne instead captures Matt's growing understanding by featuring actor George Clooney's subtle, but shell-shocked expressions. Film-viewers easily interpret Matt's widening eyes as a sign that he is figuring out the connection between Joanie's affair, Brian's ties to Don, and the land sale.

Payne relies on "Hiʻilawe" again in a scene that begins with Matt arriving at the family estate. Once again, it provides insight into the parallel relationships between Matt's multiracial identity, his marriage, and inherited estate/responsibility. Pahinui's steel guitar resonates as Matt steps inside the ancestral house and pauses to look at photos of Edward King and Princess Margaret Keʻalohilani, his great-great-grandparents. Pahinui's voice floods the scene with the song's second verse: "*Pakele mai au, i ka nui manu / Hau walaʻau nei, puni Waipiʻo,*" ("I escape all the birds chattering everywhere in *Waipiʻo,*" trans. Elbert and Mahoe 49). The birds, or gossips in this case, have nothing to do with his wife's infidelity, but instead target the media obsession with Matt's impending choice; the entire state has a stake in the sale's effects on the real estate and tourist economy. Here, Matt is more explicitly positioned in the land affair and the song suggests that a decision to sell would be a betrayal. By highlighting the land sale, Payne's second use of "Hiʻilawe" evokes the complex historical relationship between *kanaka maoli* and the land. While the King family is not exactly manipulating the system or breaking any laws, the use of the land sale for their primary benefit and in service of a tourist economy would go against cultural ties to the land. The scene ends with the songs fourth verse as the camera zooms in on family members laughing: "*He hiwahiwa au (a he milimili hoʻi) nā ka makua / A he lei ʻāʻī, nā ke kupuna*" ("I am the darling (a toy) of the parents/ And a lei for the necks of grandparents," trans. Elbert and Mahoe 49). In an assertion of self-value, the song reflects the girl's confident position, as she links her stability through both her parents and grandparents' genealogy. Clearly reflecting the King clan, this verse—in conjunction with images of the family members laughing, drinking, and voting—suggests the complicity of *hapa-haole*, biracial Native Hawaiian and Caucasian individuals who have profited accidentally, but nevertheless seem content to perpetuate the system. The song ends as the camera focuses on a contemplative Matt, who is counting votes. Matt votes to keep the land and, thus, redefines his Native Hawaiian identity. By refusing to sell the land, Matt rejects commercial and corporate development and takes on the responsibility of the family's inheritance. He stakes a claim in his loyalty to his ancestors, represented by the photos, and demonstrates the choice to revision contemporary Hawaiian relationships to the land. Although the land has the Americanized designation of property, Matt's choice upholds communal interest. Matt's choice may also suggest a need for contemporary *kanaka maoli* to acknowledge their complicity in the negative effects of land ownership. In the way Payne builds up this scene, it is clear that the combination of "Hi`ilawe" and Matt's reflection on family photos foreshadow Matt's surprising choice. He explains:

> I sign this document and something that we were supposed to protect is gone forever. Now we're haole as shit and we go to private schools and clubs and we can barely even speak pidgin, let alone Hawaiian, but we've got Hawaiian blood, and we're tied to this land. And our children are tied to this land . . . for some bullshit reason 150 years ago, we own this much of paradise, but we do (Payne, Faxon, & Rash).

As Matt reckons with his position as "haole as shit" with an obligation to the entrusted land, he astutely recognizes his family's accidental position of privilege. But he invokes an awareness of privilege based on indigeneity and genealogy through the next generation. Matt's discussion of how the family has acted *haole* is through the performance of associated privileges that code them as elite citizens. This is acted and reinforced through erasing all parts of Native Hawaiian identity except for the wealthy inheritance. In arguing for the literal "tying" of land to the family, Matt redefines *hapa-haole* identity as responsible for a collective future in a way that rejects the individualized Western notions of property as ownership and evaluated on monetary value. By family, Matt seems to include the Islands as an entity and perhaps part of a *kanaka maoli* kinship where "genealogies connect people to one another, to place, and to land: they are about relatedness" (Kauanui 64).

As a result in the novel, Hemmings seems to offer a possible version of modern *kanaka maoli* identity no longer restricted by American colonial logics of blood, citizenship, and property. Matt's emphatic description of a "bullshit reason" evokes the complicated legal politics around land divisions that have coded the King family as no longer Native Hawaiian, but at the top of an Americanized aristocracy. Tracing the history of land tenure, Halulani emphasizes how the *Ka Mahele* (division) of land in 1848 restructured their previous *"akua* [spirit]-centered communal land structure based on specialized labor and reciprocity" (57). The unprecedented separation and privatization of land not only enforced ownership rights, but also embedded Western law and regulations for land applications. The subsequent 1850 Kuleana Act allowed Native Hawaiians to "assume their rights by first applying to a land commission board for a fee-simple title claim" where applicants had to pass eligibility tests and "less than 1 percent of the total land acreage passed in fee simple to Hawaiian commoners" (Halulani 58; Kauaunui 77). In other words, the legal structures around land ultimately restricted the majority of *kanaka maoli* from becoming individual tenants. These "bullshit" colonial legal acts are what Matt obliquely references and once again, speaks to Hemmings' refusal to conform to one-dimensional and stereotypical representations of Hawai'i. Building on the significance of indigenous identity to land, Susan Najita emphasizes not only an intimate connection between Pacific indigeneity and land, but also how land embodies a cultural history that acts as living testimony to American domination; she argues: "the power of place, the active vocation of one's relation to land, is an enduring aspect of indigenous Pacific Island cultures... spaces are haunted by the everyday-ness of place (15). By refusing to sell the land, Matt recognizes and embraces his cultural history.

With "Hi`ilawe" as a mirror for Matt's decision in the film, Payne hints at the King clan's infidelity to the obligation handed down to them from their ancestors. Matt's monumental decision provides a recognition of the communal value of kinship over individualized profit in the sale. In comparison, Hemmings' novel draws out the causal effects of Joanie's affair on Matt and his decision to maintain the family legacy. Hemmings marries Matt's indigenous claim to land with an eye towards his children's future with a self-interest that derives from Joanie's imminent death. After Matt refuses to sell, he reflects, "I find myself not wanting to give it up—the land, the lush relic of our tribe, the dead. The last Hawaiian-owned land will be lost, and I will have something to do with it. Even though we don't look Hawaiian . . . my girls and I are Hawaiian and this land is ours" (Hemmings 229–230). Echoing Payne's version, Matt emphasizes the lack of physical markers of indigeneity, but also focuses on an ethical duty to the Islands' past and future inhabitants. Matt describes how the land is the "lush relic of our tribe" to stake a collective ownership and kinship in an often elided and disregarded past. Furthermore, Matt elaborates his reasons as:

> My ancestors, but no, that's not it entirely. That's what I want the reason to be, but there are other, less dignified ones: Revenge. Selfishness. A desire to see my daughters have the land. Let them make decisions about it. . . . I don't want Brian to have a part of it. I don't want his sons to have it. I don't want their history to mix with mine. Kekipi rebelled, and so will I. (Hemmings 230)

This confession, never articulated in the film, hones in on the complex emotional situation Matt is in with "revenge" and "rebellion" (the name "Kekipi" means rebel) as motivating factors. This raises the question about the target of Matt's revenge and rebellion: Brian; Joanie, for her infidelity; American imperialism. It also provides a broader critique of Matt's prior ambivalence towards land and the tourist economy. Even more revealing is Matt's impulse to exclude Brian and his sons from partaking in his family's legacy. Matt insists on an undiluted history and severs Joanie's romantic affair from not only the economic realm, but also the familial. This moment may mark the beginning Matt's catharsis, which ends when Joanie is pulled from life support. After this, he privileges his redefined *kanaka maoli* identity and its intimate marriage to the land. This becomes more evident in Matt's closing thoughts:

> I know I wouldn't have done this if my wife weren't going to die, but the fact is, she is. She is going to die and she will be gone and my daughters will not have a mother. . . . I know you understand the complicated nature of birthrights, how they're both fortuitous and undeserved. I've decided you won't be receiving any money;

but we'll all get to keep something, and we'll get to pass it on" (Hemmings 231).

Hemming connects Matt's decision on Joanie's impending death and all of the realizations unearthed by her accident. Joanie's infidelity irrefutably determines Matt's newfound valuation of land not as source of wealth or economic development, but as a protected familial entity. Joanie's accident and Matt's subsequent discovery of her affair shakes him out of his complicit state and moves him to evaluate his responsibilities to his ancestors, his children, and ultimately, the future of the Islands. This shift toward the future speaks to the ethical sakes of the land and Matt's realization that his legacy is not solely his or his family's to own or profit from. In this way, *The Descendants* resists a (colonial) blood-logic of family and underscores a larger kinship model based on land held in common and responsibility to the community. Hemmings' novel presents this as a new kind of inheritance that is more valuable than money and that is chosen rather than simply handed down or inherited. Rebecca Hogue astutely points out in her analysis of the novel: "After Matt loses his wife, he shifts his values to his family and its history, replacing his bitterness over the frivolity of modern day Hawai'i culture with recognition of his family's history" (7). Hogue identifies how Matt's change in perspective is also tied to a critique of Hawai'i's touristic culture and his need to protect his family's land. In the novel's unflinching acknowledgement of a selfish desire to keep the land as an ethical commitment, Matt emerges from his marital crisis by taking control and embracing *kanaka maoli* responsibilities. In both Hemmings' novel and Payne's adaptation of this climactic scene, the inescapable relationship between indigenous identity and responsibility to the land is undeniable and parallels Matt's coming to terms with Joanie's infidelity. As suggested earlier in Payne's use of "Hi'ilawe," this offers insight into how the passive recipients of wealth, the descendants, have been unfaithful to their inherited land.

The Descendants, in both novel and film adaptation, asserts a vision of Hawai'i that not only refuses a glossy image of paradise, but also opens up the complexity of multiracial identity and the continual struggles over land rights. Hemmings tackles the intricate nexus of part-*kanaka maoli* subjects through Matt's portrayal and uses his marital crisis as an intimate parallel to the land sale, which implies a historical relationship between indigenous identity and land. In Payne's film, the effective use of the song "Hi'ilawe" develops another layer of critique of the touristic visions of the Islands that correlates infidelity with a complacent relationship between interracial Native Hawaiian subjects and the land. While the film allows for a visual depiction of Matt's reckoning with his position as a descendant who is responsible for indigenous land, Hemmings' novel interrogates the self-interest behind Matt's choice to keep the family's legacy. In this sense, Hemmings brutally confronts how Matt is determined by his situation and history, so that his actions are not painted as purely idealistic. Still, Matt's ultimate decision reflects a valuation of communal land and provides a possibility for a modern *hapa-haole* identity. At stake in both the novel and the film are critical and timely issues in contemporary Hawai'i that will determine the use of and access to land.

Works Cited

DeLoughrey, Elizabeth M. *Routes and Roots: Navigating Caribbean and Pacific Island Literatures*. Honolulu: U of Hawai`i P, 2007.

Elbert, Samuel H., & Noelani Mahoe. *Na Mele o Hawai`i Nei*. Honolulu: U of Hawai'i P, 1970.

Gonzalez, Vernadette Vicuna. *Securing Paradise*. Durham, NC: Duke UP, 2013.

Halulani, Rona Tamiko. *In the Name of the Hawaiians*. Minneapolis: U of Minnesota P, 2002.

Hemmings, Kaui Hart. *The Descendants*. New York: Random House, 2007.

Hogue, Rebecca. "Cultural Identity and Liminal Place in Contemporary Literature of Hawai`i." *Rocky Mountain Review: Border Crossing* (Summer 2012): 144–152.

Kauanui, J. Kēhaulani. *Hawaiian Blood: Colonialism and the Politics of Sovereignty and Indigeneity* (Narrating Native Histories). Durham: Duke UP, 2008.

Lyons, Paul. *American Pacifism: Oceania in the U.S. Imagination*. New York: Routledge, 2006.

Najita, Susan Y. *Decolonizing Cultures in the Pacific: Reading History and Trauma In Contemporary Fiction*. New York: Routledge, 2006.

Pahinui, Gabby. "Hi`ilawe." *The Descendants* Soundtrack. Sony Masterworks, 2011. CD.

Payne, Alexander, Nat Faxon, & Jim Rash. *The Descendants*. Revised Final Script. 2011. *Internet Movie Script Database*. Web. 18 May 2012.

The Descendants. Dir. Alexander Payne. 2011. DVD. Fox Searchlight, 2012.

Trask, Haunani-Kay. *From a Native Daughter: Colonialism and Sovereignty in Hawai`i*. Honolulu: U of Hawai'i P, 1999.

Wilson, Rob. *Reimagining the American Pacific*. Durham, N: Duke UP, 2000.

Bridging Borders: Leslie Marmon Silko's Cross-Cultural Vision in the Atomic Age_____

Kyoko Matsunaga

Leslie Marmon Silko's novel *Ceremony* (1977) has often been discussed in terms of cultural hybridity. Native American scholar and writer Louis Owens, for instance, points out in his critical work *Mixedblood Messages* that "*Ceremony* is a novel about mixed-blood identity by a mixed-blood novelist who has declared her writing to be about mixed and relational identity" (157–58). Silko affirms Owens' comment in *Yellow Woman and a Beauty of the Spirit* when she writes, "I suppose at the core of my writing is the attempt to identify what it is to be a half-breed, or mixed-blooded person; what it is to grow up neither white nor fully traditional Indian" (41).

Like Silko, who has Laguna, Mexican, and European heritage, the novel's protagonist Tayo is a mixed-blood, the son of a white father and a Laguna mother. Throughout the novel, Tayo goes through various rituals and ceremonies, including those conducted by a mixed-blood medicine man, Betonie, and Tayo recovers and eventually regains the feeling that he "belongs." Simply put, *Ceremony* is a story about a mixed-blood man who struggles with and comes to terms with his mixed-blood identity.

Cultural hybridity in *Ceremony*, however, has mixed implications. The fact that Tayo is of mixed-blood indicates cross-cultural contact between Laguna and European peoples; Silko also demonstrates how other colonial influences, such as alcoholism, Christianity, and World War II have affected tribal culture and communities. Among the various colonial impacts, nuclear technology and industry have left an indelible mark on the American Southwest. In an interview for the University of Arizona's student literary magazine *Persona*, Silko describes the detonation of the first atomic bomb in Alamogordo, NM, as "the big dividing point for human beings":

Because after that day all human beings, whether you were a Hopi who believed in traditional ways or whether you were a Madison Avenue Lutheran, all human beings faced the same possible destruction. . . . When you can destroy the entire planet and make it uninhabitable for life for thousands and thousands of years, that's a big change. That's a change like never ever before. (Nelson 172)

Not surprisingly, then, Silko uses an abandoned uranium mine on Laguna land as the site where Tayo witnesses the most destructive power of "destroyers" or "the witchery," as she terms it. As Lawrence Buell suggests in *The Environmental Imagination*, Silko describes European conquest and technological transformation as the doings of witchery, and the production and detonation of the atomic bombs as state-of-the-art forms of witchery (287). The atomic weapons and uranium production presented in *Ceremony* are the most drastic and modernized version of destruction brought about through cross-cultural and colonial contact in the Southwest, and Tayo has to challenge them while he confronts his own identity crisis through the ceremony.

Tayo's ceremony is hybridized. In order to deal with the advanced destructive forces in the atomic age, the rituals Tayo undergoes need to be updated with new elements. But the word "new" is tricky here. Historically, according to Silko, the Laguna have adopted people from various tribes and cultures, celebrated physical differences, and included elements from outside cultures (*Yellow Woman* 67, 103). In short, "new" elements have long been part of Laguna culture. Kathleen M. Sands emphasizes this when she notes: "new blood, new ways, new ceremonies have been essential to the survival of Laguna and are at the very heart of this novel so deeply rooted in Laguna landscape and attitude" (4–5). Paradoxically, the "new" elements in Tayo's ceremony reflect the evolving nature of "traditional" Laguna culture. Silko uses cross-cultural visions, including the theme of mixed identity, as well as culturally hybridized ceremonies, to deal with the challenges posed by the "unprecedented" power of destruction in the atomic age.

Tayo's Mixed-blood Identity

Following the pattern of other male protagonists, such as Abel in N. Scott Momaday's *House Made of Dawn* and the nameless protagonist in James Welch's *Winter in the Blood*, Tayo is emotionally estranged from both mainstream and tribal society. Significantly, all three protagonists, as Judith A. Antell notes in her article, "Momaday, Welch, and Silko: Expressing the Feminine Principle through Male Alienation," are war veterans who experienced being away from home after joining the army (213). Tayo, who endured the Bataan Death March in the Philippine jungle during World War II, seemingly suffers from post-traumatic stress disorder, but like Abel in *House Made of Dawn* and the nameless protagonist in *Winter in the Blood*, his "illness" is more complex than what the white doctors usually diagnose as "war trauma." His depression and despair are strongly connected to his removal from the Laguna community and land, and this physical separation causes his mental separation from his own self.

The novel starts when Tayo returns to the reservation from the veteran's hospital in Los Angeles. While being treated by a white doctor, Tayo's mental illness has reached a critical point: he feels like he is "white smoke" or "invisible scattered smoke" (Silko, *Ceremony* 14). These are the symptoms of Tayo's loss of self: he does not know where he belongs or who he is anymore. In fact, even the racial boundaries are blurry and lost to him. This border-crossing of race and nationality becomes a positive by the end of the novel, but at this point, it is one cause of Tayo's distress. Tayo is perplexed in the Philippine jungle, where he had seen his uncle Josiah's face in a Japanese soldier's, and at the train depot in Los Angeles, where he sees his cousin Rocky's face in that of a little Japanese American boy.

Ironically, his "illness" makes Tayo more aware of the racial boundaries between mainstream Americans and American Indians that have not disappeared after the war. Other veterans, such as Emo, Harley, and Pinkie, drown themselves with liquor, dance with blonde women, and enjoy war stories, in order to create the "feeling they belong to America," but Tayo, who also resorts to alcohol "for the anger that made them hurt, for the pain of the loss" (Silko, *Ceremony* 40), feels differently:

> I am half-breed. I'll be the first to say it. I'll speak for both sides. First time you walked down the street in Gallop or Albuquerque, you knew. Don't lie. You knew right away. The war was over, the uniform was gone. All of a sudden that man at the store waits on you last, makes you wait until all the white people bought what they wanted. And the white lady at the bus depot, she's real careful now not to touch your hand when she counts your change. You watch it slide across the counter at you, and you know. Goddam it! You stupid sonofabitches! You know! (Silko, *Ceremony* 42)

Tayo emphasizes that racial discrimination exists even after the Laguna men fought for the United States because, once they take off their military uniforms, they are treated the same as before the war: as racial minorities in the hegemonic society. However, Tayo's position is special, even among the native veterans. Emo, for example, dislikes Tayo because he is "part white" and uses the fact that Tayo is of mixed-blood to target him for insult and discrimination: "You drink like an Indian, and you're crazy like one too—but you aren't shit, white trash. You love Japs the way your mother loved to screw white men" (Silko, *Ceremony* 63). Emo's attitude toward mixed-bloods and other cultures presents a clear contrast to Tayo's. Emo emphasizes the differences between the full-bloods and mixed-bloods, or Americans and Japanese, but he wants to be treated like other Americans, as if racial differences do not exist. On the other hand, Tayo sees the absurdity of racial boundaries, but he is also quite aware of existing racial boundaries that separate the American Indians from other Americans.

Even before the war, Tayo was constantly reminded of his mixed parentage. Aunt Thelma, a devout Christian, feels shame after Tayo's mother runs away with whites or Mexicans, and she wants Tayo to feel ashamed and excluded. Thelma makes sure that she treats Tayo differently from her own son, Rocky; when she kneads bread or darns socks, she gives Rocky pieces of dough, pieces of cloth, or a needle and thread to play with while making sure Tayo cannot join in the play (Silko, *Ceremony* 67). She tries to keep distance between Tayo and Rocky because, for her, raising a "dead sister's half-breed child" is a "sacrifice" (Silko, *Ceremony* 30).

Although Tayo has been reminded of his difference since he was a child, his presence has always been embraced by his maternal grandmother and his two uncles, Josiah and Robert. While Thelma always worries about how others judge her family, Grandmother, Josiah, and Robert "didn't care what the people were saying about their family" (Silko, *Ceremony* 34). Tayo feels an especially strong bond with his maternal uncle, Josiah. According to Edith Swan in "Laguna Prototypes of Manhood in *Ceremony*," an uncle is a "primary teacher," "guardian," and "disciplinarian" for his nephew in the Laguna community (41). In other words, the relationship with Josiah is essential for Tayo to gain a sense of belonging and to understand his position in the community.

Understandably, Josiah plays a key role in Tayo's education about the importance of hybridity in Laguna culture. Before Tayo joins the Army, Josiah and Tayo make a joint plan to breed cattle on Laguna land. Instead of raising Herefords, "weak" and "soft" livestock that "grew thin and died from eating thistle and burned-off cactus during the drought" (Silko, *Ceremony* 74–75), Josiah chooses Mexican cattle to raise and cross breed because "[t]hese cattle were descendants of generations of desert cattle, born in dry sand and scrubby mesquite, where they hunted water the way desert antelope did" (Silko, *Ceremony* 74). As Josiah tells Tayo, "they would grow up heavy and covered with meat like Herefords, but tough too, like the Mexican cows, able to withstand hard winters and many dry years" (Silko, *Ceremony* 80). By introducing the idea of raising mixed cattle, Josiah tries to teach Tayo that hybridity has the potential to help the Laguna community survive.

Before the plan with Josiah materializes, however, Tayo enlists in the Army with his cousin Rocky. Being away from Laguna land and his uncle has a powerful impact on Tayo. During the Bataan Death March, Rocky dies, and when Tayo returns to Laguna, Josiah is already dead and the cattle are scattered. Tayo's illness is linked to his having joined the military. Being physically away from home cut Tayo's connection with Josiah, who was not only helping Tayo understand the importance of hybridity in Laguna culture, but also helping him come to terms with his own mixed identity.

Evolving Ceremonies and Cultural Hybridization

According to Laguna writer and scholar Paula Gunn Allen, "all ceremonies, whether for war or healing, create and support the sense of community that is the bedrock of tribal life. This community is not made up only of members of the tribe but necessarily includes all beings that inhabit the tribe's universe" (63). Since the Laguna cosmos is inclusive and is made up of various elements, the ceremony Tayo undertakes is complex and consists of diverse aspects.

The "white man's medicine" at a veteran's hospital eventually brings Tayo back to a state of awareness, but fails to do more than that, so Tayo's grandmother introduces him to Ku'oosh, a traditional Laguna shaman. Ku'oosh reminds Tayo how fragile the world is and that Tayo's healing is important to the community: "It is important for all of us. Not only for your sake, but for this fragile world" (Silko, *Ceremony* 36). Ku'oosh helps other veterans with the Scalp Ceremony, but not every veteran can be healed with the traditional ceremony Ku'oosh performs. Tayo is one of them. Ku'oosh tells Tayo that "There are some things we can't cure like we used to. . . since the white people came" (Silko, *Ceremony* 38). Ku'oosh's medicine and treatment alone is not enough because Ku'oosh does not understand the war Tayo experienced:

> It was all alien to comprehend, the mortars and big guns; and even if he could have taken the old man to see the target areas, even if he could have led him through the fallen jungle trees and muddy craters of torn earth to show him the dead, the old man would not have believed anything so monstrous. Ku'oosh would have looked at the dismembered corpses and the atomic heat-flash outlines, where human bodies had evaporated, and the old man would have said something close and terrible had killed these people. Not even oldtime witches killed like that. (37)

The existing cure, or the ceremony, is not powerful enough to deal with World War II atrocities, including the destructive forces of nuclear weapons, and this is why Tayo needs to move on to the next stage of his ceremony.

Betonie, a mixed-blood medicine man, designs a novel ceremony for Tayo that takes into consideration the veteran's multicultural identity. Betonie's mixed background, of Navajo and Mexican heritage, suggests his similarity to Tayo, but there are several features that distinguish Betonie from Tayo. Where he lives is one of them. Betonie's hogan (a traditional Navajo dwelling) is located in the foothills north of the Gallup Ceremonial Grounds. This is the place where white men annually organize Indian dances, an all-Indian rodeo, and horse races for the tourists, and "where Gallup keeps Indians until Ceremonial time" (Silko, *Ceremony* 117) or where Indians who have left the reservations live. On the surface, commercialized tribal culture contrasts with the picture of impoverished Indians, but Betonie shifts this interpretation. Betonie points out that his hogan was here first, and that "It is that town down there which is out of place. Not this old medicine man" (Silko, *Ceremony* 118). From this location, Betonie and his hogan have witnessed the changes, from a traditional Navajo landscape to an industrialized and modernized one, filled with cars, electric lights, and neon signs. Gallup is a place where the old and new meet and also where different cultures intersect.

Betonie's collections at the hogan also exemplify his diverse, cross-cultural, and time-spanning perspectives. Betonie's hogan is filled with medicine bundles and healing plants as well as modern products such as telephone books, calendars, and Coke bottles. Although Tayo wants to "dismiss all of it as an old man's rubbish," the balance of diversity is well kept in Betonie's hogan: "the boxes and trunks, the bundles and stacks were plainly part of the pattern" (120). Betonie's way of living features cultural diversity as well. Betonie ties his hair in a traditional Navajo "chongo knot," but he uses "good" English and does not speak like an ordinary medicine man. Betonie's tendency to mix the old and the new and to include various cultures is incorporated into his ideas of ceremonies:

At one time, the ceremonies as they had been performed were enough for the way the world was then. But after the white people came, elements in this world began to shift and it became necessary to create new ceremonies. I have made changes in the rituals. The people mistrust this greatly, but only this growth keeps the ceremonies strong. (126)

Although Betonie tells Tayo of the importance of incorporating the new, Betonie's practices also suggest the necessity of ritual heritage. For one thing, as Valerie Harvey points out in her article "Navajo Sandpainting in *Ceremony*," he performs the traditional Navajo ritual of sandpainting or "dry painting" for Tayo. Betonie's approach to healing is modernized, but not entirely. It is effective because it evolves, changing according to the conditions warranted, and balances tradition with contemporary needs.

Spotted Cattle and Barbed Wire Fences

After participating in a series of rituals (including Navajo sand painting and Betonie's stories) at Betonie's home, Tayo proceeds to the next phase of the ceremony: searching for the spotted cattle. They are the Mexican cows Josiah bought from Ulibarri. As part of the ceremony, Tayo has to collect the scattered cattle and resume the project he started with Josiah before the war. Peter G. Beidler notes, in his article "Animals and Theme in *Ceremony*," that Tayo imitates the hardy Mexican cattle more than any other animals in the novel because, from these cattle, Tayo learns to be "closer to nature" and "survive while others perish" (Silko, *Ceremony* 21). But even before Tayo adopts these characteristics, it is easy to recognize the similarity between Tayo and the cattle. Symbolically, the scattered cattle suggest Tayo's scattered self. Just as Tayo's identity disintegrated after the war, the spotted cattle are lost after the Josiah's death. Josiah explains:

Cattle are like any living thing. If you separate them from the land for too long, keep them in barns and corrals, they lose something. Their stomachs get to where they can only eat rolled oats and dry alfalfa. When you turn them loose again, they go and they are lost. They don't stop being scared either, even when they look quiet and they quit running. Scared animals die off easily. (Silko, *Ceremony* 74)

After the death of Josiah, both Tayo and the cattle are in a vulnerable situation because they have been away from Laguna land for too long. Unless they return to where they come from, they could get lost or die. Finding the spotted cattle, therefore, signifies Tayo's return to health. And his return home with the spotted cattle is relevant to the Laguna people's relationship to the mountain.

At first, Tayo had expected to find the cattle in the South, where they had always gone, but with the help of Betonie's vision—"from the stars and the woman, the mountain and the cattle would come" (Silko, *Ceremony* 186)—Tayo finds the cattle in the north, where Mount Taylor is. Mount Taylor, or *Tse-pi'na* in the Laguna language, is important not only because it is sacred for the indigenous people, but also because it is land "stolen" from them. In the early 1900s, most of the land was "taken by the National Forest and the state which later sold it to white ranchers who came from Texas" (Silko, *Ceremony* 185), and, during the 1920s and 1930s, loggers "stripped the canyons below the rim and cut great clearings on the plateau slopes" (Silko, *Ceremony* 186) and "shot the bears and mountain lions for sport" (Silko, *Ceremony* 186). From the Laguna people's perspective, "the land had been taken, because they couldn't stop these white people from coming to destroy the animals and the land" (Silko, *Ceremony* 186), and according to the holy men at Laguna and Acoma, "the balance of the world had been disturbed and the people could expect droughts and harder days to come" (Silko, *Ceremony* 186). Mount Taylor, like the spotted cattle, represents what had been stolen from the Laguna people in the process of colonization, and Tayo learns this during his search for the cattle as he follows Betonie's vision.

Barbed wire fences are an indication of "stolen" land. The white ranchers set barbed wire fences on the land they bought to keep out Indian and Mexican "trespassers," but Silko implies that the real "trespassers" are the white ranchers because Indians and Mexicans were there first, and not the other way around (187). It is suggested that Josiah's cattle were stolen by a white Texas rancher, Floyd Lee, not by Indians or Mexicans, whom Tayo would have suspected if the cattle were found on "land-grant land" or in "some Acoma's corral" (Silko, *Ceremony* 190). When Tayo finds the cattle, they are prevented from going South by barbed wire fences that Floyd Lee built "to keep Indians and Mexicans out" and "to lock the mountain in steel wire, to make the land his" (Silko, *Ceremony* 188). Although Tayo hesitates to believe that the cattle were stolen by the white rancher, he notices that "he had learned the lie by heart—the lie which they had wanted him to learn: only brown-skinned people were thieves; white people didn't steal, because they always had the money to buy whatever they wanted" (Silko, *Ceremony* 191). When Tayo physically releases the cattle, he "cut into the wire as if cutting away at the lie inside himself" (Silko, *Ceremony* 191). Historically, barbed wire fences have been used to exclude or constrain certain groups of people, such as the fences used to contain Japanese or Japanese Americans sent to internment camps during the Second World War. But their significance in *Ceremony* is multifold. While they reflect racial divisions, they serve as reminder of the injustices and damaging impact of colonialism. The act of cutting the fence, then, is a symbolic gesture, a statement against colonialism and racism.

While searching for the cattle, Tayo meets and is aided by a woman called Ts'eh. The time Tayo spends with her is important because it is part of the healing process, and it leads to Tayo's breeding of the spotted cattle with a yellow bull. The yellow bull represents different aspects of Tayo. The bull's small, yellow eyes resemble Tayo's "hazel eyes" and the idiosyncratic features of his "mixed-bloodness." Like Tayo, too, the bull has been injured by white men and left to suffer. In an act that echoes Betonie's treatment of Tayo, Romero rescues the bull after its leg is broken at a rodeo in Prewitt. After healing the bull's leg, he sells it to Tayo. While with Ts'eh, Tayo frees the bull to let it approach the spotted cattle and, although the spotted cattle at first hesitate to go near the bull, eventually, they start to approach (Silko, *Ceremony* 226).

Tayo's recovery from his illness is reflected in the union of different breeds of cattle.

The union of the spotted cattle and the yellow bull represents the potential of a hybridized Pueblo culture. Susan Blumenthal in "Spotted Cattle and Deer: Spirit Guides and Symbols of Endurance and Healing Ceremony" argues that Tayo's cattle are modern surrogates for deer and antelope—sacred creatures for many American Indian tribes—and that the spotted cattle are symbols of "hybrid survivors": indigenous people who both maintain tribal traditions and accommodate themselves to Euro-American civilization (370–71). As Blumenthal suggests, the survival of the spotted cattle embodies the survival of the tribal community, and Tayo's recovery depends on his finding and raising the spotted cattle, developing a form of life suitable for the tribal environment.

The Witchery Narrative and the Uranium Mine

Tayo successfully finds the spotted cattle and brings them back home, but his ceremony is not over yet. Before he completes his ceremony, Tayo has to witness the actual doings of the witchery embodied by atomic destruction as well as Emo's human sacrifice on Laguna land.

Barbed wire fence plays an important role here again. Resembling the spotted cattle that escape though the hole in the fence, Tayo crawls through the barbed wire fence that surrounds an abandoned uranium mine. In this particular place, the barbed wire fence marks the work of the witchery or destroyers, as well as a site linked to the production of atomic weapons. Here, witchery takes the form of the uranium mine (the Jackpile Mine), the nuclear testing site (Trinity Site), and the nuclear laboratories (Los Alamos). These sites remind Tayo how indigenous territory has been taken away to make something as destructive as the atomic bombs:

He had been so close to it, caught up in it for so long that its simplicity struck him deep inside his chest: Trinity Site, where they exploded the first atomic bomb, was only three hundred miles to the southeast, at White Sands. And the top-secret laboratories where the bomb had been created were deep in the Jemez Mountains, on land the

Government took from Cochiti Pueblo: Los Alamos, only a hundred miles northeast of him now, still surrounded by high electric fences and the ponderosa pine and tawny sandrock of the Jemez mountain canyon where the shrine of the twin mountain lions had always been. There was no end to it; it knew no boundaries; and he had arrived at the point of convergence where the fate of all living things, and even the earth, had been laid. (Silko, *Ceremony* 245–46)

Silko uses the traditional narrative of Laguna and Navajo witchcraft to depict the destructive forces of the atomic age. As Silko explains, in her interview with Larry Evers and Denny Carr, the primary source of materials for her narrative were numerous stories of witchery and malignant magic she heard about on the Navajo reservation at Chinle, AZ, where belief in witchcraft is much more widespread and much more a part of everyday life than at Laguna (Zamir 401). But her witchery narrative is revised to reflect contemporary challenges facing indigenous people and the land. In fact, the passage quoted above is foreshadowed in an earlier part of the novel, where Silko describes the witchery narrative in poetic form. When the witches gather to show off their destructive charms and powers, the image of the uranium ore is suggested: "they will find the rocks, / rocks with veins of green and yellow and black. / They will lay the final pattern with these rocks / they will lay it across the world / and explode everything" (Silko, *Ceremony* 137). Once the pattern is completed, nuclear destruction is inevitable. The barbed wire fence surrounding the uranium mines in the American Southwest cannot contain the destruction once it is released. It goes beyond the region to obliterate the boundaries of race, culture, and countries, just as the atomic bomb detonated in Hiroshima destroyed land and killed people regardless of their race, culture, or nationality.

The barbed wire fence is also used for Emo's violent human sacrifice. Emo and two other veterans (Leroy and Pinkie), who try to make people believe that Tayo is a "crazy Indian," go to the uranium mineshaft and use Harley (Tayo's friend and another veteran) to lure Tayo. Mimicking the crucifixion of Jesus Christ, they hang Harley's naked body, covered with blood and alcohol, from the barbed wire fence. At the abandoned mine, the violence of

World War II (Emo's penchant for large mortar shells, jagged steel flakes, and the teeth removed from a Japanese soldier is repeated in the text) and the destructive power of the atomic bombs is projected by Emo's ceremonial brutality. Emo, Tayo's archenemy, represents multilayered forms of destruction: the atrocity of the war in the Pacific, the destruction of nuclear weapons, and the power of the tribal witchery narrative. Tayo almost succumbs to the witchery narrative by killing Emo with a screwdriver, but he narrowly escapes. Tayo does not yield to violence, despite Emo's final temptation: "Look at this, you half-breed! White son of a bitch! You can't hide from this! Look! Your buddy, Harley" (Silko, *Ceremony* 252).

Silko's witchery narrative signifies the destructive forces of the atomic age that cross cultures as well as the hybridity of tribal narratives in the American Southwest. But witchery is also a tactic of tribal subversion because it enables Tayo and his community to reinterpret the imposition of the destructive "white" narrative on their own terms. Betonie tells Tayo that "white people are only tools that the witchery manipulates" and that "we invented white people; it was Indian witchery that made white people in the first place" (Silko, *Ceremony* 132). Betonie's view of the world incorporates even the war stories and the atomic age into the narrative of Laguna history, since they were created by tribal witchery. The "new" narrative of destruction is not "new," then, as Tayo's Grandmother says at the end of the novel: "It seems like I already heard these stories before . . . only thing is, the names sound different" (Silko, *Ceremony* 260).

Conclusion

Just as hybrid witchery is used to subvert the narrative of the destruction in the atomic age, the culturally, racially, and geographically diverse features of Tayo's ever-evolving ceremony enable him to reenact hybridized tribal realities. Cultural hybridity then offers Tayo a tool for survival as well as the cross-cultural visions to combat the destructive forces established by the Military Industrial Complex. In a memorable scene at the abandoned uranium mine, Tayo finds a gray rock striped with yellow uranium ore:

He knelt and found an ore rock. The gray stone was streaked with powdery yellow uranium, bright and alive as pollen; veins of sooty black formed lines with the yellow, making mountain ranges and rivers across the stone. But they have taken these beautiful rocks from deep within earth and they had laid them in a monstrous design, realizing destruction on a scale only they could have dreamed. (Silko, *Ceremony* 246)

In the black and yellow lines of the stone, Tayo sees the mountain ranges and rivers; this is appropriate because Tayo views uranium ore not only as a resource to be modified by technology, but as something life-affirming and naturally occurring. As Rachel Carson points out in *Silent Spring* (1962), the natural aspect of substances have been changed into something "unnatural" through human technology (17); however, Tayo manages to form a positive view towards the ore, even after its power has been harnessed by humans for destructive purposes. By having her protagonist realize that the uranium appropriated by "the destroyers" actually has another design in nature, Silko succeeds in showing how Tayo's multilayered perception is a counterforce against the narratives of war and violence, and ultimately, against the colonial forces in the atomic age.

Works Cited

Allen, Paula Gunn. *The Sacred Hoop: Recovering the Feminine in American Indian Tradition*. Boston: Beacon, 1986.

Beidler, Peter G. "Animals and Theme in *Ceremony*." *Leslie Marmon Silko's Ceremony: A Case Book*. New York: Oxford UP, 2002. 17–22.

Blumenthal, Susan. "Spotted Cattle and Deer: Spirit Guides and Symbols of Endurance and Healing Ceremony." *American Indian Quarterly* 14 (1990): 367–78.

Buell, Lawrence. *The Environmental Imagination*. Cambridge: Belknap of Harvard UP, 1995.

Carson, Rachel. *Silent Spring*. 1962. New York: Mariner, 2002.

Harvey, Valerie. "Navajo Sandpainting in *Ceremony*." *Critical Perspectives on Native American Fiction* 96 (1993): 256–59.

Nelson, Robert. *Place and Vision: The Function of Landscape in Native American Fiction*. New York: Lang, 1993.

Mitchell, Carol. "Ceremony as Ritual." *American Indian Quarterly* 5 (1979): 27–36.

Owens, Louis. *Mixedblood Messages: Literature, Film, Family, Place*. Norman: U of Oklahoma P, 1998.

_____. *Other Destinies: Understanding the American Indian Novel*. Norman: U of Oklahoma P, 1992.

Sayler, Gregory. *Leslie Marmon Silko*. New York: Twayne, 1997.

Silko, Leslie Marmon. *Ceremony*. New York: Viking, 1977.

_____. *Yellow Woman and a Beauty of the Spirit*. New York: Simon & Schuster, 1996.

Swan, Edith. "Laguna Prototypes of Manhood in Ceremony" *MELUS* 17.1 (1991–92): 39–61.

Zamir, Shamoon. "Literature in a National Sacrifice Area: Leslie Marmon Silko's *Ceremony*." *New Voices in Native American Literary Criticism*. Ed. Arnold Krupat. Washington: Smithsonian, 1993. 396–413.

A Tent of One's Own: Negotiating Mourning Dove's Authorial Identity

John C. Orr & Enid R. Spitz

In 1928, Virginia Woolf delivered a series of lectures that would compose her influential analysis of the restrictions placed on women writers, *A Room of One's Own*. Woolf argued that, in order for a woman to be able to succeed as a writer, she must have "money and a room of her own" (4). Her tract continues to provide insight into the struggles faced by women writers. Despite the upper middle-class, even bourgeois perspective of her analysis, she recognized the further struggles class deprivations created, noting, for instance, that "a poor child in England has little more hope than had the son of an Athenian slave to be emancipated into that intellectual freedom of which great writings are born" (Woolf 123). Yet, as Alice Walker so strikingly notes in her essay "In Search of Our Mother's Gardens," Woolf barely noted the implications of race and ethnicity.

At the same time that Woolf was lecturing, a woman a world away was hawking copies of her one and only novel, a book that had taken over a decade to see print. This woman lived out the circumscriptions that Woolf identified, though her race and decidedly non-bourgeois status meant that multiple forces conspired to keep her from attaining her dream of being a writer. Her pen name was Mourning Dove, and her status as an impoverished Native American woman from the outback of eastern Washington speaks to the ways in which, to borrow Margo Crawford's phrase, "race, gender, class, sexuality, and, also, region cannot be separated" (1). Woolf's diagnosis was accurate as far as it went, but Mourning Dove's situation included elements that Woolf could never imagine. Hers was a condition compromised by multiple forces, and her one novel, *Cogewea*, depicts the travails of a mixed-blood woman attempting to negotiate her way in a world fraught with multiple obstacles. Both Mourning Dove and her heroine mediated between cultures, and though each was, in her own way, victimized, neither allowed herself to remain a victim. Instead, each redefined herself in the face of the dominant cultural expectations that confronted her, and through her journey, Mourning Dove expanded Woolf's definition of the barriers facing the female author.

This essay's title references a 1917 letter from Fairview, BC, where Mourning Dove noted, "I intend writing those stories in due time. As soon as I get my tent finished and can be strictly alone."[1] The twelve-by-fourteen-foot tent in this ecrie echo of Woolf was her winter home that year and likely the same tent she mentioned in letters over the next two decades. In addition to offering a corrective to Woolf's bourgeois perspective, Mourning Dove's experience calls into question the stable sense of place that is inherent in Woolf's room. Ultimately, the two categories (social class and place) are inseparable, as Woolf's privileged status affords her the stability of a room she can call her own. Place, for the impoverished Native person—particularly one whose life was made even more challenging by the onset of the Great Depression—implies a region rather than a fixed dwelling in a specific town or city. The migratory component is evident from the multiple originating sites of her letters. Likewise, her quest for survival saw Mourning Dove undertake a series of seasonal and menial jobs: washing dishes, picking and boxing apples, harvesting hops, farming, and cooking and cleaning for a family with six children. Ultimately, Mourning Dove did not have the place, the time, or the money that Woolf claimed were necessary for a woman to write, yet she continued pursuing her dream despite the odds. *Cogewea* is significant for being only the second novel written by a Native American woman, while its development and eventual publication speak to the constrained situation of Mourning Dove as well as her determination to succeed as an author. Yet amid the many disappointments, her letters to her white mentor also indicate the strength of her character and her attempts to mediate cultures, in order to explain to him cultural aspects he could never truly grasp.

Numerous dates have been given for Mourning Dove's birth, ranging from 1882 to 1888. Likewise, questions remain about her racial and ethnic heritage. Was her mother a full-blood Colville tribal member or of mixed Colville and Arrow Lakes ancestry? Was Mourning Dove's father half Irish, the son of a Hudson Bay employee who had abandoned Mourning Dove's paternal grandmother (Viehmann 220.1)? What is known is that her birth name was Christine (also appearing as "Christal") Quintasket, though she later took the pen name Mourning Dove. After attending various schools for Indians beginning in 1894, she spent time in Montana, where she entered into what would prove to be a failed marriage in 1909, and by 1912, she moved to Portland, OR, to escape her marriage and to begin writing her novel (Miller xvii). From there, she migrated to Calgary to attend secretarial school, apparently in hopes of improving her opportunities as a writer by learning to type (Brown 275). Initially, she misspelled her adopted pseudonym "Morning Dove" until she saw an exhibit in a Spokane, WA, museum in 1921 and realized that the true spelling of the bird was "Mourning Dove" (Miller xvii). The switch to the bitter-sweet "Mourning" was an apt symbol for her difficult life. As she noted in her autobiography, while discussing childhood fantasies, "I never imagined the many hardships and shattered dreams my life had in store" (Mourning Dove, *Salishan* 16).

In 1914, she met Lucullus Virgil McWhorter, an amateur anthropologist, who was translating Yakima oral legends, and the two entered into a long working relationship. McWhorter, who was sympathetic to the plight of Native Americans—he published *The Crime Against the Yakimas* in 1913—encouraged her writing aspirations, though he was more concerned with transcribing oral legends, while she aspired to write frontier romances. The results of their collaboration were *Cogewea*, published in 1927, and *Coyote Stories*, a collection of Native oral legends, published in 1933.

She completed a draft of *Cogewea* during World War I, but the form the book took in 1927 continues to be the source of much scholarly debate. McWhorter undertook—without the assent of Mourning Dove—to make changes to the novel. Some were relatively minor, such as correcting grammatical errors and adding quite a few footnotes to lend credence to aspects of Mourning Dove's narrative. But he also used this opportunity to add various invectives against white hypocrisy and malfeasance, while at times giving the heroine a more lofty voice than seemed authentic. Mourning Dove saw his changes only after the book was printed in 1927 and wrote to McWhorter in the summer of 1928 from Omak, WA, that she was "surprised at the changes that you made." She went on to write: "I felt like it was some one elses book and not mine at all." She concluded the letter, "Oh my Big Foot [his adopted Yakima name], you surely roasted the Shoapees [whites] strong. I think a little too strong to get their sympathy. I wish we had not gone too strong now."

Understandably, scholars have argued that hers was a "Trilby-like relationship with the Svengali McWhorter" (Green 221). Likewise, critics have noted that the alterations McWhorter made to *Cogewea* indicate the manner in which their narrative collaboration "in striking ways emulated the paternalistic stance encoded in broader Euro-American and Native American relations" (Bernardin 494). Such a characterization cannot be easily dismissed, but it provides only a partial portrait of the aspirant writer and her relationship with her white benefactor, a relationship fleshed out in her letters to McWhorter. Whether or not she was herself a person of mixed blood, Mourning Dove clearly understood and identified with the dilemmas the heroine of her novel faced, as she attempted to mediate between two worlds. It is fitting that a novel detailing the travails of a heroine negotiating her status of hybridity should also be itself a hybrid construction.

Set on a Montana ranch, the novel begins with Cogewea pondering her fate. Despite struggling hard via education to "equip herself for a useful career," she fears that "there was but one trail for her—that of mediocrity and obscurity. Regarded with suspicion by the Indian; shunned by the Caucasian; where was there any place for the despised breed?" (Mourning Dove, *Cogewea* 17). The remainder of the book is largely an attempt to answer this question as Cogewea negotiates between the Natives and Anglo Americans. Her unsettled double-consciousness is graphically depicted early in the book, when Cogewea competes in the horse races held in conjunction with the Fourth of July Celebration; first, there is the "ladies race" and, then, the "squaw race." When dressed in a blue corduroy riding habit, she enters the ladies race, only to be met with cries of, "'Why is this *squaw* permitted to ride? This is a *ladies* race!'" (Mourning Dove, *Cogewea* 63). After winning that race, she changes into a buckskin dress and emerges from a tipi with "her face artistically decorated with varied paints" (Mourning Dove, *Cogewea* 65) in preparation for the squaw race. Yet she is again the object of disdain. "'You have no right to be here,'" says one of the Kootenai girls. "You are half-white! This race is for Indians and not for *breeds*!'" (Mourning Dove, *Cogewea* 66). Belonging wholly to neither group, Cogewea demonstrates the ability to maintain a fluid identity that allows her to migrate between both groups.

Cogewea's cultural negotiation is likewise played out within a romance, which revolves around the pursuit of Cogewea by the unscrupulous Easterner, Alfred Densmore, a hired hand on her brother-in-law's ranch. Quickly smitten, he becomes even more intrigued when Cogewea tells him the story of how her father abandoned her mother and their children, in order to seek gold in the Yukon, arousing "his latent passion for wealth. It was the one god of his ambition, to go back home a rich man" (Mourning Dove, *Cogewea* 84). His strategy to win the young woman's affection is by feigning interest in her Native culture, which leads to a meeting with her grandmother, the Stemteemä, in her tipi. But the old grandmother is not fooled and immediately warns the young woman of Densmore's motives, declaring, "His eye speaks the lie. You must not be so much with him. If his intentions were good, he would want to take you to the priest and marry you. All that the pale faces desire of Indian women, is pleasure and riches. When they get these, they marry back among their own race" (Mourning Dove, *Cogewea* 103). And of course, we quickly learn that Densmore is interested in marrying Cogewea in a Native ceremony, just as the Stemteemä predicted, a rite that would have the effect of rendering the young woman little more than a mistress in his eyes and in the eyes of US legal and social culture.

Despite the warnings and her own misgivings, Cogewea continues to fall victim to Densmore's charms. The dilemma she faces is choosing between the two cultures. Later, after hearing the

Stemteemä's refusal to grant her permission to marry, Cogewea replies, "I know that the Stemteemä's judgment is always good, but I cannot think the Shoyahpee bad" (Mourning Dove, *Cogewea* 247–48). Cogewea, in essence, rejects her Indian heritage by failing to adhere to her grandmother's warnings and agreeing to elope with Densmore. The Stemteemä's early warning identifies the white man's desire for riches as well as pleasure, and we come to learn how apt her warning is. After agreeing to elope with Densmore, Cogewea is subjected to an act of violence when Densmore punches her in the face before gagging her and tying her to a tree in the middle of the woods. He erupts in violence when he learns that, in fact, she owns very little, and his dreams of becoming rich will not be realized should he marry her.

Ultimately, Cogewea triumphs rather than remaining victimized. But her triumph depends upon a key transformation in her sense of self: embracing her Indian heritage. Cogewea's rescue by Jim LaGrinder, her mixed-blood suitor, occurs only after her grandmother has a dream of "a lonely wood" where "the body of the grandchild was bruised, her hair torn and tangled with fallen autumn leaves" (Mourning Dove, *Cogewea* 271). When Jim finds her, Cogewea is, in essence, saved by the culture that she had rejected in eloping with Densmore. It takes two years before she fully embraces her Native heritage and accepts Jim's proposals, and when she does, she hears "the Voice as it comes only to the Indian: '*The Man! The Man! The Man!*'" (Mourning Dove, *Cogewea* 284). Her final reward occurs in a happy-ending coda, where we learn that she inherited millions when her father died. Though he attempted to leave little to his mixed-blood daughters, an error in the will left them the entirety of his gold mine investments.

Martha L. Viehmann identifies *Cogewea* as a "multivoiced text reflecting different approaches to the material and to the audience," with Mourning Dove seeking to persuade with stories and McWhorter with facts (206). In many cases, the different voices are distinct, but the text remains forever a product of an uneasy collaboration. In terms of structure, *Cogewea* owes more to the Anglo tradition that precedes it than it does to an Indian aesthetic, though it does contain chapters in which Okanogan legends are presented

Critical Insights

as alternative and corrective means of understanding history and accessing reality. Most critics agree that those are the sections that come solely from the hand of Mourning Dove, relatively untouched by McWhorter. The book obviously draws on the popular form of the Western romance and is complete with elements taken directly from that form. In fact, *Cogewea* can be read as Mourning Dove's response to Therese Broderick's novel *The Brand*, which appeared in 1909 and is set on the Flathead Reservation, a novel Cogewea reads and ponders early in her novel. That book also addresses the dilemmas faced by mixed-race Indians, though the young Native man in love with a white woman eventually curses his hybrid status (Viehmann 207). An element of McWhorter's justification for his alterations to Mourning Dove's draft was his fear that, without them, the book might disappear as just another western novel (Bernardin 488). Susan K. Bernardin, however, believes that Mourning Dove's desire was not so much to exploit a form in order to make money, but instead "to intervene in dominant constructions of Indian identity and to validate Okanogan culture and make it accessible to an outside reader" (490). In short, Mourning Dove "appropriated popular literary forms in order to reshape the discourse surrounding Indians in the early twentieth century" (Bernardin 490). Mourning Dove's comment to McWhorter concerning the reaction of white readers to the finished novel speaks to her desire for the book to function as a means of cultural transformation.

That Mourning Dove, at times, depended upon and deferred to McWhorter is unassailable. When they met, she had already completed an early draft of her novel, but had no opportunity to publish it. So, meeting McWhorter was fortuitous, since he already possessed knowledge of the publishing industry, a crucial avenue to her authorial aspirations. Without McWhorter's knowledge of the publication process and without his constant efforts with multiple presses to see it into print, the novel would likely have never been published.

But just as she needed him for her preferred project, so he also needed her for his: the quest to record Indian oral legends and myths before they were forever lost. At the time, many anthropologists, whether professional or amateur, like McWhorter, believed that Native cultures would disappear when confronted with the dominant Anglo culture—thus the trope of the Vanishing American, creating a sense of urgency that informed the field work (Lamont 369). McWhorter's true desire in working with Mourning Dove was for her to gather oral materials from members of the Okanogan Nation—materials he would never otherwise have access to—in order to preserve them in written form. And as his diatribes that appear so randomly in the completed edition of *Cogewea* indicate, had he written what he wanted, it most certainly would not have been a sentimental love story complete with stock characters from western romances.

Like her heroine, Mourning Dove was in a culturally liminal position because she stood astride oral and chirographic, or print, cultures. That position furthermore provided her with an authority she otherwise would not have had in her relationship with McWhorter. As she says in her autobiography, "No foreigner could possibly penetrate or research these [Native customs] because of the shy reluctance of the Indian when it comes to giving information to whites" (Mourning Dove, *Salishan* 12). Despite McWhorter's sympathies for his Indian neighbors, Mourning Dove's letters reveal the extent to which he remained forever the foreigner, who constructed his own version of Native life and who was, therefore, dependent upon the mediating explanations of his mentee to provide him a glimpse into the world she inhabited.

In order to grasp the nuances of Mourning Dove's relationship with McWhorter, one must note that, in response to his view of her and her people, she constructed what Mary Louise Pratt deems an autoethnographic representation of self. In effect, Pratt notes, "people undertake to describe themselves in ways that engage with representations others have made of them," a depiction of self that is constructed "*in response to* or in dialogue with" the ethnographic texts of the dominant culture (5). McWhorter's sympathetic attempts to support and promote his mentee inevitably led to misrepresentation. At times, Mourning Dove initially resisted conforming to McWhorter's perspective before ultimately acquiescing. In a letter sent from Polson, MT, in September 1916, an era when McWhorter was proposing the idea of having her go on a speaking tour, she thanked him for the head dress that he sent to her, before noting, "Altho' I never fancied wearing them. They make me look funny I imagine, but I will wear it to please you all."

Likewise, Mourning Dove was self-conscious about her limited command of English, and her letters contain countless apologies to McWhorter for those limitations. She consistently misspelled words and worried over other minor problems. In 1915, she responded from Napoleon, WA, to McWhorter's query about her translation of a Native story. She explained to him, "I wrote that story by pencil first, and *than* I typed and found out that I had made a mistake, so I wrote it over again and I still have all the first writings in my *pocession*."

A measure of her failure to adhere to the rules of standard written English can be attributed to her poor education; she was, in many ways, an autodidact. But many of her writing problems occurred as a consequence of her existence on the cusp between an oral and a chirographic culture. For instance, she consistently misspelled certain words because of their homophonic qualities. She often used "been" when she meant "being," and she regularly substituted "than" for "then." Likewise, she often exhibited qualities that Walter Ong identifies as characteristic of oral cultures, including constructing additive sentences by stringing together a series of clauses with simple coordination (Ong 37). In a 1915 letter from Napoleon, she informed McWhorter that she was having some foot problems that made it hard for her to get around, "and don't expect my MSS to soon and I will try to write about what you asked about my life or whatever it is, but I have no typewriter at the present but will it be alright to use just pen and ink for the matter."

Her position negotiating between an oral and a print culture allowed her an understanding of each that McWhorter seemingly failed to grasp, and she consistently attempted to explain to him the differences between the two. In that way, she reconstructed a version of herself and her culture that confronted McWhorter's limited understanding of both. In one of the few surviving fragments of a letter to her, he urged her in 1917 to find the correct spelling for the term "Shoo-yah-poo," the Okanogan term for "white man":

> I want to be sure and get it correct. I suggest that you pronounce the word to some well educated white man or woman, a teacher or other person, and let them spell it as they think it should be. Speak it often to them. Also have some Indian do the same for you. If I was with you now, I could determine which is the correct way of spelling this word. Perhaps your priest can give you the proper spelling. In writing me be sure and tell me which you think is correct. I have great faith in *your* judgement. I wish that you would do this soon as you can.

His demands exposed his lack of understanding of the fluidity of spelling when transcribing from an oral cultural, an intellectual issue that she grasped and attempted to explain to him.

Numerous letters from Mourning Dove answered questions he asked about spellings and word choice, and though she sent him the requested material, she also tried to explain why the answers were not so simple. For instance, her branch of the tribe is, as she noted in a letter mailed from Boyds, WA, in 1916, "called 'Swe lapa' or some such word. It is hard to write it proper, but no doubt you recollect how much trouble we hade before we could write it near proper." Likewise, Sho-ya-poo, she informed him in a 1917 letter from Fairview, "is no word of translation in our language, but a foreign word also, and how it came to be applied to the whiteman I do not know." Yet his demands for precision continued. Finally, in a 1930 letter from Omak, she explained that Indians "are not accurate like white people with their support of writing and putting down to correct type on their meanings. We have no books, and have only sounds and words, which sometimes are misprounced and we have to figure the correct words and meaning of it." She understood, given her position mediating the oral and typographic worlds, that an oral culture is not simply a culture without writing, but one with a different way of retaining and organizing knowledge. Thus, her identity as a person conversant with two very different cultures, one print and one oral, highlights for us the awareness and insight she gains from her liminal position between two cultures.

She also perceptively concluded another letter from the same season, one in which she answered numerous questions from McWhorter about the origin of certain names, by asserting, "I think I am beganing to understand the ways of the Shuppwaps after coming incontact with them all these years. They are great for searching for knowledge and any thing with mystery is never left unsolved by the whiteman if they can help it. Ain't I correct?" McWhorter's demands made her more conscious of her weaknesses, but his constant quest for precision indicates that he was much less informed of her cultural norms than she was of his. His quest for accuracy colors, as Viehmann notes, the ways in which he edited and transformed *Cogewea*. In addition to offering him a platform to vent his hostility at the Indian Bureau for their transgressions, the added footnotes attest that "his main concern seems to be factual accuracy" (Viehmann 216), a point not lost on Mourning Dove.

Her simultaneous inhabitance of cultures caused her to be in an uncomfortable position among her own people. From the start of their relationship, McWhorter urged her to become the voice of the Okanogans by recording their legends, a role she reluctantly accepted even though her true interests lay elsewhere. In response to his visionary letter in 1915, outlining his version of her future as a recorder of her peoples' heritage, she wrote back from Fairview that he should "know and understand our natural Indian suspicious nature, a born nature we inherit from our forefathers, against our White Brother." That suspicious nature extended to books and writing in general. A year later, she wrote from Spokane that she was having some trouble obtaining stories from Indians and that it is "one good thing they do not know I am writing outside of my own family." Although she did not elaborate, the telling of secrets seems to have been the cause of the hostility, as was confirmed when she noted that, in order to get old people to tell her legends, she could not reveal that she would include them in a book. "Of course it looks sneaky," she noted in a 1930 letter from Omak, "but it was the only means that I could be able to collect datas." She ultimately felt that her attempts to obtain oral legends were equivalent to a betrayal of her people. The manuscript preface to *Coyote Stories* contains a disclaimer that did not see its way into print: "It has been," she declares, "with the greatest reluctance that I consented to attempt this chronicling of the few legends now available of the once profuse oral philosophy of the Okanogans. And now, on the threshold of publication there is a heart-shrinking from what I realize must be regarded by the older members of my fast dwindling tribe, as irreverent sacralege on my part" (Box 46, Folder 440). Once again, she must sacrifice something of what she feels she owes her Okanogan community to maintain her identity as a writer and interpreter of her people to outsiders.

Among her family, her need to write was generally accepted, though she was something of an oddity. She informed McWhorter in a 1916 letter mailed from Polson that her father was illiterate and "does not know the value of books as I do." Other members of her family clearly could read, but they still were seemingly perplexed by the habits of a writer and did little to afford her the space and time to write. More than a few of her letters came to abrupt conclusions, like one sent from Napoleon in 1915 that ends, "Oh dear, Every body is talking around me and asking me questions so I can't write at all." In order to steal a few moments for writing, she, at different times, took to writing late into the night, causing family members to think that she was, as she reported from Fairview in 1919, "looney or have too much company, because I use too much lamp oil."

Inseparable from Mourning Dove's economic status and race was her having been born female. Not surprisingly, time to write was often stolen from domestic and other chores, as is clear from a 1929 letter from Omak, in which she casually remarks, "I have wrote this letter while the potatoes are cooking for our dinner." A few months later, she reported that she thinned apples for ten hours before coming home and cooking a meal. Likewise, Mourning Dove often found herself amid numerous relatives, and though childless herself, she routinely mentioned taking care of her sister's children. In 1916, she reported from Spokane that "I am in no position to do any writing at the present. The children will bother me to death even if I should attempt." She also cared for sick relatives, prompting her to lament to McWhorter from her home in Spokane, "honestly I feel discouraged it seems I am never going to get started with my

Critical Insights

own work and whenever I do reach it, I am worn out and need a rest instead of new field of work."

In 1919, she married Fred Galler, who was generally tolerant of her literary goals. Along with his increased unemployment in the early 1930s came difficulties in their marriage, brought on partially by his abuse of alcohol. But the men in her immediate family were not the only ones she occasionally depicted in an antagonistic manner. Her relationship with McWhorter contained numerous conflicts. In a 1916 letter from Polson, she referred to a letter from him "where you mentioned of being roasted and fried in my letter to you. Now admit you deserve it, I mean a little of it." Late in their collaboration, her relationship with him sounded, at times, contractual. After answering his string of queries about legends and spelling, she dryly remarked in a letter mailed from Omak in 1930, "This ends your questions. I hope that I have fulfilled my duty."

Clearly, she felt that her ability to determine what she wrote was compromised by various men in her life, one of whom was McWhorter. In a letter from Spokane in 1916, after mentioning that her sister had invited her to come to Montana to write, she remarked, "but you know I am not all together my own *Boss*. You savey Injun. I have you and McLean [a collaborator with McWhorter] to ask besides the *redman*," the "redman" apparently being her husband. Why would she need permission from McWhorter and MacLean, if not because what she would be writing in Montana would take away from what they were demanding of her? A letter from MacLean to Mourning Dove a few months later made clear that such was the case. He urged that "Big Foot is right in recommending that you should spend the summer in finishing the collection of Indian legends and stories. This should be done without delay. This is a very great and very important work" (Box 46, Folder 446). It was not the work that she wanted to pursue, but as she noted, she was not always her own boss.

Mourning Dove's literary ambitions remained largely unfulfilled, since she suffered from the limitations Woolf defined combined with others that Woolf could never anticipate. Yet her letters make clear that those ambitions provided her a voice that she came to use in local politics to "help my poor defendless old uneducated Indians." She may have lacked the forum and other advantages afforded Woolf, but she found opportunities to explain and defend herself and her people. And she managed to do the unthinkable: write and publish two books that, though compromised each in its own way, stand as testimonials to her strength of character and determination to transcend the cultural limitations placed upon her by her own Okanogan people and by representatives of white America.

Note

1. Mourning Dove's letters are located in Box 46 of the Lucullus Virgil McWhorter Papers, housed in the archives of Washington State University. All letters quoted here are found in Folder 444. No further citation for individual letters will appear in the text. Original spelling and grammar are maintained in the transcription of the letters.

Works Cited

Bernardin, Susan K. "Mixed Messages: Authority and Authorship in Mourning Dove's *Cogewea, The Half-Blood: A Depiction of the Great Montana Cattle Range*." *American Literature* 67 (September 1995): 487–509.

Brown, Alanna Kathleen. "Looking Through the Glass Darkly: The Editorialized Mourning Dove." *New Voices in Native American Literary Criticism*. Ed. Arnold Krupat. Washington, DC: Smithsonian, 1993. 274–290.

Crawford, Margo. "Preface: Erasing the Commas: RaceGenderClassSexualityRegion." *American Literature* 77 (March 2005): 1–5.

Green, Rayna. Untitled Review of *Cogewea*. *Tulsa Studies in Women's Literature* 1 (Autumn, 1982): 217–221.

Lamont, Victoria. "Native American Oral Practice and the Popular Novel; Or, Why Mourning Dove Wrote a Western." *Western American Literature* 39 (Winter 2005): 368–393.

Miller, Jay. "Introduction." *Mourning Dove: A Salishan Autobiography*. Ed. Jay Miller. Lincoln: U of Nebraska P, 1990.

Mourning Dove. *Cogewea: The Half-Blood*. Lincoln: U of Nebraska P, 1981.

_____. *Mourning Dove: A Salishan Autobiography*. Ed. Jay Miller. Lincoln: U of Nebraska P, 1990.

Ong, Walter J. *Orality and Literacy: The Technologizing of the Word*. London: Routledge, 1982.

Pratt, Mary Louise. "Arts of the Contact Zone." *Professing in the Contact Zone: Bringing Theory and Practice Together*. Ed. Janice M. Wolff. Urbana: NCTE, 2002. 1–18.

Viehmann, Martha L. "'My People...My Kind': Mourning Dove's *Cogewea, The Half-Blood* as a Narrative of Mixed Descent." *Early Native American Writing: New Critical Essays*. Ed. Helen Jaskoski. Cambridge: Cambridge UP, 1996. 204–222.

Woolf, Virginia. *A Room of One's Own*. New York: Harcourt, 1929.

"All growth involves change, all change involves loss": Modernism, Mourning, and Social Change in Gish Jen's *Mona in the Promised Land*

Conor Picken

> They told him, "Nothing can stop you now except one thing: don't let the people at home hold you back." Rocky understood what he had to do to win in the white outside world … [Auntie] wanted him to be a success. She could see what white people wanted in an Indian, and she believed this way was his only chance. She saw it as her only chance too, after all the village gossip about their family. When Rocky was a success, no one would dare to say anything against them anymore."
>
> (Leslie Marmon Silko, *Ceremony*)

> "Fu-li-sah-kah Soo." He said "Fleishhacker Zoo" to himself in Chinatown language, just to keep a hand in, so to speak, to remember and so to keep awhile longer words spoken by the people of his brief and dying culture.
>
> (Maxine Hong Kingston, *Tripmaster Monkey*)

> "You know what I've come to realize about you kindly rich liberals who own the world? Nothing is further from your understanding than the nature of reality."
>
> (Philip Roth, *American Pastoral*)

In her intellectual autobiography, *Tiger Writing: Art, Culture, and the Interdependent Self* (2013), Chinese American author Gish Jen writes, "Culture is not fate; it only offers templates, which individuals can finally accept, reject, or modify, and do" (7). The ethos behind this statement—that one possesses agency in how forces in the world shape self and ideology—penetrates the heart of her novel *Mona in the Promised Land* (1996). Many critics ascribe to Jen "the burden of representation" (Byers 114), choosing to view the novel's protagonist Mona Chang as the author's literary doppelgänger. Jen states publicly that she, unlike Mona, did not convert to Judaism as an adolescent to assimilate into Scarshill's liberal, bourgeois Jewish sect, though one quickly sees how "culture," for a second-generation Chinese American, occupies centrality in her narrative project. Mona's marriage to Seth Mandel and the tearful reunion with her disapproving mother Helen after years of estrangement at the novel's end reflect what can be defined as a new, decidedly ethnic, and ultimately recuperative version of the American Dream, one that relies importantly on ideas of mourning and loss. This essay argues that Jen uses her characters' antagonism toward and acceptance of American cultural assimilation both to critique the ethos of privileged cultural liberalism and to illustrate how Mona's path as a Chinese American reflects a particular kind of experience endemic to ethnic minorities. Also argued here is that the American Dream unfurls differently according to generation, and the divergent assimilationist route that Mona takes, relative to that of her parents', points to something *lost* along the way, namely the cultural foundations of their Chinese ethnicity, which once stabilized family relations. As an immigrant family struggling to reconcile its Chinese and American identities, the Changs might one day find a comfortable spot in this Promised Land, but the casualties along these roads to assimilation belie notions that the American Dream applies in the same way to everyone.

The novel's setting serves as a petri dish for all things "progressive" about a 1960s America embroiled in radical social and political change. Along with her older sister Callie, Mona and her parents, Ralph and Helen, relocate to Scarshill, New York and become "the New Jews . . . a model minority and Great American Success. They know they belong in the promised land" (Jen, *Mona* 3). Scarshill residents are the perfect combination of educated and affluent, traits that drew Mona's parents to this desirable community. As Ivy-educated and rich as this predominantly-Jewish population may be, it is shown to exist in a state of blissful unawareness next to the surrounding tumult generated from the Civil Rights Movement and the countercultural revolution. Despite it being 1968, "the blushing dawn of ethnic awareness has yet to pink up their inky suburban night. They have an idea about the blacks because poor Martin Luther King" (Jen, *Mona* 3). Tongue in cheek, the narrator boasts that locals are socially aware "what with civil rights on TV," though their liberal purview is hardly limited to African Americans, since "[i]n another ten years, there'll be so many Orientals [living there] they'll turn into Asians; a Japanese grocery store will buy out that one deli too many" (Jen, *Mona* 6). For the Changs, not Jewish, educated, or rich, "they're not so much accepted as embraced. Especially by the Jewish part of town" (Jen, *Mona* 6). It comes as no surprise when, later, Mona converts to Judaism, setting in motion Jen's broader critique of blind ascription to Scarshill's unqualified liberalism.

While Scarshill represents the ideal community for Mona in its embrace of her ethnic differences, it is also attractive to Ralph and Helen for economic reasons. Their American Dream includes both personal goals related to work and money, as well as opportunities for the future, specifically regarding their daughters' education. Speaking to the former, the Changs own a moderately successful pancake house that they frequently daydream of franchising. What little profit margins are found between stacked pancakes are earned with stubborn hard work. At the end of each day, Helen returns home exhausted, and the only thing keeping her from much needed sleep is her preoccupation with her family back in China (Jen, *Mona* 26). Hard work though this may be, Helen and Ralph remain committed to the equation that hard work + perseverance = success, if not for them, then at least for their "American" children. Scarshill's accepting social climate allows Ralph and Helen to focus considerable time and energy on a nest egg, rather than their daughters' social-cultural development. Fully committed to pancakes, they judge Scarshill solely on the high quality public schools and are too busy working to foresee the seductive forces of liberalism pulling Mona away her native ethnicity.

It is in competing versions of the American Dream that Jen shows intergenerational fissures appearing in the Chang family, particularly between Mona and Helen. Author and critic Bharti Mukherjee identifies this tension within first- and second-generation immigrant families, stating that "immigrants are determined to remake their identities, or at least their children's, even if the larger society fails to recognize the goal" (689). In the novel, the "larger society" is replaced by Mona herself, for she, as a poly-ethnic Chinese-American-Jew, does not identify with her parents' myopic subscription to financial prosperity as the future endgame. Late in the story, Mona tells her friend Sherman, "'But for my parents, it's the whole point of life . . . Jews believe in the here and now; Catholics believe in heaven; the Chinese believe in the next generation'" (Jen, *Mona* 231). Indeed, where Mona subscribes to the American notion that we can choose who we want to be, her parents believe that we should have the means to buy what we want to buy. Ralph encourages Callie to attend medical school after she graduates from Harvard despite her having no desire to practice medicine: *"Life is about work, and since when is work supposed to be interesting?"* (Jen, *Mona* 233). But what is the fun in that? For Ralph and Helen, the goal is to ascend the ladder of social-economic class; for Callie and Mona, it is to become "American" on their own terms.

Although Ralph and Helen chase the dream in an "American" way (through sacrifice and hard work), they never lose sight of the culture from which they came. By virtue of having moved here, Ralph and Helen offer their children opportunities that they themselves will never have, and it is they who have lost something fundamental in the process: cultural hallmarks of their homeland. Much of this loss was to be expected. Mukherjee states that if persons of Ralph and Helen's generation "wanted to resist self-transformation, if they wanted to remain immured from their adoptive society and unmolested by its familiar culture . . . they would be exiles or expatriates, not immigrants" (689). Accounting in large part for the intergenerational disagreement is that Mona, attending Temple with Barbara Gugelstein or smoking pot with Seth Mandel, sees her newfound pluralist ethnicity as an entitlement, and this attitude naturally undercuts the value her parents see in her Chinese heritage. Mona's particular American aspirations vary fundamentally from those of her parents,' highlighting what critic Werner Sollors sees as the differences between ethnicities of descent and consent. First-generation immigrants, like Ralph and Helen, adhere to descent relations, which emphasize "our positions as heirs, our hereditary qualities, liabilities, and entitlements" (Sollors 6). In short, ethnicities of descent value "blood" and "substance." Conversely, those of the second-generation, like Callie and Mona, struggle with assimilationist pressures that their parents do not, and they, therefore, adhere to Sollors' model of consent relations, which "stresses our abilities as mature free agents and 'architects of our fates' to choose our spouses, destinies, and our political systems" (6). Following Sollors' model, the Changs are not unique in ethnic American literature as an immigrant family wrestling with identity formation in the so-called Promised Land. While the descent-consent model highlights useful distinctions between generations, it is limited in defining what else—beyond order of birth—separates Mona from her parents and, specific to the plot of the novel, causes such a deep rift between mother and daughter.

A brief theoretical aside is necessary to contextualize how the Changs mourn something lost. Seth Moglen argues that American modernist writing emerged as a reaction to the advent of global monopoly capitalism and all of its destructive and disorienting tendencies. Modernist writers responded to a profound and collective sense of loss, as monopoly capitalism cracked longstanding pillars upholding the American social and cultural psyches. Capitalism produced a pervasive anxiety—both in the authors and in their works—whereby modernist writers forked into one of two categories (borrowed from Freud) in response, mourning or melancholia. Melancholic modernists thought that resistance to the unseen forces of monopoly capitalism was futile, and the tenor of their work reflects this despair (think Jake Barnes' skeptical response to Brett Ashley's deluded fantasy at the end of *The Sun Also Rises*: "Isn't it pretty to think so?"). Modernists of mourning, on the other hand, remained "practitioners of a modernism committed to political resistance and to a chastened social hopefulness" (Moglen 9). Mourning and melancholia can emerge "'in reaction to the loss of a loved person, or to the loss of some abstraction which has taken the place of one, such as one's country, liberty, and so on'" (Freud qtd. in Moglen 243). Gish Jen might not fit chronologically into Moglen's mourning-melancholia paradigm (he cites writers from the first half of the twentieth-century), but the model can still be applied to *Mona*, particularly since it can be argued that the tensions informing the Changs' ethnicities of descent and consent are rooted in divergent concepts of the American Dream, ones that are split along the lines of capital and social class and, consequently, produce a sense of loss that the entire family mourns in different ways.

At the heart of Mona's disagreements with her parents is what it means to "be" American. Where Ralph and Helen see Americanness as an offshoot of one's ability to contribute meaningfully to the wheels of capitalism, Mona attaches herself more to precepts of ethnic self-identity, and Jen shows these viewpoints to be mutually exclusive. By immigrating to America, Ralph and Helen effectively leave their Chinese selves half a world away, so that they might flourish in America. Not so much Mona, since the Changs "don't have their ready alert. They don't have their friends' institutions, or their ways of reminding themselves who they are, that they might not be lulled by a day in the sun. Prescriptions and rituals, holidays and recipes, songs. They have catalogs. And soon, G-d willing, so will Mona" (Jen, *Mona* 36). Ralph and Helen have swapped the ability to express their ethnicity in America for the privilege to work here, whereas Mona only has catalogs from which to choose how she will identify herself (a fitting metaphor, given Scarshill's laughable materialism). To this end, Mona sees no problem referring to herself as "Chi-Am" and her parents as "*immigrants*." Language and culture barriers, along with long hours flipping pancakes, have blinded Mona's parents to the seductive forces of American assimilationism. Slowly, Mona becomes something foreign to her mother. After she converts, Mona, now called "Mona-also-known-as-Ruth, a more or less Catholic Chinese Jew," (Jen, *Mona* 44) and Helen's relationship magnifies the gap between how each conceives of her ethnicity relative to her identity as an American. One fight in particular highlights this divide. Mona reminds Helen that she stated the family was not "pure Chinese anymore." Helen responds that they are "'American, not Jewish'" before Mona replies that "'Jewish is American [and] American means being whatever you want, and I happened to pick being Jewish'" (Jen, *Mona* 49). Of note in this exchange is how Helen dissociates "American" from "Jewish." For her, substituting one minority (Chinese) for another (Jewish) is not acceptable, or rather not American.

That Mona can "pick being Jewish" speaks as much to what is lost as it does to what is gained. Andrew Furman notes that Mona's desire to be Jewish resists a broader form of cultural homogenization: "Jen's characters cling to whatever cultural identity might distance themselves from the increasingly nebulous, and toothless, 'mainstream,'" against whom he contrasts late twentieth-century Americans who wanted "exceedingly little to do with embracing whatever religion or ethnicity one wanted and everything to do with sacrificing that element of one's identity, often at a tremendous spiritual cost" (215, 216). True though this may be, what Mona's fight with Helen illustrates is that the choice to "be" Jewish and, therefore in Mona's eyes, "American," presupposes that Mona must be *not* Chinese. Contrary to Helen's protestations against Mona's newfound Judaism is that Helen and Ralph themselves are drawn to what Furman describes as the "assimilationist impulse" more so than their daughters. Furman distinguishes first- and second-generation immigrants differently from Sollors, noting that "Mona's parents do not subscribe to the multicultural rage" and "find it incredible that their children wish to adopt an ethnic, rather than a mainstream, identity" (Furman 214). In this respect, both generations seek identities of consent, albeit consenting to different things. This begs the question: If neither Helen nor Mona is "pure Chinese anymore," then why is Helen so angry with Mona?

The answer lies in the nature of Ralph and Helen's assimilationist impulse, which is markedly different from Mona's. Their impulse is economic (capitalist, more specifically), an American one to be sure, but not one that requires the shedding of everything Chinese. Critic and scholar Fu-Jen Chen reads the novel like much of Jen's fiction, as a study in how social class influences characters; rather than ask "Who's Irish?" a better understanding of what motivates Jen's characters comes from answering "Which class?" (Chen 5). Thus, Ralph and Helen's constant anxiety about the success of the pancake house signifies their Americanness—how better to perform the American WASP identity than to obsess about work? Jen's portrayal of immigrants aspiring to economic assimilation reveals something different between generations. Chen notes:

> In her arguments with her mother on her performing a Jew, Mona . . . avoids aiming at the unspeakable thing: class antagonism. Although their argument about performing identity ranges from being an American to being a tree, they skirt the central issue of class, an issue that is the cause of deep anxiety as far as Helen is concerned. (20)

Chen correctly identifies social class as the locus of stress for Helen and Mona, though mother and daughter conceive of it differently. Mona's conversion may seem important to her identity formation, but her parents are the ones bearing the brunt of America's harsh capitalist forces. Ralph and Helen sell pancakes so Mona can indulge herself in what they perceive as trivialities. Each side of the generational divide adheres to the tenets of its American Dream—capitalist success and ethnic self-identification—but such unfettered (American) ambition necessitates a sacrifice. Something is lost, not the least of which is the once-close relationship between Helen and Mona, and their competing ideas of being American belie their common Chinese heritage. The capitalist impulse to assimilate blinds Helen to what she surrenders for stable economic footing: her ethnicity and, perhaps more importantly, her family. In addition, her assimilationist impulse makes it impossible for her to see—fairly or not—Mona's version of "being" American as anything other than an insult to her hard work and sacrifice as well as something economically unproductive. Callie's decision to become "more" Chinese through her studies at Harvard and Mona's decision to be Jewish (and, therefore, in Helen's eyes, *less* American) are viewed as decisions that will potentially exempt them from the economic opportunities promised by another decidedly American trait: capitalism. Mona's being Jewish, then, is seen not as a decision to exert the American choice to self-identify, but rather as the naïve and uninformed choice *not* to work tirelessly toward material prosperity.

Intergenerational differences exacerbate the Changs' collective sense of loss. Ralph and Helen's tireless pursuit of material stability embroils them in the exhausting cycle of American capitalism and commerce. Long work days magnify their domestic stressors, particularly as Mona's version of the American Dream has little to do with dollars and cents. As Helen's assimilationist impulses show the harsh fallout from hard work, Mona's bellying up to the ethnic buffet must also be seen as something contributing to the family's loss. Once again, Moglen's model of modernism and mourning is useful for further contemplation of how Jen's 1960s America contributes to this sense of loss. Moglen evolves Freud's dyadic model—where the subject (the mourner) mourns the loss of an object (a person, ideal, social-cultural transformation)—into a triadic one, where the *social forces* responsible for the loss must be taken into account (15). He holds these social forces as responsible for having "destroyed that object or made it unavailable" (Moglen 15). As shown in this essay, intergenerational difference illustrates the loss of ethnic identity and family relations. While sympathies can vary, Helen often comes off as antagonistic; her rage toward Mona results from a myopic, capitalist interpretation of American identity. This essay's interpretation does not seek to excuse Helen's behavior—Jen portrays her as very unlikeable—but it is necessary to show that Mona and her brand of Americanness are equally complicit in this loss.

Jen's Scarshill "is a liberal place" (6), which accounts for a specific social climate resulting in the Changs' sense of loss. This liberalism promotes religious, racial, and ethnic pluralism inside the community's gated confines, though Jen portrays Scarshill's tolerance ironically—Callie connects back to her ethnic heritage only while studying Chinese at Harvard, Mona converts to Judaism, and Barbara Gugelstein's nose job plants her firmly within Jewish and Gentile sects of society. As much as Scarshill's acceptance of diversity seems positive, it also needs to be understood as the cultural homogenizer that it is. Jen shows how this seemingly enlightened population inadvertently smears meaningful cultural and ethnic signifiers that should have value despite what America's commodity and cultural markets suggest. Sociologist Michele Byers points to the power of the "hyphen" in a novel where hybridity is often championed over and above one's native ethnicity: "By the late 1960s and 1970s, ethnicity was commodified," which "represents a longing for belonging, a desire to find a true self rooted in an anterior and fully meaningful identity outside the myth of transcendental assimilation into American culture" (103). For Mona and others, then, to be Jewish *and* Chinese *and* American is to enact "a desire to stand in the performative space of the hyphen" (Byers 103). While this hyphenation surely represents a node of social progress in the late 1960s, Jen's appropriation of it suggests that this space is often a stage for folly. For example, Callie learns "high" Chinese (a privileged dialect spoken by neither Ralph nor Helen), which Ralph—ever the capitalist—deems "a waste of time" (Jen 129). What good will Peking Chinese do for Ralph's Ivy-educated, medical school-bound daughter? However, the narrator then remarks "Of course . . . even Ralph will be affirming his heritage [and] celebrating diversity in this, our country the melting pot—no, mosaic—no, salad bowl. Mostly this will mean writing checks . . . . Community? What community?" (Jen, *Mona* 129). In Scarshill, the trendy flaunting of diversity for the sake of diversity comes across as disingenuous.

Callic's academic interest in Chinese reflects the cultural ethos of which Jen is critical, one where self-identity (always hyphenated) is spun tightly around political correctness (liberalism), resulting in a loss of ethnic authenticity. The confluence of a socially changing America with liberal political correctness in hyper-drive simultaneously obscures what is lost (Ralph's working-class, Shanghai Chinese) and trivializes what is gained (Callie's academic, Peking Chinese). For Mona, Barbara, and Seth, the steps they take to self-identify within the performative space of the hyphen spurs them into social action. When Ralph and Helen fire Alfred, the African American cook/dishwasher at the pancake house, Mona, Barbara, and Seth offer the Gugelsteins' uninhabited house as a commune for the newly unemployed. Seth sees the post-racial possibilities of this utopian experiment, but when a piece of art goes missing and Alfred and company are blamed for its disappearance, "Camp Gugelstein" closes. One African American man crashing at the house reacts strongly: "Later Luther will proclaim it to be no wonder blacks don't believe in liberals anymore, look at Seth—your typical paternalistic motherfucker who cannot stand blacks talking for themselves, much less acting in their own self-defense" (Jen, *Mona* 202). For her part, Mona shrugs off the failed experiment: "Sure, things fell apart and they got called racist bastards. But even she's got the social-action bug now, who knows but that she'll be out getting arrested pretty soon?" (Jen, *Mona* 207). Mona's reaction here deserves pause: What point does "liberalism" serve to the greater good when it is performed half-heartedly, a bug only to be "caught"? If Alfred and the rest of the kitchen proletariat have only Mona, Seth, and Barbara to advocate on their behalves, then Scarshill's brand of social "progress" will never exceed hyphenation. Luther's disgust at Camp Gugelstein's counselors seems warranted.

As Mona tries to settle her differences with Helen, Jen hints at an end to the mourning. For the planets of mother and daughter to align, what each mourns must be gotten over, reconciled, recuperated. Moglen writes that "any community that suffers grave harm must find or invent practices of grieving in order to understand what its members have lost, in order to affirm those aspects of the self that have been denied . . . in order to survive" (xviii). While *Mona* does not depict actual life and death, it is worthwhile to view the novel's conclusion as Mona's and Helen's surviving the forces guiding America through social and political upheaval, and, finally, recuperating the Changs', for lack of a better term, *Chang*-ness. Toward the end of the story, Mona is privy to two enlightening conversations with adults whose age and wisdom redirect her über-liberal hyphenating tendencies toward more productive ends. The first is with Bea, Seth's stepmother, often criticized because of her bourgeois liberalism: "'And what's the matter with liberal guilt anyway?'" Bea asks. "'Better to feel guilty than to feel nothing, that's my opinion. I write my letters, I'm doing my best. The rest

I'll have to leave to the great leaders of our age'" (Jen, *Mona* 258). Sure, it is easy to criticize Scarshill's wealthy elite as little more than capitalist do-gooders whose altruism is solely guided by current trends in political correctness, but at least they act. Later, Mona encounters the former Rabbi Horowitz, who tells her, "'It's not so easy to get rid of your old self. On the other hand, nothing stands still. All growth involves change, all change involves loss'" (Jen, *Mona* 268). Horowitz excuses Mona's obsession with the hyphen—her "old self" now becomes something that can never be truly lost, only pluralized, and this necessitates a reexamination of how enduring the social forces are that catalyze Mona's sense of loss. Her ethnic identity is never fixed, but rather remains in constant, evolving flux. In order to, in Moglen's words, "survive" one must necessarily *grow*, and this signals something gained (not lost).

If Jen argues that culture is not fate, then the Changs must rectify their incompatible positions relative to the assimilationist impulses responsible for the family dysfunction. To overcome what each side of the generation split privileges as being American, Ralph and Helen require a better understanding of how their work-life balance (or lack thereof) runs counter to a sustainable fruition of their American Dream, while Mona must come to understand her brand of liberalism as the punch line that Jen intends it to be. Speaking to the former, Ralph and Helen have employed and promoted Chinese workers at the pancake house simply because they are Chinese, despite the fact that some of the African Americans running the kitchen are far better employees. Mona has long protested her parents' cronyism as being racist. By the end of the novel, Ralph's stance has softened considerably, and he hires a black cook named Moses to run his second restaurant. This decision signifies more than good business sense: "By Ralph's own admission, Julio and Moses are people he probably would have overlooked ten years ago; they take some getting used to, is his explanation for the change . . . Of course, relying on blacks is not the only thing Ralph's learned. He's also learned to keep the Chinese help in back" (Jen, *Mona* 300–1). Ralph's change of heart exemplifies the overcoming of mourning, shown "as the renewed capacity for dynamic object relation: as the capacity to experience new people and relations with spontaneity, with a receptivity to difference, to newness, to changes in oneself and others" (Moglen 22–3). The shift shows an emerging acceptance of racial difference that coincides with personal capitalist expansion (the second pancake house). He fulfills his economic American Dream, but not in a way that alienates or oppresses (as when he only hired Chinese workers).

For the novel to truly demonstrate a renewed capacity for hope over and against the mourning of a loss, Mona and Helen have to settle their differences. The story concludes "some years later," the day on which Mona is to marry Seth Mandel, the father of their young daughter Io. Age and motherhood have tempered Mona's hyphenated enthusiasm. When asked if Mona will change her last name to match Seth's, she silently demurs, prompting her Aunt Theresa to inquire, "'No more women's lib?'" Jen continues, "Mona smiles. She thinks how she really could change her name if she wanted to and she thinks how at one point in her life that was what mattered more than anything" (Jen, *Mona* 303). Moglen notes that "while the work of mourning takes place slowly, it comes to an end after a finite 'lapse of time'" (13). The severing of family bonds has long separated Mona and Helen, setting the stage for Jen to punctuate the recovery from this loss. When Helen shows up on the wedding day, the emotional release from mother and daughter points to the renewal at the end of Jen's ethnic modernism of mourning, where consent and descent converge in a tearful reunion: "Helen exclaims as Mona turns, adjusting her illusion veil—and even before she sees her mother, she's glad she finally got contact lenses; also that she doesn't wear mascara. For the way she's crying, anyone would think that Helen is the person Mona's taking in sickness or in health" (Jen, *Mona* 304).

In Jen's progressing America, the Changs all mourn something lost. Ralph and Helen's blind pursuit of the American Dream polarizes the family. Mona's desire to self-identify further exacerbates the ethnic consent-descent divide between generations born from the pressures of assimilation. Recall Jen's assertion that "culture is not fate"; for all of its self-righteousness and the eye-rolling it induces, Jen's America allows trans-generational ethnicity to flower in dynamic, unexpected ways. Despite casualties along the way, the novel offers an end to mourning. The wedding day reunion reconciles the intra-familial discord as well as the divergent trajectories experienced by first- and second-generation immigrants. When Helen decides that her stubborn withdrawal from Mona's life has persisted long enough, she ends mourning the loss of the relationship with her daughter and, by doing so, accepts Mona's choices of identity and spouse. Consider the closing lines. As Mona goes toward her mother, Io falls down: "everyone expects her to start crying like Mona. But instead she stands right back up on her own two feet, and like a fine little witness, claps" (Jen, *Mona* 304). Io is the next generation—truly a Chinese-American-Jew—whose parents identified themselves according to their social-political battles, fought in the name of progress. Unlike her parents, Io will not merely perform the hyphen. Io *is* the hyphen, or rather the necessary dismissal of it, for this third-generation identifies as American in a way that eschews the need for hyphenation.

Works Cited

Byers, Michele. "Material Bodies and Performative Identities: Mona, Neil, and the Promised Land." *Philip Roth Studies*. Fall (2006): 102–120.

Chen, Fu-Jen. "Performing Identity in Gish Jen's *Mona in the Promised Land*." *The International Fiction Review*. 34.1–2 (2007): n.p.

Furman, Andrew. "Immigrant Dreams and Civic Promises: (Con-)Testing Identity in Early Jewish American Literature and Gish Jen's *Mona in the Promised Land*." *MELUS*. 25.1 (2000): 209–226.

Hemingway, Ernest. *The Sun Also Rises*. 1926. New York: Scribner, 2006.

Jen, Gish. *Mona in the Promised Land*. 1996. New York: Vintage Contemporaries, 1997.

_____. *Tiger Writing: Art, Culture, and the Interdependent Self*. Cambridge: Harvard UP, 2013.

Kingston, Maxine Hong. *Tripmaster Monkey: His Fake Book*. 1987. New York: Vintage International, 1990.

Moglen, Seth. *Mourning and Modernity: Literary Modernism and the Injuries of American Capitalism*. Stanford: Stanford UP, 2007.

Mukherjee, Bharti. "Immigrant Writing: Changing the Contours of a National Literature." *American Literary History*. 23.3 (2011): 680–696.

Roth, Philip. *American Pastoral*. 1997. New York: Vintage International, 1998.

Silko, Leslie Marmon. *Ceremony*. 1977. New York: Penguin, 1986.

Sollors, Werner. *Beyond Ethnicity: Consent and Descent in American Culture*. New York: Oxford UP, 1986.

RESOURCES

Works on American Multicultural Identity_____

Novels

Adichie, Chimamanda Ngozi. *Americanah*, 2013

Alexie, Sherman. *Indian Killer*, 1996

Álvarez, Julia. *How the García Girls Lost Their Accents*, 1991

Butler, Octavia. *Kindred*, 1979

Castillo, Ana. *Sapogonia: An Anti-Romance in 3/8 Meter*, 1990

Chabon, Michael. *The Amazing Adventures of Kavalier and Clay*, 2000

Cisneros, Sandra. *The House on Mango Street*, 1984

Cisncros, Sandra. *Caramelo*, 2003

Danticat, Edwidge. *Breath, Eyes, Memory*, 1994

Díaz, Junot. *The Brief Wondrous Life of Oscar Wao*, 2007

Erdrich, Louise. *Love Medicine*, 1984

Erdrich, Louise. *Tracks*, 1987

Erdrich, Louise. *The Last Report on the Miracles at Little No Horse*, 2001

Hosseini, Khaled. *The Kite Runner*, 2003

Jen, Gish. *Typical American*, 1998

Keller, Nora Okja. *Comfort Woman*, 1997

Kingston, Maxine Hong. *The Woman Warrior: Memoirs of a Girlhood Among Ghosts*, 1976

Kingston, Maxine Hong. *China Men*, 1980

Lahiri, Jhumpa. *The Namesake*, 2003

Larsen, Nella. *Passing*, 1929

Morrison, Toni. *Beloved*, 1987

Morrison, Toni. *The Bluest Eye*, 1970

Morrison, Toni. *Song of Solomon*, 1977

Mukherjee, Bharati. *Jasmine*, 1989

Myenne Ng, Fae. *Bone: A Novel*, 1993

Okada, John. *No-No Boy*, 1957

Roth, Henry. *Call It Sleep*, 1934

Silko, Leslie Marmon *Gardens in the Dunes*, 1999

Tan, Amy. *The Joy Luck Club*, 1989

Walker, Alice. *The Color Purple*, 1982

Short Stories

Alexie, Sherman. *The Lone Ranger and Tonto Fistfight in Heaven*, 1993

Alexie, Sherman. *Ten Little Indians*, 2003

Alexie, Sherman. *War Dances*, 2010

Cisneros, Sandra. *Woman Hollering Creek and Other Stories*, 1991

Danticat, Edwidge. *Krik? Krak!*, 1995

Lahiri, Jhumpa. *Interpreter of Maladies*, 1999

Proulx, Annie. *Close Range: Wyoming Stories*, 1999

Poetry

Alexie, Sherman. *The Business of Fancydancing*, 1992

Cisneros, Sandra. *Loose Woman*, 1994

Dove, Rita. *Sonata Mulattica*, 2007

Finney, Nikki. *Head Off & Split*, 2011

Harjo, Joy. *How We Became Human: New and Selected Poems, 1975–2001*, 2004

Harper, Michael S. *Songlines in Michaeltree: New and Collected Poems*, 2000

Komunyakaa, Yusef. *Copacetic*, 1984

Komunyakaa, Yusef. *Neon Vernacular*, 1993

Lee, Li-Young. *Rose*, 1986

Rose, Wendy. *Bone Dance: New and Selected Poems, 1965–1992*, 1994

Song, Cathy. *Picture Bride*, 1983

Trethewey, Natasha. *Native Guard*, 2006

Plays

Hansberry, Lorraine. *A Raisin in the Sun*, 1959

Hwang, David Henry. *M. Butterfly*, 1988

Parks, Suzan-Lori. *Topdog/Underdog*, 2001

Shange, Ntozake. *for colored girls who have considered suicide/when the rainbow is enuf*, 1975

Wilson, August. *The Piano Lesson*, 1990

Memoir

Abu-Jabar, Diana. *The Language of Baklava*, 2005

Alexander, Meena. *Fault Lines: A Memoir*, 1993

Baca, Jimmy Santiago. *A Place to Stand: The Making of a Poet*, 2001

Bulosan, Carlos. *America is in the Heart: A Personal History*, 1946

Dumas, Firoozeh. *Funny in Farsi: A Memoir of Growing Up Iranian in America*, 2004

Hongo, Garrett Kaoru. *Volcano*, 1995

Jemison, Mary. *Narrative of the Life of Mrs. Mary Jemison*, 1824

McBride, James. *The Color of Water: A Black Man's Tribute to His White Mother*, 1996

Pham, Andrew X. *Catfish and Mandala: A Two-Wheeled Voyage through the Landscape and Memory of Vietnam*, 1999

Rodriguez, Richard. *Hunger of Memory*, 1982

Segrest, Mab. *Memoir of a Race Traitor*, 1994

Thomas, Piri. *Down These Mean Streets*, 1967

Bibliography

Adichie, Chimimanda Ngozi. "The Danger of a Single Story." *TED*. TEDGlobal, Jul. 2009. Web. 10 May 2014.

Aguilar-San Juan, Karin. *Little Saigons: Staying Vietnamese in America*. Minneapolis: U of Minnesota P, 2009.

Anzaldúa, Gloria. *Borderlands/La Frontera*. 2nd ed. San Francisco: Aunt Lute, 1999.

Ashcroft, Bill, Gareth Griffiths, & Helen Tiffin. *Post-Colonial Studies: The Key Concepts*. London: Routledge, 2003.

_____. *The Post-Colonial Reader*. London: Routledge, 1995.

Baker, Houston A., ed. *Three American Literatures: Essays in Chicano, Native American, and Asian-American Literature for Teachers of American Literature*. New York: Modern Language Association of America, 1982.

Bernheimer, Charles, eds. *Comparative Literature in the Age of Multiculturalism*. Baltimore: Johns Hopkins UP, 1995.

Bolaki, Stella. *Unsettling the Bildungsroman: Reading Contemporary Ethnic American Women's Fiction*. New York: Rodopi, 2011.

Brown, Julie, ed. *Ethnicity and the American Short Story*. New York: Garland, 1997.

Calderón, Héctor, & José David Saldívar, eds. *Criticism in the Borderlands: Studies in Chicano Literature, Culture, and Ideology*. Durham, NC: Duke UP, 1991.

Chan, Jeffrey Paul, Frank Chin, Lawson Fusao Inada, & Shawn Wong, eds. *The Big Aiiieeeee! An Anthology of Chinese American and Japanese American Literature*. New York: Meridian, 1991.

Clark, Keith, ed. *Contemporary Black Men's Fiction and Drama*. Urbana & Chicago: U of Illinois P, 2001.

Coulombe, Joseph L. "The Efficacy of Humor in Sherman Alexie's Flight: Violence, Vulnerability, and the Post-9/11 World." *MELUS* 39.1 (Spring 2014): 130–148.

Cowart, David. *Trailing Clouds: Immigrant Fiction in Contemporary America*. Ithaca, NY: Cornell UP, 2006.

Crawford, Margo. "Preface: Erasing the Commas: RaceGenderClassSexualityRegion." *American Literature* 77 (March 2005): 1–5.

Cunningham, John. *Race-ing Masculinity: Identity in Contemporary U.S. Writings.* New York: Routledge, 2002.

Cutter, Martha, ed. *Rescripting Ethnic Bodies and Subjectivites.* Special Issue, *MELUS* 39.1 (Spring 2014): 1–232.

Du Bois, W. E. B. *The Souls of Black Folk.* 1903. New York: Tribeca, 2011.

Gates, Henry Louis, Jr. *The Signifying Monkey: A Theory of Afro-American Literary Criticism.* New York: Oxford U, 1988.

Gordon, Avery F., & Christopher Newfield, eds. *Mapping Multiculturalism.* Minneapolis: U of Minnesota P, 1996.

Grassian, Daniel. *Hybrid Fiction: American Literature and Generation X.* Jefferson, NC: McFarland, 2003.

Kanellos, Nicholás, ed. *Herencia: The Anthology of Hispanic Literature of the United States.* New York: Oxford UP, 2002.

Karem, Jeff. *The Romance of Authenticity: The Cultural Politics of Regional and Ethnic Literatures.* Charlottesville: U of Virginia P, 2004.

Lape, Noreen Groover. *West of the Border: The Multicultural Literature of the Western American Frontiers.* Athens: Ohio UP, 2000.

McRuer, Robert. *The Queer Renaissance: Contemporary American Literature and the Reinvention of Lesbian and Gay Identities.* New York: NYU P, 1997.

Madsen, Deborah L. *Beyond the Borders: American Literature and Post-Colonial Theory.* London: Pluto, 2003.

Martin, Holly E. *Writing Between Cultures: A Study of Hybrid Narratives in Ethnic Literature of the United States.* NC: McFarland, 2011.

Morrison, Toni. *Playing in the Dark: Whiteness and the Literary Imagination.* Cambridge, MA: Harvard UP, 1992.

Moya, Paula M. L. *Learning from Experience: Minority Identities, Multicultural Struggles.* Berkeley, CA: U of California P, 2002.

Mukherjee, Bharti. "Immigrant Writing: Changing the Contours of a National Literature." *American Literary History.* 23.3 (2011): 680–696.

Ottery, James R. "'Who Are They and What Do They Have To Do with What I Want to Be': The Writing of Multicultural Identity and College Success Stories for First-Year Writers." *Identity Papers: Literacy and Power in Higher Education*. Ed. Bronwyn T. Williams. Logan: Utah State UP, 2006. 122–137.

Owens, Louis. *Mixedblood Messages: Literature, Film, Family, Place*. Norman: U of Oklahoma P, 1998.

Pearl, Monica B. *AIDS Literature and Gay Identity: The Literature of Loss*. New York: Routledge, 2013.

Pérez-Firmat, Gustavo. *Life on the Hyphen: The Cuban-American Way*. Austin, TX: U of Texas P, 2012.

Powell, John A. *Racing to Justice: Transforming Our Conceptions of Self and Other to Build an Inclusive Society*. Bloomington: Indiana UP, 2012.

Pratt, Mary Louise. "Arts of the Contact Zone." *Profession* (1991): 33–40.

Reed, Ishmael, ed. *MultiAmerica: Essays on Cultural Wars and Cultural Peace*. New York: Penguin, 1997.

Reesman, Jeanne Campbell, ed. *Trickster Lives: Culture and Myth in American Fiction*. Athens: U of Georgia P, 2001.

Renshon, Stanley A. *The 50% American: Immigration and National Identity in an Age of Terror*. Washington, DC: Georgetown UP, 2005.

Ruoff, A. LaVonne Brown, & Jerry Washington Ward., eds. *Redefining American Literary History*. New York: Modern Language Association of America, 1990.

Saldívar, José David. *Border Matters: Remapping American Cultural Studies*. Berkeley: U of California P, 1997.

Shell, Marc, ed. *American Babel: Literatures of the United States from Abnaki to Zuni* Cambridge, MA: Harvard UP, 2002.

Smith, Jeanne Rosier. *Writing Tricksters: Mythic Gambols in American Ethnic Literature*. Berkeley: U of California P, 1997.

Sollors, Werner. *Beyond Ethnicity: Consent and Descent in American Culture*. New York: Oxford UP, 1986.

_____. *The Invention of Ethnicity*. New York: Oxford UP, 1989.

_____. *Neither Black nor White yet Both: Thematic Explorations of Interracial Literature*. New York: Oxford UP, 1997.

Spillers, Hortense J. *Comparative American Identities: Race, Sex, and Nationality in the   Modern Text*. New York: Routledge, 1991.

Stanley, Sandra. *Other Sisterhoods: Literary Theory and U.S. Women of Color*. Urbana & Chicago: U of Illinois P, 1998.

Takaki, Ronald. *A Different Mirror: A History of Multicultural America*. Boston: Little, Brown, 1993.

_____. *A Larger Memory: A History of Our Diversity, with Voices*. New York: Little, Brown, 1998.

Taylor, Christopher. "North America as Contact Zone: Native American Literature and the Cross-Cultural Dilemma." *Studies in American Indian Literatures* 22.3 (Fall 2010): 26–44.

Teuton, Sean Kicummah. *Red Land, Red Power: Grounding Knowledge in the American Indian Novel*. Durham, NC: Duke UP, 2008.

About the Editors

Linda Trinh Moser is professor of English at Missouri State University, where she teaches multicultural American literature, world literature, and women's literature. She co-edited, with Kathryn West, *Research Guide to American Literature: Contemporary Literature, 1970 to Present*, to which she contributed essays on "Feminism and Women's Writing," "Literature and the Environment," "Multiculturalism and Globalization," and "Vietnam War (And Anti-war) Literature." She has also edited and introduced the work of Onoto Watanna in *Me: A Book of Remembrance* and *"A Half Caste" and Other Writings*. In 2011, the National Academic Advising Association recognized her with an Outstanding Faculty Advisor Award.

Kathryn West is professor and chair of the department of English at Bellarmine University in Louisville, Kentucky. She teaches primarily twentieth- and twenty-first century American literature, women's literature, and women's and gender studies. With Linda Trinh Moser, she published *Contemporary American Literature, 1970 to the Present*, part of the Research Guides to American Literature series. To that volume, she contributed entries on "African American Literature," "The Native American Renaissance," and "Postmodernism," as well as essays on a number of contemporary writers. She is co-author of *Women Writers in the United States: A Timeline of Literary, Cultural, and Social History* (Oxford, 1994), and she has published articles on contemporary American literature and women's literature.

Contributors

Jessica Boykin is a PhD student and teaching associate at Arizona State University, studying ethnic American literature and assistant teaching in film and media studies. Her research examines identity and self-representation in American literature, particularly African American writing from 1850 to the Harlem Renaissance. She looks at various forms of literature, including autobiographies, journals, speeches, and comics, as well as poetry and fiction, with a recent project discussing representations of slavery in graphic novels. Boykin has presented on the narrator in Margaret Atwood's *Surfacing* as well as the pop music star Rihanna in her examination of race and gender identity politics.

Joanna Davis-McElligatt is assistant professor of ethnic studies in the department of English at the University of Louisiana at Lafayette. She is currently at work on her first monograph, entitled *Black and Immigrant: The New African Diaspora in Twentieth-Century American Literature*. In this project, she explores literature by and about US immigrants of African descent and makes the case that their experiences challenge long-held assumptions about both immigrant and African American identities. She has also written about comics, race, and gender for *The Comics Journal, MELUS,* and the edited collection *The Comics of Chris Ware: Drawing is a Way of Thinking* (U of Mississippi P, 2010). Her chapter, co-written with Forrest Roth, on conceptions of racialized male genius in Gus Van Sant's 2000 film *Finding Forrester* appears in the collection *The Pedagogy of Pop: Theoretical and Practical Strategies for Success* (Lexington Books, 2012).

Leanne P. Day is a doctoral student in English literature at the University of Washington. She has taught English in Hawai'i, Thailand, and Washington. Her research interests focus on the racial, social, and political dynamics of Hawai'i and the complicated effects of neocolonial and neoliberal power on Asian Americans and Native Hawaiians. She has presented at the Pacific Ancient and Modern Language Association Conference in 2012 and 2013 as well as the 2012 Asian American Association Studies conference. Her work has been published in *New Ways in Teaching Reading*, and she was a co-editor for a custom textbook for the University of Washington, *A Guide to Research and Writing at the University of Washington*.

Michael Gorman is associate professor at Hiroshima City University in Japan. His teaching and research interests include rural American civilization as well as multicultural, environmental, and transnational literatures. Co-author of *Listening to Alternative Voices: Reading Literature from the Perspective of Ethnicity and Gender* [*orutanatibu boisu o kiku: esunishitii to jendaa de yomu*], he has also recently published articles in *Bloom's Modern Critical Interpretations: Willa Cather's My Ántonia*, *The Journal of Genbaku [Atomic Bomb] Literature* [*Genbaku bungaku kenkyuu*], *Studies in English Language and Literature* [*Hiroshima jogakuin daigaku eigo eibei bungaku kenkyuu*], and *Counter-Narratives and American Literature* [*Kauntaa naratibu de yomu amerika bungaku*]. His current projects include a book about Willa Cather and first Americans.

Gad Guterman is assistant professor in the Conservatory of Theatre Arts at Webster University, where he heads the theatre studies and dramaturgy program. He is the author of *Performance, Identity, and Immigration Law: A Theatre of Undocumentedness*, published by Palgrave Macmillan. His essays, focused generally on connections between theatre and law, have appeared in *Theatre Survey*, *Theatre Journal*, the *Journal of American Drama and Theatre*, and *Contemporary Theatre Review*. He received his PhD from the Graduate Center, City University of New York.

Jessica Labbé is honored to serve her community and state as a teacher at Guilford Technical Community College in North Carolina, after having taught at universities including Florida State, South Carolina, and Francis Marion, as well as a private liberal arts college. Labbé teaches a wide range of composition, literature, theory, gender, and cultural studies courses and seminars. Over her fourteen years of college instruction, she has garnered just as many awards recognizing her teaching and service. Her publications can be seen in *Meridians*, *College Literature*, and various encyclopedias and essay collections. She is a deeply engaged teacher, writer, and scholar who believes that lifelong success begins with the acquisition of knowledge.

Rickie-Ann Legleitner is a PhD candidate at the University of South Dakota. She specializes in American literature, focusing on women writers, identity politics, and the *Bildungsroman*. Her dissertation, *The Artist Embodied: Female Creativity and Development in American Literature from 1850–1940,* explores the development of the female artist in American literature by women writers, including the work of E.D.E.N Southworth, Elizabeth Stuart Phelps, Willa Cather, Jessie Fauset, and Zelda Fitzgerald.

Kyoko Matsunaga is an associate professor at Kobe City University of Foreign Studies, Japan, and a former Fulbright fellow at the University of Nebraska-Lincoln. She specializes in American Indian literature, nuclear/atomic literature, and environmental literature. She is co-author of *Listening to Alternative Voices: Reading Literature from the Perspective of Ethnicity and Gender* [*orutanatibu boisu o kiku: esunisitii to jendaa de yomu*] (2011). Her essays have appeared in such books and journals as *Counter-Narratives and American Literature* [*kauntaa naratibu de yomu amerika bungaku*] (2012); *Sovereignty, Separatism, and Survivance: Ideological Encounters in the Literature of Native North America* (2009); *Southwestern American Literature*; and *Journal of Genbaku* [Atomic Bomb] *Literature* [*Genbaku bungaku kenkyu*]. She is currently working on a book about American Indian Literature and nuclear issues.

John C. Orr teaches nineteenth- and early twentieth-century American literature at the University of Portland, where he also oversees the Honors Program and advises students applying for major competitive scholarships. In addition to continued research on Henry Adams, he investigates American women writers from the American West who were writing in the early decades of the twentieth century. Beyond the essay in this volume on Mourning Dove's *Cogewea*, he has spent time in archives exploring her relationship with her mentor, Lucullus McWhorter, as demonstrated in their correspondence.

Conor Picken teaches English and Interdisciplinary Studies at Bellarmine University in Louisville, Kentucky. His research and teaching focus on American literature, modernism, Southern literature, and social change. He has presented papers on the works of William Faulkner, Robert Penn

Warren, and Cormac McCarthy. He has two publications forthcoming: "'There Ought to Be a Law': Prohibition in Faulkner and Warren" and "Drunk and Disorderly: Alcoholism in William Faulkner's *Sanctuary*."

Annette Harris Powell is associate professor of English, with a specialization in rhetoric and writing, at Bellarmine University. Her research and teaching interests include rhetorics of place, memory, and epistemology as well as the representation of culture through language, images, and structures, specifically, how memory is impacted by surrounding structures of meaning-making and how it influences contemporary discourses. She is also interested in how place shapes civic engagement both in and outside the writing classroom and public memory as a site for teaching writing. Powell has served as a consultant, contributor, and member of the Scholars Advisory Committee for the Frazier History Museum's exhibit, *Spirits of the Passage: The Story of the Transatlantic Slave Trade* (2013). Her on-going project focuses on identity, memory, and place in the preservation of indigenous Sea Islands culture. Powell's most recent publication on memory and place is "Discourses of Preservation: The Gullah Community and Rhetorical Construction" in *Practicing Research in Writing Studies* (Hampton Press).

Tina Powell is a PhD candidate at Fordham University. Her dissertation examines how Vietnamese American fiction incorporates American tropes, myths, and literature to relay the trauma, racial melancholia, and racial and class struggles that complicate the relationship between Vietnamese refugees and American society.

Enid R. Spitz majored in English and was a member of the honors program at the University of Portland. She graduated in 2013 and is looking forward to graduate studies.

Index
